25892

D1095772

Library
Oakland S.U.M.

SERMONS PREACHED IN MANCHESTER

SECOND SERIES

SERMONS PREACHED IN MANCHESTER by

Alexander Maclaren D.D.

Second Series

NEW YORK

FUNK & WAGNALLS COMPANY

30 LAFAYETTE PLACE

1902

CONTENTS

CONTENTS.

CONTENTS.

THE TWO AWAKINGS.

PSALM xvii. 15.

I shall be satisfied, when I awake, with Thy likeness.

PSALM lxxiii. 20.

As a dream when one awaketh ; so, O Lord, when Thou awakest, Thou shalt despise their image.

BOTH of these Psalms are occupied with that standing puzzle to Old Testament worthies—the good fortune of bad men, and the bad fortune of good ones. The former recounts the personal calamities of David its author. The latter gives us the picture of the perplexity of Asaph its writer, when he "saw the prosperity of the wicked."

And as the problem in both is substantially the same, the solution also is the same. David and Asaph both point onwards to a period when this confusing distribution of earthly good shall have ceased, though the one regards that period chiefly in its bearing upon himself as the time when he shall see God and be at rest, while the other thinks of it rather with reference to the godless rich as the time of their destruction.

2ND SER. B

In the details of this common expectation, also, there is a remarkable parallelism. Both describe the future to which they look as an awaking, and both connect with it, though in different ways and using different words, the metaphor of an image or likeness. In the one case, the future is conceived as the Psalmist's awaking, and losing all the vain show of this dream-land of life, while he is at rest in beholding the appearance, and perhaps in receiving the likeness of the one enduring Substance, God. In the other, it is thought of as God's awaking, and putting to shame the fleeting shadow of well-being with which godless men befool themselves.

What this period of twofold awaking may be is a question on which good men and thoughful students of Scripture differ. Without entering on the wide subject of the Jewish knowledge of a future state, it may be enough for our present purpose to say that the language of both these Psalms seems much too emphatic and high-pitched, to be fully satisfied by a reference to anything in this life. It certainly looks as if the great awaking which David puts in immediate contrast with the death of "men of this world," and which solaced his heart with the confident expectation of beholding God, of full satisfaction of all His being, and possibly even of wearing the Divine likeness, pointed onwards, however dimly, to that "within the veil." And as for the other psalm, though the awaking of God is, no doubt, a Scriptural phrase for His ending of any period of probation and indulgence by an act of judgment, yet the strong words in which the context describes this awaking, as the "destruction" and the "end" of the godless, make it most natural to take it as here referring to the final close of the probation of life. That conclusion appears to be strengthened by the contrast which in subsequent verses is drawn between this "end" of the worldling, and the poet's hopes for himself of Divine guidance in life, and afterwards of being taken (the same word as is used in the account of Enoch's translation) by God into His presence and glory—hopes whose exuberance it is hard to confine within the limits of any changes possible for earth.

The doctrine of a future state never assumed the same prominence, nor possessed the same clearness in Israel as with us. There are great tracts of the Old Testament where it does not appear at all. This very difficulty, about the strange disproportion between character and circumstances, shows that the belief had not the same place with them as with us. But it gradually emerged into comparative distinctness. Revelation is progressive, and the appropriation of Revelation is progressive too. There is a history of God's self-manifestation, and there is a history of man's reception of the manifestation. It seems to me that in these two Psalms, as in other places of Old Testament Scripture, we see inspired men in the very course of being taught by God, on occasion of their earthly sorrows, the clearer hopes which alone could sustain them. They stood not where we stand, to whom Christ has "brought life and immortality to light;" but to their devout and perplexed souls, the dim regions beyond were partially opened, and, though they beheld there a great darkness, they also "saw a great light." They saw all this solid world fade and melt, and behind its vanishing splendours they saw the glory of the God whom they loved, in the midst of which they felt that there *must* be a place for them, where eternal realities should fill their vision, and a stable inheritance satisfy their hearts.

The period, then, to which both David and Asaph look, in these two verses, is the end of life. The words of both, taken in combination, open out a series of aspects of that period which carry weighty lessons, and to which we turn now.

I. The first of these is that *to all men the end of Life is an Awaking*. The representation of death most widely diffused among all nations is that it is a sleep. The reasons for that emblem are easily found. We always try to veil the terror and deformity of the ugly thing by the thin robe of language. As with reverential awe, so with fear and disgust, the tendency is to wrap their objects in the folds of metaphor. Men prefer not to name plainly their god or their dread, but find round-about phrases for the one, and coaxing flattering titles for the other. The furies and the fates of heathenism, the supernatural beings of modern superstition, must not be spoken of by their own appellations. The recoil of men's hearts from the thing is testified by the aversion of their languages to the bald name—death. And the employment of this special euphemism of sleep is a wonderful witness to our weariness of life, and to its endless toil and trouble. Everywhere that has seemed to be a comforting and almost an attractive name, which has promised full rest from all the agitations of this changeful scene. The prosperous and the wretched alike have owned the fatigue of living, and been conscious of a soothing expectance which became almost a hope, as they thought of lying still at last with folded hands and shut eyes. The wearied workers have bent over their dead, and felt that they are blessed in this at all events, that they rest from their labours; and, as they saw them absolved from all their tasks, have sought to propitiate the power that had made this ease for them, as well as to express their sense of its merciful aspect, by calling it not death, but sleep.

But that emblem, true and sweet as it is, is but half the truth. Taken as the whole, as indeed men are ever tempted to take it, it is a cheerless lie. It is truth for the senses—"the foolish senses," who "crown" Death, as "Omega," the last, "the Lord," because "*they* find no *motion* in the dead." Rest, cessation of consciousness of the outer world, and of action upon it, are set forth by the figure. But even the figure might teach us that the consciousness of life, and the vivid exercise of thought and feeling, are not denied by it. Death is sleep. Be it so. But does not that suggest the doubt—"in that sleep, what dreams may come?" Do we not all know that, when the chains of slumber bind sense, and the disturbance of the outer world is hushed, there are faculties of our souls which work more strongly than in our waking hours? We are all poets, "makers" in

our sleep. Memory and Imagination open their eyes
when flesh closes it. We can live through years in the
dreams of a night; so swiftly can spirit move when even
partially freed from "this muddy vesture of decay." That
very phrase, then, which at first sight seems the opposite
of the representation of our text, in reality is preparatory
to and confirmatory of it. That very representation
which has lent itself to cheerless and heathenish thoughts
of death as the cessation not only of toil but of activity,
is the basis of the deeper and truer representation, the
truth for the spirit, that death is an awaking. If, on the
one hand, we have to say, as we anticipate the approach-
ing end of life, "The night cometh, when no man can
work;" on the other the converse is true, "The night is
far spent; the day is at hand."

We shall sleep. Yes; but we shall wake too. We
shall wake just because we sleep. For flesh and all its
weakness, and all its disturbing strength, and craving im-
portunities—for the outer world, and all its dissipating
garish shows, and all its sullen resistance to our hand—
for weariness, and fevered activity and toil against the
grain of our tastes, too great for our strength, disappoint-
ing in its results, the end is blessed calm sleep. And
precisely because it is so, therefore for our true selves,
for heart and mind, for powers that lie dormant in the
lowest, and are not stirred into full action in the highest,
souls; for all that universe of realities which encompass
us undisclosed, and known only by faint murmurs which
pierce through the opiate sleep of life, the end shall be
an awaking.

The truth which corresponds to this metaphor, and which David felt when he said, "I shall be satisfied when I awake," is that the spirit, because emancipated from the body, shall spring into greater intensity of action, shall put forth powers that have been held down here, and shall come into contact with an order of things which here it has but indirectly known. To our true selves and to God we shall wake. Here we are like men asleep in some chamber that looks towards the eastern sky. Morning by morning comes the sunrise, with the tender glory of its rosy light and blushing heavens, and the heavy eyes are closed to it all. Here and there some lighter sleeper, with thinner eyelids or face turned to the sun, is half conscious of a vague brightness, and feels the light, though he sees not the colours of the sky nor the forms of the filmy clouds. Such souls are our saints and prophets, but most of us sleep on unconscious. To us all the moment comes when we shall wake, and see for ourselves the bright and terrible world which we have so often forgotten, and so often been tempted to think was itself a dream. Brethren, see to it that that awaking be for you the beholding of what you have loved, the finding, in the sober certainty of waking bliss, of all the objects which have been your visions of delight in the sleep of earth!

This life of ours hides more than it reveals. The day shows the sky as solitary, but for wandering clouds that cover its blue emptiness. But the night peoples its waste places with stars, and fills all its abysses with blazing glories.

"If light so much conceals, wherefore not life?" Let us hold fast by a deeper wisdom than is born of sense; and though men, now-a-days, seem to be willing to go back to the "eternal sleep" of the most unspiritual heathenism, and to cast away all that Christ has brought us concerning that world where He has been and whence He has returned, because positive science and the anatomist's scalpel preach no gospel of a future, let us try to feel as well as to believe that it is life, with all its stunted capacities and idle occupation with baseless fabrics, which is the sleep, and that for us all the end of it is—to awake.

II. The second principle contained in our text is that *death is to some men the awaking of God.*

"When Thou awakest, Thou shalt despise their image." Closely rendered, the former clause would read simply "in awaking," without any specifying of the person, which is left to be gathered from the succeeding words. But there is no doubt that the English version fills the blank correctly by referring the awaking to God.

The metaphor is not infrequent in the Old Testament, and, like many others applying to the Divine nature, is saved from any possibility of misapprehension by the very boldness of its materialism. It has a well-marked and uniform meaning. God "awakes" when He ends an epoch of probation and long-suffering mercy by an act or period of judgment. So far, then, as the mere expression is concerned, there may be nothing more meant here than the termination by a judicial act in this life, of the transient "prosperity of the wicked."

Any Divinely-sent catastrophe which casts the worldly rich man down from his slippery eminence would satisfy the words. But the emphatic context seems, as already pointed out, to require that they should be referred to that final crash which irrevocably separates him who has "his portion in this life," from all which he calls his "goods."

If so, then the whole period of earthly existence is regarded as the time of God's gracious forbearance and mercy; and the time of death is set forth as the instant when sterner elements of the Divine dealings start into greater prominence. Life here is predominantly, though not exclusively, the field for the manifestation of patient love, not willing that any should perish. To the godless soul, immersed in material things, and blind to the light of God's wooing love, the transition to that other form of existence is likewise the transition to the field for the manifestation of the retributive energy of God's righteousness. Here and now His judgment on the whole slumbers. The consequences of our deeds are inherited, indeed, in many a merciful sorrow, in many a paternal chastisement, in many a partial exemplification of the wages of sin as death. But the harvest is not fully grown nor ripened yet; it is not reaped in all its extent; the bitter bread is not baked and eaten as it will have to be. Nor are men's consciences so awakened that they connect the retribution, which does befall them, with its causes in their own actions, as closely as they will do when they are removed from the excitement of life and the deceit of its dreams. "Sentence against an evil work is not executed speedily." For the long years of our stay here, God's seeking love lingers round every one of us, yearning over us, besetting us behind and before, courting us with kindnesses, lavishing on us its treasures, seeking to win our poor love. It is sometimes said that this is a state of probation. But that phrase suggests far too cold an idea. God does not set us here as on a knife edge, with abysses on either side ready to swallow us if we stumble, while He stands apart watching for our halting, and unhelpful to our tottering feebleness. He compasses us with His love and its gifts, He draws us to Himself, and desires that we should stand. He offers all the help of His angels to hold us up. "He will not suffer thy foot to be moved; He that keepeth thee will not slumber." The judgment sleeps; the loving forbearance, the gracious aid wake. Shall we not yield to His perpetual pleadings, and, moved by the mercies of God, let His conquering love thaw our cold hearts into streams of thankfulness and self-devotion?

But remember that that predominantly merciful and long-suffering character of God's present dealings affords no guarantee that there will not come a time when the slumbering judgment will stir to waking. The same chapter which tells us that "He is long-suffering to us-ward, not willing that any should perish, but that all should come to repentance," goes on immediately to repel the inference that therefore a period of which retribution shall be the characteristic is impossible, by the solemn declaration, "*But* the day of the Lord shall come as a thief in the night." His character remains ever the same, the principles of His government are unalterable, but there may be variations in the prominence given in His acts, to the several principles of the one, and the various though harmonious phases of the other. The method may be changed, the purpose may remain unchanged. And the Bible, which is our only source of knowledge on the subject, tells us that the method *is* changed, in so far as to intensify the vigour of the operation of retributive justice after death, so that men who have been compassed with "the loving-kindness of the Lord," and who die leaving worldly things, and keeping worldly hearts, will have to confront "the terror of the Lord."

The alternation of epochs of tolerance and destruction is in accordance with the workings of God's providence here and now. For though the characteristic of that providence as we see it is merciful forbearance, yet we are not left without many a premonition of the mighty final "day of the Lord." For long years or centuries a nation or an institution goes on slowly departing from truth, forgetting the principles on which it rests, or the purposes for which it exists. Patiently God pleads with the evil-doers, lavishes gifts and warnings upon them. He holds back the inevitable avenging as long as restoration is yet possible—and *His* eye and heart see it to be possible long after men conclude that the corruption is hopeless. But at last comes a period when He says, "I have long still holden my peace, and refrained Myself · now will I destroy " and with a crash one more hoary iniquity disappears from the earth, which it has burdened so long. For sixty times sixty slow, throbbing seconds, the silent hand creeps unnoticed round the dial, and then, with whirr and clang, the bell rings out, and another hour of the world's secular day is gone. The billows of the thunder-cloud slowly gather into vague form, and slowly deepen in lurid tints, and slowly roll across the fainting blue; they touch—and then the fierce flash, like the swift hand on the palace-wall of Babylon, writes its message of destruction over all the heaven at once. We know enough from the history of men and nations since Sodom till to-day, to recognize it as God's plan to alternate long patience and "sudden destruction :"—

> "The mill of God grinds slowly,
> But it grinds exceeding small ;"

and every such instance confirms the expectation of the coming of that great and terrible day of the Lord, whereof all epochs of convulsion and ruin, all falls of Jerusalem and Roman empires, Reformations, and French Revolutions, and American wars, all private and personal calamities which come from private wrong-doing, are but feeble precursors. "When Thou awakest, Thou wilt despise their image."

Brethren, do we use aright this goodness of God which is the characteristic of the present? Are we ready for that judgment which is the mark of the future?

III. Death is the *annihilation of the vain show of worldly life.* The word rendered *image* is properly shadow, and hence copy or likeness, and hence image. Here, however, the simpler meaning is the better. "Thou shalt despise their shadow." The men are shadows, and all their goods are not what they are called, their "substance," but their *shadow*, a mere appearance, not a reality. That show of good, which seems but is not, is withered up by the light of the awaking God. What He despises cannot live.

So there are the two old commonplaces of moralists set forth in these grand words—the unsatisfying character of all merely external delights and possessions, and also their transitory character. They are non-substantial and non-permanent.

Nothing that is without a man can make him rich or restful. The treasures which are kept in coffers are not real, but only those which are kept in the soul. Nothing which cannot enter into the substance of the life and character can satisfy us. That which we are makes us rich or poor, that which we own is a trifle.

There is no congruity between any outward thing and man's soul, of such a kind as that satisfaction can come from its possession. "Cisterns that can hold no water," "that which is not bread," "husks that the swine did eat" —these are not exaggerated phrases for the good gifts which God gives for our delight, and which become profitless and delusive by our exclusive attachment to them. There is no need for exaggeration. These worldly possessions have a good in them, they contribute to ease and grace in life, they save from carking cares and mean anxieties, they add many a comfort and many a source of culture. But, after all, a true, lofty life may be lived with a very small modicum. There is no proportion between wealth and happiness, nor between wealth and nobleness. The fairest life ever lived on earth was that of a poor man, and with all its beauty it moved within the limits of narrow resources. The loveliest blossoms do not grow on plants that plunge their greedy roots into the fattest soil. A little light earth in the crack of a hard rock will do. We need enough for the physical being to root itself in ; we need no more.

Young men ! especially you who are plunged into the busy life of our great commercial centres, and are tempted by everything you see, and by most that you hear, to believe that a prosperous trade and hard cash are the realities, and all else mist and dreams, fix this in your mind to begin life with—God is the reality, all else is shadow. Do not make it your ambition to get *on*, but to get *up*. Having food and raiment, let us be content. Seek for your life's delight and treasure in thought, in truth, in pure affections, in moderate desires, in a spirit set on God. These are the realities of our possessions. As for all the rest, it is sham and show.

And while thus all without is unreal, it is also fleeting as the shadows of the flying clouds ; and when God awakes, it disappears as they before the noonlight that clears the heavens. All things that are, are on condition of perpetual flux and change. The cloud-rack has the likeness of bastions and towers, but they are mist, not granite, and the wind is every moment sweeping away their outlines, till the phantom fortress topples into red

ruin while we gaze. The tiniest stream eats out its little
valley and rounds the pebble in its widening bed, rain
washes down the soil, and frost cracks the cliffs above.
So silently and yet mightily does the law of change work
that to a meditative eye the solid earth seems almost
molten and fluid, and the everlasting mountains tremble
to decay.

"Wilt thou set thine eyes upon that which is not?"
Are we going to be such fools as to fix our hopes and
efforts upon this fleeting order of things, which can give
no delight more lasting than itself? Even whilst we are
in it, it continueth not in one stay, and we are in it for
such a little while! Then comes what our text calls
God's awaking, and where is it all then? Gone like a
ghost at cockcrow. Why! a drop of blood on your brain
or a crumb of bread in your windpipe, and, as far as you
are concerned, the outward heavens and earth "pass
away with a great" *silence*, as the impalpable shadows
that sweep over some lone hill-side.

> "The glories of our birth and state
>   Are shadows, not substantial things;
> There is no armour against fate,
>   Death lays his icy hand on kings."

What an awaking to a worldly man that awaking of God
will be! "As when a hungry man dreameth, and behold
he eateth, but he awaketh and his soul is empty." He
has thought he fed full, and was rich and safe, but in one
moment he is dragged from it all, and finds himself a
starving pauper, in an order of things for which he has
made no provision. "When he dieth, he shall carry

nothing away." Let us see to it that not in utter nakedness do we go hence, but clothed with that immortal robe,
and rich in those possessions that cannot be taken away
from us, which they have who have lived on earth as
heirs of God and joint-heirs with Christ. Let us pierce,
for the foundation of our life's house, beneath the shifting
sands of time down to the Rock of Ages, and build
there.

IV. Finally, death is for some men the *annihilation of
the vain shows in order to reveal the great reality*.

"I shall be satisfied, when I awake, with Thy likeness."

"Likeness" is properly "form," and is the same word
which is employed in reference to Moses, who saw "the
similitude of the Lord." If there be, as is most probable,
an allusion to that ancient vision in these words, then the
"likeness" is not that conformity to the Divine character
which it is the goal of our hopes to possess, but the
beholding of His self-manifestation. The parallelism of
the verse also points to such an interpretation.

If so, then, we have here the blessed confidence that
when all the baseless fabric of the dream of life has faded
from our opening eyes, we shall see the face of our ever-
loving God. Here the distracting whirl of earthly things
obscures Him from even the devoutest souls, and His
own mighty works which reveal do also conceal. In
them is the hiding as well as the showing of His power.
But there the veil which draped the perfect likeness, and
gave but dim hints through its heavy swathings of the
outline of immortal beauty that lay beneath, shall fall
away. No longer befooled by shadows, we shall possess

the true substance; no longer bedazzled by shows, we shall behold the reality.

And seeing God we shall be satisfied. With all lesser joys the eye is not satisfied with seeing, but to look on Him will be enough. Enough for mind and heart, wearied and perplexed with partial knowledge and imperfect love; enough for eager desires, which thirst, after all draughts from other streams; enough for will, chafing against lower lords and yet longing for authoritative control; enough for all my being—to see God. Here we can rest after all wanderings, and say, "I travel no further; here will I dwell for ever—*I shall be satisfied.*"

And may these dim hopes not suggest to us too some presentiment of the full Christian truth of assimilation dependent on vision, and of vision reciprocally dependent on likeness? "We shall be like Him, for we shall see Him as He is,"—words which reach a height that David but partially discerns through the mist. This much he knows, that he should in some transcendent sense behold the manifested God; and this much more, that it must be "in righteousness" that he should gaze upon that face. The condition of beholding the Holy One was holiness. We know that the condition of holiness is trust in Christ. And as we reckon up the rich treasure of our immortal hopes, our faith grows bold, and pauses not even at the lofty certainty of God without us, known directly and adequately, but climbs to the higher assurance of God within us, flooding our darkness with His great light, and changing us into the perfect copies of His express Image, His only-begotten Son. "I shall be satisfied, when I

2ND SER. C

awake, with Thy likeness," cries the prophet Psalmist. " It is enough for the disciple that he be as his master," responds the Christian hope.

Brethren ! take heed that the process of dissipating the vain shows of earth be begun betimes in your souls. It must either be done by Faith, whose rod disenchants them into their native nothingness, and then it is blessed; or it must be done by death, whose mace smites them to dust, and then it is pure, irrevocable loss and woe. Look away from, or rather look through, things that are seen to the King eternal, invisible. Let your hearts seek Christ, and your souls cleave to Him. Then death will take away nothing from you that you would care to keep, but will bring you your true joy. It will but trample to fragments the "dome of many-coloured glass" that "stains the white radiance of eternity." Looking forward calmly to that supreme hour, you will be able to say, "I will both lay me down in peace and sleep, for Thou, Lord, only makest me dwell in safety." Looking back upon it from beyond, and wondering to find how brief it was, and how close to Him whom you love it has brought you, your now immortal lips touched by the rising Sun of the heavenly morning will thankfully exclaim, "When I awake, I am still with Thee."

THE HEAVENLY WORKERS AND THE EARTHLY
WATCHERS.

ISAIAH lxii. 1, 6, 7.

For Zion's sake will I not hold my peace, and for Jerusalem's sake
I will not rest. . . . I have set watchmen upon thy walls, O
Jerusalem, which shall never hold their peace day nor night : ye
that make mention of the Lord, keep not silence, and give Him
no rest.

TWO remarks of an expository nature will prepare
the way for the consideration of these words.
The first is that the speaker is the personal Messiah.
The second half of Isaiah's prophecies forms one great
whole, which might be called The Book of the Servant
of the Lord. One majestic figure stands forth on its
pages with ever-growing clearness of outline and form
The language in which He is described fluctuates at first
between the collective Israel and the one Person who
is to be all that the nation had failed to attain. But
even near the beginning of the prophecy we read of " My
servant whom I uphold," whose voice is to be low and
soft, and whose meek persistence is not to fail till He
have set judgment in the earth. And as we advance the

reference to the nation becomes less and less possible, and the recognition of the person more and more imperative. At first the music of the prophetic song seems to move uncertainly amid sweet sounds, from which the true theme by degrees emerges, and thenceforward recurs over and over again with deeper, louder harmonies clustering about it, till it swells into the grandeur of the choral close.

In the chapter before our text we read, "The Spirit of the Lord God is upon me, because the Lord hath anointed me to preach good tidings unto the meek." Throughout the remainder of the prophecy, with the exception of one section which contains the prayer of the desolate Israel, this same person continues to speak; and who he is was taught in the synagogue of Nazareth. Whilst the preceding chapter, then, brings in Christ as proclaiming the great work of deliverance for which He is anointed of God, the following chapter presents Him as treading the wine-press alone, which is a symbol of the future judgment by the glorified Saviour. Between these two prophecies of the earthly life and of the still future judicial energy, this chapter of our text lies, referring, as I take it, to the period between these two—that is, to all the ages of the Church's development on earth. For these Christ here promises His continual activity, and His continual bestowment of grace to His servants who watch the walls of His Jerusalem.

The second point to be noticed is the remarkable parallelism in the expressions selected as the text: "I will not hold *My* peace;" the watchmen "shall never hold *their* peace." And His command to them is literally, " Ye that remind Jehovah—no *rest* (or silence) to you ! and give not *rest* to Him."

So we have here Christ, the Church, and God all represented as unceasingly occupied in the one great work of establishing " Zion " as the centre of light, salvation, and righteousness for the whole world. The consideration of these three perpetual activities may open for us some great truths and stimulating lessons.

I. First, then, *The glorified Christ is constantly working for His Church.*

We are too apt to regard our Lord's real work as all lying in the past, and, from the very greatness of our estimate of what He has done, to forget the true importance of what He evermore does. " Christ that died " is the central object of trust and contemplation for devout souls—and that often to the partial hiding of Christ that is risen again, who is even at the right hand of God, who also maketh intercession for us. But Scripture sets forth the present glorious life of our ascended Lord under two contrasted and harmonious aspects—as being rest, and as being continuous activity in the midst of rest. He was received up into heaven, and sat on the right hand of God. In that session on the throne manifold and mighty truths are expressed. It proclaims the full accomplishment of all the purposes of His earthly ministry; it emphasizes the triumphant completion of His redeeming work by His death; it proclaims the majesty of His nature, which returns to the glory which He had with the Father before the world was; it shows to the world, as on some coronation day, their King on His throne, girded with power and holding the far-reaching sceptre of the universe; it prophesies for men, in spite of all present sin and degradation, a share in the dominion which manhood has in Christ attained, for though we see not yet all things put under Him, we see Jesus crowned with glory and honour. It prophesies, too, His final victory over all that sets itself in unavailing antagonism to His love. It points us backward to an historical fact as the basis of all our hopes for ourselves and for our fellows, giving us the assurance that the world's deliverance will come, from the slow operation of the forces already lodged in its history by Christ's finished work. It points us forwards to a future as the goal of all these hopes, giving us that confidence of victory which He has who, having kindled the fire on earth, henceforward sits at God's right hand, waiting in the calm and sublime patience of conscious omnipotence and clear foreknowledge until His enemies become His footstool.

But whilst on the one side Christ rests as from a perfected work which needs no addition nor repetition, on the other He rests not day nor night. And this aspect of His present is as distinctly set forth in Scripture as that is. Indeed the words already quoted as embodying the former contain the latter also. For is not "the right hand of God" the operative energy of the Divine nature? And is not "sitting at the right hand of God" equivalent to possessing and wielding that unwearied, measureless power? Is there not blended together in this pregnant phrase the idea of profoundest calm and of intensest action, that being expressed by the attitude, and this by the situation? Therefore does the Evangelist who uses the expression expand it into words which wonderfully close his Gospel, with the same representation of Christ's swift and constant activity as he had been all along pointing out as characterizing His life on earth. " They went forth," says he, " and preached everywhere." So far the contrast between the Lord seated in the heavens and His wandering servants fighting on earth is sharp and almost harsh. But the next words tone it down, and weave the two apparently discordant halves of the picture into a whole: "the Lord *working* with them." Yes! in all His rest He is full of work, in all their toils He shares, in all their journeys His presence goes beside them. Whatever they do is His deed, and the help that is done upon the earth He doeth it all Himself.

Is not this blessed conviction of Christ's continuous operation in and for His Church that which underlies, as has often been pointed out, the language of the introduction to the Acts of the Apostles, where mention is made of the former treatise that told "all which Jesus *began* both to do and teach?" The Gospel records the beginning; the Book of the Acts the continuance; it is one biography in two volumes. Being yet present with them He spoke and acted. Being exalted He "speaketh from heaven," and from the throne carries on the endless series of His works of power and healing. The whole history is shaped by the same conviction. Everywhere "the Lord" is the true actor, the source of all the life which is in the Church, the arranger of all the providences which affect its progress. The Lord adds to the Church daily. His name works miracles. To the Lord believers are added. His angel, His Spirit, bring messages to His servants. He appears to Paul, and speaks to Ananias. The Gentiles turn to the Lord because the hand of the Lord is with the preachers. The Lord calls Paul to carry the Gospel to Macedonia. The Lord opens the heart of Lydia, and so throughout. Not the Acts of the Apostles, but the Acts of the Lord in and by His servants, is the accurate title of this book. The vision which flashed angel radiance on the face, and beamed with Divine comfort into the heart, of Stephen, was a momentary revelation of an abiding reality, and completes the representation of the Saviour throned beside Almighty Power. He beheld his Lord, not seated, as if careless or resting, while His servant's need was so sore, but as if risen with intent to help, and ready to defend—"*standing* on the right hand of God."

And when once again the heavens opened to the rapt eyes of John in Patmos, the Lord whom he beheld was not only revealed as glorified in the lustre of the inaccessible light, but as actively sustaining and guiding the human reflectors of it. He "holdeth the seven stars in His right hand," and "*walketh* in the midst of the seven golden candlesticks."

Not otherwise does my text represent the present relation of Christ to His Church. It speaks of a continuous forth-putting of power, which it is, perhaps, not over fanciful to regard as dimly set forth here in a twofold form —namely, work and word. At all events, that division stands out clearly on the pages of the New Testament, which ever holds forth the double truth of our Lord's constant action on, in, through, and for His Zion, and of our High Priest's constant intercession.

"I will not rest." Through all the ages His power is in exercise. He inspires in good men all their wisdom, and every grace of life and character. He uses them as His weapons in the contest of His love with the world's hatred; but the hand that forged, and tempered, and sharpened the blade is that which smites with it; and the axe must not boast itself against him that heweth. He, the Lord of lords, orders providences, and shapes the course of the world for that Church which is His witness: "Yea, He reproved kings for their sake, saying, Touch not Mine anointed, and do My prophets no harm." The ancient legend which told how, on many a well-fought field, the ranks of Rome discerned through the battle-dust the gleaming weapons and white steeds of the Great Twin Brethren far in front of the solid legions, is true in loftier sense in our Holy War. We may still see the vision which the leader of Israel saw of old, the man with the drawn sword in his hand, and hear the majestic word, "As captain of the Lord's host am I now come." The Word of God, with vesture dipped in blood, with eyes alit with His flaming love, with the many crowns of un- limited sovereignty upon His head, rides at the head of the armies of heaven; "and in righteousness doth He judge and make war." For the single soul struggling with daily tasks and petty cares, His help is near and real, as for the widest work of the collective whole. He sends none of us tasks in which He has no share. The word of this Master is never " Go," but " Come." He unites Himself with all our sorrows, with all our efforts. " The Lord also working with them " is a description of all the labours of Christian men, be they great or small.

Nor is this all. There still remains the wonderful truth of His continuous intercession for us. In its widest meaning that word expresses the whole of the manifold ways by which Christ undertakes and maintains our cause. But the narrower signification of prayer on our behalf is applicable, and is in Scripture applied, to our Lord. As on earth, the climax of all His intercourse with His disciples was that deep yet simple prayer which forms the Holy of Holies of John's Gospel, so in heaven His loftiest office for us is set forth under the figure of His intercession. Before the Throne stands the slain Lamb, and therefore do the elders in the outer circle bring acceptable praises. Within the veil stands the Priest, with the names of the tribes blazing on the breastplate, and on the shoulders of His robes, near the seat of love, near the arm of power. And whatever difficulty may surround that idea of Christ's priestly intercession, this at all events is implied in it, that the mighty work which He accomplished on earth is ever present to the Divine mind as the ground of our acceptance and the channel of our blessings ; and this further, that the utterance of Christ's will is ever in harmony with the Divine purpose. Therefore His prayer has in it a strange tone of majesty, and, if we may so say, of command, as of one who knows that He is ever heard: "*I will* that they whom Thou hast given Me, be with Me where I am."

The instinct of the Church has, from of old, laid hold of an event in His earthly life to shadow forth this great truth, and has bid us see a pledge and a symbol of it in that scene on the Lake of Galilee: the disciples toiling in the sudden storm, the poor little barque tossing on the waters tinged by the wan moon, the spray dashing over the wearied rowers. They seem alone, but up yonder, in some hidden cleft of the hills, their Master looks down on all the weltering storm, and lifts His voice in prayer. Then when the need is sorest, and the hope least, He comes across the waves, making their surges His pavement, and using all opposition as the means of His approach, and His presence brings calmness, and immediately they are at the land.

So we have not only to look back to the Cross, but up to the Throne. From the cross we hear a voice, "It is finished." From the Throne a voice, "For Zion's sake I will not hold My peace, and for Jerusalem's sake I will not rest."

II. Secondly, *Christ's servants on earth derive from Him a like perpetual activity for the same object.*

The Lord, who in the former portion of these verses declares His own purpose of unwearied action for Zion, associates with Himself in the latter portion the watchmen, whom He appoints and endows for functions in some measure resembling His own, and exercised with constancy derived from Him. "I have set watchmen upon thy walls, O Jerusalem, which shall never hold their peace day nor night." On the promise follows, as ever, a command, (for all Divine gifts involve the responsibility of their use, and it is not His wont either to bestow without requiring, or to require before bestowing,) "Ye that remind Jehovah, keep not silence."

There is distinctly traceable here a reference to a two-fold form of occupation devolving on these Christ-sent servants. They are watchmen, and they are also God's remembrancers. In the one capacity as in the other, their voices are to be always heard. The former meta-phor is common in the Old Testament, as a designation of the prophetic office, but, in accordance with the genius of the New Testament, as expressed on Pentecost, when the Spirit was poured out on the lowly as well as on the high, on the young as on the old, and all prophesied, may be fairly extended to designate not some select few, but the whole mass of Christian people. The watch-man's office falls to be done by all who see the coming peril, and have a tongue to echo it forth. The remem-brancer's priestly office belongs to every member of Christ's priestly kingdom, the lowest and least of whom has the privilege of unrestrained entry into God's pre-sence-chamber, and the power of blessing the world by faithful prayer. What should we think of a citizen in a beleaguered city, who saw the enemy mounting the very ramparts, and gave no alarm because that was the sentry's business? In such extremity every man is a soldier, and women and children can at least keep watch and raise shrill shouts of warning.

The gifts then here promised, and the duties that flow from them, are not the prerogatives or the tasks of any class or order, but the heritage and the burden of the Lord to every member of His Church.

Our voices should ever be heard on earth. A solemn message is committed to us, by the very fact of our belief in Jesus Christ and His work. With that faith come responsibilities of which no Christian can denude himself. To warn the wicked man to turn from His wickedness; to blow the trumpet when we see the sword coming; to catch ever gleaming on the horizon, like the spears of an army through the dust of the march, the out-riders and advance-guard of the coming of Him whose coming is life or death to all, and to lift up our voices with strength and say, " Behold your God;" to peal into the ears of men, sunken in earthliness and dreaming of safety, the cry which may startle and save; to ring out in glad tones to all who wearily ask, " Watchman, what of the night? Will the night soon pass?" the answer which the slow dawning east has breathed into our else stony lips, "The morning cometh;" to proclaim Christ, who came once to put away sin by the sacrifice of Him-self, who comes ever, through the ages, to bless and uphold the righteousness which He loves, and to destroy the iniquity which He hates, who will come at the last to judge the world: this is the never-ending task of the watchmen on the walls of Jerusalem. The New Testa-ment calls it " preaching;" proclaiming as a herald does.

And both metaphors carry one common lesson of the manner in which the work should be done. With clear loud voice, with earnestness and decision, with faithfulness and self-oblivion, forgetting himself in his message, must the herald sound out the will of his King, the largess of his Lord. And the watchman who stands on his watch-tower whole nights, and sees foemen creeping through the gloom, or fire bursting out among the straw-roofed cottages within the walls, shouts with all his might the short sharp alarum, that wakes the sleepers to whom slumber were death. Let us ponder the pattern.

Our voices should ever be heard in heaven. They who trust God remind Him of His promises by their very faith ; it is a mute appeal to His faithful love, which He cannot but answer. And, beyond that, their prayers come up for a memorial before God, and have as real an effect in furthering Christ's kingdom on earth as is exercised by their entreaties and proclamations to men.

How distinctly these words of our text define the region within which our prayers should ever move, and the limits which bound their efficacy! They *remind* God. Then the truest prayer is that which bases itself on God's uttered will, and the desires which are born of our own fancies or heated enthusiasms have no power with Him. The prayer that prevails is a reflected promise. Our office in prayer is but to receive on our hearts the bright rays of His word, and to flash them back from the polished surface to the heaven from whence they came.

These two forms of action ought to be *inseparable.* Each, if genuine, will drive us to the other, for who could fling himself into the watchman's work, with all its solemn consequences, knowing how weak his voice was, and how deaf the ears that should hear, unless he could bring God's might to his help? and who could honestly remind God of His promises and forget his own responsibilities ?   Prayerless work will soon slacken, and never bear fruit; idle prayer is worse than idle.   You cannot part them if you would.   How much of the busy occupation which is called "Christian work" is detected to be spurious by this simple test!   How much so-called prayer is reduced by it to mere noise, no better than the blaring trumpet or the hollow drum !

The power for both is derived from Christ. He sets the watchmen ; He commands the remembrancers. From Him flows the power, from His good Spirit comes the desire, to proclaim the message.   That message is the story of His life and death.   But for what He does and is we should have nothing to say; but for His gift we should have no power to say it; but for His influence we should have no will to say it.   He commands and fits us to be intercessors, for His mighty work brings us near to God ; He opens for us access with confidence to God. "All the promises are in Him yea, and Amen."   He inspires our prayers.   He hath made us priests to God.

And, as the Christian power of discharging these twofold duties is drawn from Christ, so our pattern is His manner of discharging them, and the condition of receiving the power is to abide in Him.   He proposes Himself as our example.   He calls us to no labours which he has not Himself shared, not to any earnestness or continuance in prayer which He has not Himself shown forth. This master works in front of His men. The farmer that goes first among all the sowers, and heads the line of reapers in the yellowing harvest-field, may well have diligent servants. Our Master went forth, weeping, bearing precious seed, and has left it in our hands to sow in all furrows. Our Master is the Lord of the harvest, and has borne the heat of the day before His servants. Look at the amount of work, actual hard work, compressed into these three short years of His ministry. Take the records of the words He spake on that last day of His public teaching, and see what unwearied toil they represent. Ponder upon that life till you catch the spirit which breathed through it all, and, like Him, embrace gladly the welcome necessity of labour for God, under the sense of a vocation conferred upon you, and of the short space within which your service must be condensed. "I must work the work of Him that sent me, while it is day: the night cometh, when no man can work."

Christ asks no romantic impossibilities from us, but He does ask a continuous, systematic discharge of the duties which depend on our relation to the world, and on our relation to Him. Let it be our life's work to show forth His praise ; let the very atmosphere in which we move and have our being be prayer. Let two great currents set ever through our days, which two, like the great movements in the ocean of the air, are but the upper and under halves of the one movement—that beneath with constant energy of desire rushing in from the cold poles to be warmed and expanded at the tropics, where the all-moving sun pours his directest rays; that above charged with rich gifts from the Lord of light, glowing with heat drawn from Him, and made diffusive by His touch, spreading itself out beneficent and life-bringing into all colder lands, swathing the world in soft warm folds, and turning the polar ice into sweet waters.

In the tabernacle of Israel stood two great emblems of the functions of God's people, which embodied these two sides of the Christian life. Day by day, there ascended from the altar of incense the sweet odour, which symbolized the fragrance of prayer as it wreathes itself upwards to the heavens. Night by night, as darkness fell on the desert and the camp, there shone through the gloom the hospitable light of the great golden candlestick with its seven lamps, whose steady rays outburned the stars that paled with the morning. Side by side they proclaimed to Israel its destiny to be the light of the world, to be a kingdom of priests.

The offices and the honour have passed over to us, and we shall fall beneath our obligations unless we let the light shine constantly before men, and let our voice "rise like a fountain night and day" before God—even as He did who, when every man went to his own house, went alone to the Mount of Olives, and in the morning, when every man returned to his daily task, went into the Temple and taught. By His example, by His gifts, by the motive of His love, our resting, working Lord says to each of us, "Ye that remind God, keep not silence."

2ND SER.   D

Let us answer, " For Zion's sake will I not hold my peace, and for Jerusalem's sake I will not rest."

III.   Finally, *The constant activity of the servants of Christ will secure the constant operation of God's power.*

" *Give* Him no rest :" let there be no cessation to Him.   These are bold words, which many people would not have been slow to rebuke, if they had been anywhere else than in the Bible.   Those who remind God are not to suffer Him to be still.   The prophet believes that they can regulate the flow of Divine energy, can stir up the strength of the Lord.

It is easy to puzzle ourselves with insoluble questions about the co-operation of God's power and man's ; but practically, is it not true that God reaches His end, of the establishment of Zion, through the Church ?   He has not barely willed that the world should be saved, nor barely that it should be saved through Christ, nor barely that it should be saved through the knowledge of Christ ; but His will is that the world shall be saved, by faith in the person and work of Christ, proclaimed as a gospel by men who believe it.   And, as a matter of fact, is it not true that the energy, with which God's power in the Gospel manifests itself, depends on the zeal and activity and prayerfulness of the Church ?   The great reservoir is always full—full to the brim ; however much may be drawn from it, the water sinks not a hair's-breadth ; but the bore of the pipe and the power of the pumping-engine determine the rate at which the stream flows from it.   " He could there do no mighty works because of their unbelief."   The obstruction of indifference dammed back the water of life. The city perishes for thirst if the long line of aqueduct that strides across the plain towards the home of the mountain torrents be ruinous, broken down, choked with rubbish.

God is always the same—equally near, equally strong, equally gracious. But our possession of His grace, and the impartation of His grace through us to others, vary, because our faith, our earnestness, our desires vary. True, these no doubt are also His gifts and His working, and nothing, that we say now, touches in the least on the great truth that God is the sole originator of all good in man; but while believing that, as no less sure in itself than blessed in its message of confidence and consolation to us, we also have to remember, "If any man open the door, I will come in to him." We may have as much of God as we want, as much as we can hold, far more than we deserve. And if ever the victorious power of His Church seems to be almost paling to defeat, and His servants to be working no deliverance upon the earth, the cause is not to be found in Him, who is "without variableness," nor in His gifts, which are "without repentance," but solely in us, who let go our hold of the eternal might. No ebb withdraws the waters of that great ocean; and if sometimes there be sand and ooze where once the flashing flood brought life and motion, it is because careless warders have shut the sea-gates.

An awful responsibility lies on us. We can resist and refuse, or we can open our hearts and draw into ourselves His strength. We can bring into operation those energies which act through faithful men faithfully proclaiming the faithful saying; or we can limit the Holy One of Israel. "Why could not we cast him out? Because of your unbelief."

With what grand confidence, then, may the weakest of us go to his task. We have a right to feel that, in all our labour, God works with us; that, in all our words for Him, it is not we that speak but the Spirit of our Father that speaks in us; that if humbly and prayerfully, with self-distrust and resolute effort to crucify our own intrusive individuality, we wait for Him to enshrine Himself within us, strength will come to us, drawn from the deep fountains of God, and we, too, shall be able to say, "Not I, but the grace of God in me."

How this sublime confidence should tell on our characters, destroying all self-confidence, repressing all pride, calming all impatience, brightening all despondency, and ever stirring us anew to deeds worthy of the exceeding greatness of the power which worketh in us—I can only suggest.

On all **sides** motives for strenuous toil press in upon us—chiefly those great examples which we have now been contemplating. But, besides these, there are other forms of activity which may point the same lesson. Look at the energy *around* us. We live in a busy time. Life goes swiftly in all regions. Men seem to be burning away faster than ever before, in an atmosphere of pure oxygen. Do we work as hard for God as the world does for itself? Look at the energy *beneath* us: how evil in every form is active; how lies and half-truths propagate themselves quick as the blight on a rose-tree; how prof ligacy, and crime, and all the devil's angels are busy on his errands. If *we* are sitting drowsy by our camp-fires, the enemy is on the alert. You can hear the tramp of their legions and the rumble of their artillery through the night, as they march to their posts on the field. It is no time for God's sentinels to nod. If they sleep, the adversary does not, but glides in the congenial darkness, sowing his baleful tares. Do we work as hard for God as the emissaries of evil do for their master? Look at the energy *above* us. On the throne of the universe is the immortal Power who slumbereth not nor sleepeth. Before the altar of the heavens is the Priest of the world, the Lord of His Church, "who ever liveth to make intercession for us." Round Him stand perfected spirits, the watchmen on the walls of the New Jerusalem, who "rest not day and night, saying, Holy, Holy, Holy, Lord God Almighty." From His presence come, filling the air with the rustle of their swift wings, and the light of their flame-faces, the ministering spirits who evermore do His commandments, hearkening to the voice of His word. And we, Christian brethren, where are we in all this magnificent concurrence of activity, for purposes which ought to be dear to our hearts as they are to the heart of God? Do we work for Him as He and all that are with Him do? Is His will done by us on earth, as it is in heaven?

Alas! alas! have we not all been like those three Apostles whose eyes were heavy with sleep, even while the Lord was wrestling with the tempter under the gnarled olives in the pale moonlight of Gethsemane? Let us arouse ourselves from our sloth. Let us lift up our cry to God : " Awake, awake, put on strength, O arm of the Lord, as in the ancient days, in the generations of old ;" and the answer shall sound from the heavens to us as it did to the prophet, an echo of his prayer turned into a command: " Awake, awake, put on *thy* strength, O Zion."

MEMORY, HOPE, AND WORK.

PHILIPPIANS iii. 13, 14.

This one thing I do, forgetting those things that are behind, and reaching forth unto those things which are before, I press toward the mark for the prize.

HOPE is usually the gift of the young. They naturally look forward to the long years before them, and think comparatively little of the brief space through which they have already passed. But the centre of interest changes with alarming, though imperceptible, rapidity; and, almost before we know it, we find ourselves beginning to look more frequently and more tenderly backwards, and to think less of the possibilities that lie in that swiftly-narrowing tract between us and the grave. So, the future for the young; the present for the middle-aged; the past for the old.

But these words of my text, so full of hope and unflagging energy, are the words of "Paul the aged:" are written in the very last year of his life. A few months more and he will be saying, "I have fought the good fight; I have finished my course." A little while after that, he will be a martyr.   He is a prisoner already. For thirty years he has been at work ; his work is almost done.   And yet he says, "I think nothing of all that, that is behind me : I forget it all ; and here, old and worn and broken as I am, with the light of unquench-able hope in me, I press toward the mark, and forget everything that is behind, to reach out to that which is before."   A grand picture !   Whether it be a true prin-ciple upon which he acted or not, at least it worked well in his life, and made it to the very end the noble thing that it was, "bringing forth fruit in old age, to show that the Lord was upright."

But I think that these words carry with them broad practical lessons for us all, dear friends, as to the way in which you and I should order the scheme of our lives, and I venture to put them just into three advices, three counsels : Live in the future ; let that bright, certain, infinite future dwarf the imperfect past ; and let hopes for the future and the lessons of the past unite in strenuous concentration of effort in the present.   "This one thing I do, forgetting those things which are behind me, reach-ing forth to the things before, I press toward the mark."

I. First, then, take this as the advice commended to us by the example here taught us : *Live in the future.*

Look at that image, "I press toward the mark, reach-ing forth unto the things that are before."   Of course the reference is to a runner.   And there is great emphasis and power in that word translated "reaching forth unto." The idea is that of a man stretching himself out towards something as a runner does, with his body straining forward, the hand and the eye drawn onward toward the goal. He does not think of the furlongs that he has passed, he heeds not the nature of the ground over which he runs. The sharp stones in the path do not stay him, nor the flowerets in the grass catch his glance. The white faces of the crowd around the course are seen as in a flash as he rushes past them to the winning-post, and the parsley-garland that hangs there is all that he is conscious of. "They do it to obtain a corruptible crown, but we an incorruptible." Let us, with eye and hand flung forward, "stretch out towards the things that are before," and imitate that example,—not in the fierce whirl of excitement, indeed, but in fixed regard to, and concentrated desire of, the mark and the prize.

These two objects of hope and effort seem to be distinct, though inseparably connected ; and it is, perhaps, not over-interpreting a metaphor to see a separate meaning in each. The mark is reached by the runner's effort : the prize is the reward given for victory. If we are to distinguish between them, which seems probable, we may say that the former stands for " being made conformable unto Christ's death," and the latter for "attaining unto the resurrection of the dead ;" or, in other words, that the mark is the absolute and thorough moral likeness to our Lord, which ought to be the goal and aim of all Christian effort, while the prize is whatsoever of glory and felicity, besides, the great Judge of the race may be pleased to bestow on us, unworthy, who by His grace have been kept from falling.

If we are right in this distinction, the language of the

text suggests important principles about the relation of these two things. There is to be a distinct recognition of moral perfection as our conscious aim. Our efforts after it are allowably stimulated by the hope of the fair reward which it ensures. We hear a great deal from some folk at present of the selfishness of having any "respect to the recompense of reward." Paul, at any rate, gives no adhesion to such exaggerations, but knows enough of the difficulties of the race to be thankful that he can stir his flagging energies, by the vision of the prize. But he will insist that it is to be reached only through attaining to the mark; that is to say, if you want to be blessed, you must be good; if you want to get to heaven, you must be like Christ. Do you press toward the mark, and the moment that you toe the line where the winning-post stands, at that moment on your brow will fall the amaranthine garland. "The man shall be crowned if he have striven lawfully." Set your efforts towards the goal, and God will give you the reward.

But, passing by such considerations, let us look a little more closely at that thought of living in the future, as the true attitude for Christian men. Our highest condition in this world (and I believe we might leave out the words, in *this* world) is not the attainment of perfection, but the recognition of heights above us which are as yet unreached.

Such recognition is the condition of all progress of all sorts. The artist that is satisfied with his transcript of his ideal will not grow any more   There is a touching story, I remember, told of a modern sculptor, who was found standing in front of his masterpiece, sunk in sad reverie; and when they asked him why he was so sad, "Because," he answered, "I am satisfied with it." "I have embodied," he would say, "all that I can think or feel. There it is. And because there is no discord between what I dream and what I can do, I feel that the limit of my growth is reached." Unless we saw an ideal far above us, the actual would never approximate toward it. Therefore dissatisfaction and unrest, born of the contrast between these two, are the very prerogative of man, by which he is marked off from the happy contentment of the brutes beneath him, and from the happy peacefulness of the angels of God. We may venture to apply Christ's words to this subject, "The foxes have holes, and the birds of the air have nests, but" man "has not where to lay his head." If he could rest, he could not grow. And so from generation to generation, for the individual and for the species, the condition of our progress is a distance beckoning us, and a feeling that we have not already attained, neither are already perfect.

And that is eminently true of the moral and spiritual progress which make the Christian conception of "growth in grace." The very characteristic of that idea is the indefinite approximation to an infinite perfection. The type for us is the express image of God, the complete man, Jesus Christ. To that supreme beauty our nature is capable of unlimited approach. No man knows how much of goodness, nobleness, and wisdom are possible for any man, or for himself. No bounds can be set to that progress of growth. There is no point on that happy voyage, beyond which icy cliffs and a frozen ocean forbid a passage ; but before us, to the verge of our horizon of to-day, stretch the open waters; and when that furthest point of vision lies as far astern as it now gleams ahead, the same boundless sapphire sea will draw our yearning desires, and bear onwards our advancing powers.

There are two ideas in that notion of "perfection." The one is extirpation of sin, the other is the attainment to the likeness of the infinite God. Sin may be extirpated, and yet the second process may be but in its infancy. A man may have no transgression, no blot, no stain upon his nature, and yet his nature may not have expanded to all the width which is possible for it. He may have "a clean heart," and yet the elastic walls of his heart may not have widened by their pulsations to their utmost capacity. He may be pure, and in that sense perfect, and yet may have lying before him a dazzling path of light along which he may travel through all eternity, and beyond its furthest bound he may know that there lie leagues, and that if he got to what now seems the furthest possible point, he will still have to say, "Not as though I had already attained, neither were already perfect, but I follow after."

Even the former of these two elements of perfection is not fully attained on earth, and how much less the latter! Our task, then, can never be completed here, and our eyes must ever be directed to what still remains unfinished of the Divine purpose in us. Such is the law of our condition on earth. Is it confined to earth? Shall we stop growing in heaven, or is our entrance there not much rather the beginning of a new stage in that growth, which has no end? There, too, will not our loftiest attainments be as a platform on which we can stand to reach up to what is still higher? Will not the attitude of spirit which is inseparable from all advancement and all health here, be the attitude for the other world too? Shall we sit there, with nothing to wish for, drowsy amid languid contentments? or shall we there, as now, feel the truest sense of life in aspiration and motion towards unattained but possible good and goodness? Shall we not then possess all that hope by which now we are saved, with only the loss of the painful sense of incompleteness? May not a fair vision of what we shall be gleam before us, which shall excite wishes without tumult, consciousness of non-possession without pain, aspiration without the pang of yearning, certainty without fear, and work without effort? Will not the glories that are to be revealed exercise their attraction over us then? Will not this still be the description of our Being—"reaching forth unto those things that are before"? I believe that thus we shall live through all the eternities that are before us, growing wiser, nobler, stronger, greater; plunging deeper into God, and being more and more filled with more and more of Him. So we shall move for ever as in ascending spirals that rise ever higher, and draw ever closer to the throne we compass and to Him that dwells alone ; ever perfect, yet ever growing, **for we have an** inexhaustible Saviour to absorb into our hearts, and we have hearts that never reach the ultimate term and bound of their indefinite possibility of receiving.

This grand future should draw our thoughts all the more to itself, because it is not only grand but certain. For this is the difference between the Christian man's hope and any other, that it is not an air-blown bubble, that it is not a dream, a fancy, a peradventure, that it has a "Verily, verily, I say unto you" to rest upon, that all the promises of God "in Him are Yea and Amen." Unrest comes with anticipation, when it has only possibilities to cleave to. Terror accompanies even Hope when her sunny eyes try to pierce the future by their own power alone. Ordinary experience tells us that we can be sure of the past because it is dead, and that it is folly to reckon upon the future; and that thus, between yesterday that has ceased to be anything to us, and to-morrow which we cannot see, our poor life is saddened and dwarfed to one fleeting point. But, believing on Him who was and is to come, we may reverse that bitter experience. To our thankful memory the past will live. And to our instructed hopes there is a certain future on which we can build, far more glorious, far more beautiful, than anything in the past. "We *know* that when He shall appear we shall be like Him." We have a future which is an object, not of dim expectation and trembling hope, but of knowledge. Our word is not "it may be," but "it will be." We have a certainty, not a possibility or a probability, for our hope. That which is to be becomes as firm reality as that which has been. Hope is truer than history. The future is not cloudland, but solid fruitful soil on which we can plant a firm foot.

And therefore that habit of living in the future should make us glad and confident. We should not keep the contemplation of another state of existence to make us sorrowful, nor allow the transiency of this present to shade our joys. Our hope should make us buoyant, and should keep us firm. It is an anchor of the soul. All men live by hope, even when it is fixed upon the changing and uncertain things of this world. But the hopes of men, who have not their hearts fixed upon God, try to grapple themselves on the cloudrack that rolls along the flanks of the mountains, and *our* hopes pierce within that veil and lay hold of the Rock of Ages, that towers above the flying vapours. Let us then be strong, for our future is not a dim peradventure, nor a vague dream, nor a fancy of our own, nor a wish turning itself into a vision, but it is made and certified by Him who is the God of all the past and of all the present. It is built upon His word, and the brightest hope of all its brightness is the enjoyment of more of His presence, and the possession of more of His likeness. That hope is certain. Therefore let us live in it, and "reach forth unto the things that are before."

And that is the true temper, dear friends, depend upon it, for wider interests than our own. Live in the future for yourselves; live in the future for the world. Believe in a millennium of some sort or other, in better times than we have ever seen, or than the world has ever seen; because that faith is wrapped up and involved in

the confidence that God loves us all, and is shaping this
earth's history to His own perfect aim.   And instead of
looking back and lamenting, and saying, "The former
days were better than now," let us for ourselves and for
those whom we love, for the Church, for the world, gaze
into the future with bold, bright, hopeful eyes like the
prophets of old, and see as the one figure that towers
above all the dimness of the unknown generations the
conquering Servant of the Lord, and as the last result of
the perplexed history of the race—"the tabernacle of
God is with men."   For us let the Cross be the central
point of the world, from which are evolved the powers
that will lead to that blessed time when, after all stum-
blings and wanderings, our brethren with us will have
reached the mark, and the purposes of God will be
finished, in a redeemed humanity and a perfected world.
Thus, "reach forth unto the things that are before."

II. Then secondly, side by side with this piece of
advice, practically illustrated by the Apostle himself,
there comes another.   *Let that bright, certain, infinite*
future dwarf for us the narrow and stained past—"forgetting the things that are behind."

It seems a strange advice, and one which goes dead
in the teeth of a great deal that calls itself experimental
Christianity.   But it is a very wise advice for all that,
and reaches, I think, very deep into the secret of the
strength of the Christian character.

Paul meant, I suppose, only, "I don't count that these
past efforts are complete, I don't build anything upon
what I have done already; I recognize the mark of

imperfection over it all, I fling it behind me and press onwards." But I think we may widen the application a little further than that, and include all sorts of backward looking, as being (except under very special conditions and in a very limited degree) a positive weakness and impediment to a man in running the race that lies before him. Why? Well, for one thing, plainly and simply enough, time given to such an occupation is time withdrawn from the actual work of life. A man cannot run with his eyes looking over his shoulder; he is sure to knock against somebody, and so be delayed and hindered. There may have been floating in the Apostle's mind, combined with the image of the racer, some remembrance of the old story in the Book of Genesis about Lot's wife. She looked back, and as she stood there gazing behind her, precious time was irrevocably lost, the fugitives swept on in front, and the swift-flying death that struck her with terror, as she saw it pressing close behind, caught her up. She was whelmed in the fiery destruction that filled the air; and as the shower of ashes at Pompeii moulded themselves over the forms of the poor wretches that were smothered by them, and preserved till to-day the print of the very waves of their hair and the texture of their dress, "salt" was crusted round that living core, and she perished, because she wasted in trembling retrospect the flying moments which, rightly used, would have set her in safety. And if you stand there, looking backwards instead of making the best of your way out of evil, the evil will catch *you* up, or, at least, will be so much the nearer you by all the time wasted.

Remembering always tends to become a substitute for Doing. The temperament which is perpetually looking back, the praiser of a past period, is in all respects the antithesis of his who takes occasion by the forelock, and is vigorous just because he is full of hope. Politically and socially, the great things are done by the men whose minds are full of "all the wonder that shall be." Their visions impel to labour that their visions may become realities. You get little work out of the people whose fond regrets dwell in the good old times, and whose word of command is "as you were." The same thing is true for the individual life. "The native hue of resolution is sicklied o'er by the pale" pensive light cast upon the Past, and he who lives in his former self is a dreamer, not a worker.

But then take the injunction more specifically, and think whether it does not especially hold with reference to our Christian life, and that in all its aspects.

Forget past failures. They are apt to weaken you. We are prone to take them as measures of the future, and say, "Oh, I shall never be any better; I have always broken down just at that point, and it is no use trying to expect I shall ever get beyond it. Experience teaches me my limits."

Yes, experience does teach us our limits. It teaches us, if I might use such a phrase, the limits of our possible "lateral extension:" that there are certain things we never shall be able to do if we try all our lives, and all eternity as well; but it does not say anything about the limits in *our* line of things. It teaches us what is not congruous to our temperament and character, but not what perfection our temperament and character can reach. There is no limit in that respect; and to look back and say, "I take the past, with all my blunders, and weaknesses, and sins, as the measure of my possible future," is to deny the infinite power of God's gospel, the indefinite expansibility of the human soul, and the sure promise of the Divine Spirit. "Forget the things that are behind." The failures do *not* indicate what we shall be. In reference to me it is not true, "that which is to be hath already been," but it is true that I may day by day grow liker my Lord. "The path of the just is as a shining light, that shineth more and more until the noon of the day."

Then I would say again, *be sure to forget past attainments.* They are apt to become food for complacency, for every vain confidence. We are tempted to look back to past religious emotions and experiences as grounds of our hope. We are apt to say, "At such and such a time I saw clearly God's truth, I felt deeply the love of Christ, I was profoundly conscious of my own sin. Then I was converted, or then I was growing in Christian attainments. I *did* conquer evil. Then my heart was cleaving to the Lord, and filled with His fulness." Yes, and you ate your dinner twenty years ago; will that serve to strengthen you for to-day? And the rain fell on the young spring wheat when you and I were boys; will that do anything towards this year's harvest? These past emotions were good for the time. If you turn them into the occasion for complacent confidence, as to the present and as to the future, they are simply bad. "Forget the things that are behind." And still further remember, too, that these attainments in the past, like the failures in the past, do very often become practically to us the measure of our notion as to what we shall be able to do in the future. You find some certain type of Christian character, or exercise of Christian grace, that is easy and natural to you, and you come to know how to do it. It becomes your special habit, which is all right, but it also tends to become your limit, which is wrong. Habits are like fences, very good to guard the soul from sudden incursions of trespassers, but very bad when the trunk has grown up and presses against their stubborn rings. And many of us simply keep on doing the narrow round of things that we fancy we can do well, or have always been in the way of doing, like barrel-organs, grinding our poor little set of tunes, without any notion of the great sea of music that stretches all round about us, and which is not pegged out upon our cylinders at all.

"Forget, then, the things that are behind,"—your failures, lest they should seem the measure of your future, and teach despair; your successes, lest they should be the measures of your future, and so teach you either a vain confidence, or a limitation of that noble ambition which ought to impel every Christian heart "to fulfil all the good pleasure of His goodness and the work of faith."

But I venture to say still further, *forget your past circumstances,* whether they be sorrows or joys. The one are not without remedy, the other not perfect. " God is able to give thee much more than these ;" to bring again blessednesses which surpass all those joys, and compensations which shall make the sorrows seem like a dream. Both are past; why remember them ? Why should you carry about parched corn when you dwell among fields white unto harvest? Why carry putrid water in the bottom of a rancid skin, when living in a land of fountains and brooks that run among the hills ? Why clasp a handful of poor withered flowers, when the grass is sown with their bright eyes opening to the sunshine? Why live in the Past, which, after all, was not so precious when it was a Present, since we have God and Christ now as then, and in them may find peace for to-day, and endless hope for every morrow ? " Forget the things that are behind."

Well, of course, one need not exaggerate this advice. To cut oneself utterly loose from the past is revolutionary madness in a nation, and it is quite as bad in a man. To teach oneself nothing out of it would be to fall below the level of our dogs ; or to prove oneself untameable as flies, that have not, I suppose, any memory to speak of.

But God gives us Remembrance in order that we may make great and blessed use of it. It may teach us humility and hopeful thankfulness. Often in our hearts may shine an after-glow of uncoruscating light from a sun that has set, more lustrous, more calm, more mellow than when its hot fervours were falling on our heads—a pensive, clear, and still Indian summer of memory after the sultry

autumn has gone.   But when we have given memory its
rights, and learned its lessons of practical wisdom and of
softened hearts, let us take care of letting sentimental
indulgence in it sap our souls, and eat out our energy for
the strenuous work of the moment.   That "brook by the
way" is but to refresh us as we go on to the fight.   A
few drops caught up in the palm as we run will help
us, but if we fall on our knees to slake our thirst, we
have to fling down our sword and unbrace our helmet,
and we prove ourselves too self-indulgent for the army
of God.

Some of you may say, "Ah, easy to say, Forget.   How
can I forget?"   The Apostle tells us : not by resolving
to do it.   Such efforts simply deepen the impression in
our minds of the thought which we want to get out of our
minds.   The way is, as he says, "reaching forth unto
the things that are before."   That is to say, this wise
oblivion is to be won, not so much by forcing ourselves
to forget as by letting ourselves anticipate.   If we will
occupy mind and heart with that sunlit future, it will
dim the past, however bright it may be.   The billows
are white on the long track astern, but he does not see
them who stands at the bow, and marks the foam of the
sparkling waves that leap up to meet the good ship as
she comes onward.   It is when you turn your *face* to the
sun, that a golden path of light stretches across the sea,
right before your feet.   It is when we look forward and
Christward, letting Him fill the future and the future
fill our hearts, and it is only then, that we can forget
the things that are behind.

III. And then, to come to that final piece of practical wisdom that lies in this text : *Let hopes for the Future and lessons from the Past alike lead to strenuous work in the Present.* "This one thing I do." Be the past what it may, be the future what it may, I know that I cannot reach the one nor forget the other, except by setting myself with all my might and main to present duties, and by reducing all duties to various forms of one great life-purpose. Concentration of all our strength on a single aim, and that aim pursued through all our days with their varying occupations—what a grand ideal of life that is! Such concentration has for its complement a wise diffusion, which two are practically hard to reconcile, and yet, if separated, tend to evil, the one to rigid narrowness, the other to desultory frivolity. But when the "many things" are regarded as branches of "the one thing needful," and the choice of that for ours consecrates and restrains within bounds the care about these, then the life will become serene and harmonious, and we shall be able to mingle in all active duties, nor move from our place at His feet. We shall work hard and heartily at various tasks, and yet the good part shall not be taken away from us by outward activity, any more than our possession of it will sequester us from vigorous service of God and man.

What a noble thing any life becomes, that has driven through it the strength of a uniting single purpose, like a strong shaft of iron bolting together the two tottering walls of some old building!

"But," you say, "how is that possible? My life is cut

up into bits, frittered away into fragments. I cannot bring it into a unity, even apart from the breach that is made in it by the difference between things secular and things sacred. I cannot make even the week-days one whole, and how can I bring them and Sunday into harmony?"

Well, it is the spirit in which, not the thing at which, we work, that makes life one. The accident of occupation may vary, but the purpose and goal may remain the same. A hundred processes may go to the manufacture of one article, though it were only a pin, and all the multitude of our engagements may, if we will, be stages in one great journey.

We may always be trying to be like Jesus Christ, whatever be the material at which we toil. He was subject to His parents; He, I suppose, worked in a carpenter's shop; He had passed through all varieties of 'earthly life. Whether we eat or drink, or whatever we do, we may do all to the glory of God.

Such work will be the natural issue of Christian hope for the future, and of Christian oblivion of the past.

Take that as the test of your Christian hope. If it makes you work, it is right; if it does not, there is something wrong with it. If it makes you think that it does not matter how you scramble though this life, because you are going to another, you mistake the relations of the two lives. If it makes you restless, impatient, uneasy here, for ever sickening to get out of this place where God has set you, in order to sink into some restful region beyond, you have not yet learned the nobleness and greatness, either of the region to which you go, or the region in which you live. But if your hope proves itself by the patience that comes from it, and your faith by the work which it produces, and your love by the labour which is its result, then you may believe that the hope and faith and love are of God, and will abide for ever. Being in Christ, it is safe to forget the past, it is possible to be sure of the future, it is possible to be diligent in the present. Then how blessed such a life ! For the past—"I was the chief of sinners, but I obtained mercy ;" for the future—"We shall bear the image of the heavenly ;" for the present—"I press toward the mark."

And all our course, if we have Him with us in the vessel, will be like sailing down some fair widening stream amongst rocky mountains and vine-clad slopes, with the blue sky above, every now and then seeming to be landlocked, and yet, as each rocky headland is rounded, the shining river stretches itself into another reach, and, laving the base of another verdant hill, slides broader and deeper to the great sea to which we come. "Wherefore, forgetting the things that are behind, and reaching forth unto those that are before, let us press toward the mark for the prize of the high calling of God in Christ Jesus."

Tell His disciples, and Peter, that He goeth before you into Galilee.

THE prevailing tradition of Christian antiquity ascribes this Gospel to John Mark, sister's son to Barnabas, and affirms that in composing it he was in some sense the "interpreter" of the Apostle Peter. Some confirmation of this alleged connection between the Evangelist and the Apostle may be gathered from the fact that the former is mentioned by the latter, as with him when he wrote his First Epistle. And, in the Gospel itself, there are some little peculiarities which seem to look in the same direction. A certain speciality is traceable here and there, both in omissions of incidents in the Apostle's life recorded by some of the other Evangelists, and in the addition of slight facts concerning him unnoticed by them.

Chief among these is the place which his name holds in this very remarkable message, delivered by the angels to the women who came to Christ's tomb on the resurrection morning. Matthew, who also reports the angels' words, has only "tell His disciples." Mark adds the words, which must have come like wine and oil to the bruised heart of the denier, "tell His disciples *and Peter*." To the others, it was of less importance that his name should have been named then ; to him it was life from the dead, that he should have been singled out to receive a word of forgiveness and a summons to meet his Lord ; as if He had said through His angel messengers—" I would see them all ; but whoever may stay behind, let not *him* be wanting to our glad meeting again."

We find, too, that the same individualizing of the Apostle, which led to his being thus greeted with the first thoughts of his risen Lord, led also to an interview with Him on that same day, about which not a syllable of detail is found in any Gospel, though the fact is known to the whole body of the disciples. For when the two friends who had met Christ at Emmaus came back in the night with their strange tidings, their eagerness to tell their joyful news is anticipated by the eagerness of the brethren to tell *their* wonderful story. "The Lord is risen indeed, and hath appeared to Simon." Paul, too, gives that meeting, when the Lord was alone with the penitent, the foremost place in his list of the evidences of Christ's resurrection, "He was seen of Cephas." What passed then is hidden from all eyes. The secrets of that hour of deep contrition and healing love Peter kept secretly curtained from sight, in the innermost chamber of his memory. But we may be sure that then forgiveness was sought and granted, and the bond that fastened him to his Lord was welded together again, where it had snapped, and was the stronger because it had been broken, and at the point of fracture.

The man must be first re-united to his Saviour, before the Apostle can be reinstated in his functions. In secrecy, not beheld by any, is the personal act of restoration to love and friendship effected : and then in public, before his brethren, who were concerned in his official position, but not in his personal relation to his Lord, the reappointment of the pardoned disciple to his apostleship takes place. His sin had had a public aspect, and his threefold denial must, in so far as it was an outward act, be effaced by his threefold confession. Then he becomes again "Peter,"—not merely "Simon Bar Jonas ;" and, as the Book of the Acts shows, never ceases to hear the Divine commissions, "Feed my sheep," "Follow me ;" nor ever forgets the lessons he had learned in these bitter hours of self-loathing, and in the rapturous moments when again he saw his Lord.

Putting all these things together—this message from Christ, the interview which followed it, and the subsequent history of the Apostle—we have a connected series of facts which may illustrate for us, better than many dry words of mine could do, the triumph over sin of the forgiving love of Christ.

I. Notice, then, first the *loving message with which He beckons the wanderer back.*

If we try to throw ourselves back into the Apostle's black thoughts during the interval between his denial and the resurrection morning, we shall better feel what this love-token from the grave must have been to him. His natural character, as well as his real love for his Master, ensured that his lies could not long content him. They were uttered so vehemently because they were uttered in spite of inward resistance. Overpowered by fear, beaten down from all his vain-glorious self-confidence by a woman-servant's sharp tongue and mocking eye, he lied— and then came the rebound. The same impulsive vehemence which had hurried him into the fault, would swing him back again to quick penitence when the cock crew, and that Divine face, turning slowly from before the judg- ment-seat with the sorrow of wounded love upon it, silently said, "Remember." We can fancy how that bitter weeping, which began so soon, grew more passionate and more bitter when the end came. We are singularly happy if we do not know the pang of remembering some fault to the loved dead—some hasty word, some momentary petulance, some selfish disregard of their happiness, some sullen refusal of their tenderness. How the thought that it is all irrevocable now embitters the remorse! How passionately we long that we could have one of the moments again, which seemed so trivial while we pos- sessed them, that we might confess and be forgiven, and atone! And this poor, warm-hearted, penitent denier had to think that his very last act, to the Lord whom he loved so well, had been such an act of cowardly shrinking from acknowledging Him; and henceforward his memory of that dear face was to be for ever saddened by that last look! That they should have parted so! that that sad gaze was to be the last he should ever have, and that *it* was to haunt him for the rest of his life! We can understand

how heavily the hours passed on that dreary Saturday.
If, as seems probable, he was with John in his home,
whither the latter had led the mother of our Lord, what
a group were gathered there, each with a separate pang
from the common sorrow !

Into this sorrow come the tidings that all was not over,
that the irrevocable was not irrevocable, that perhaps
new days of loyal love might still be granted, in which the
doleful failure of the past might be forgotten ; and then,
whether before or after his hurried rush to the grave we
need not here stay to inquire, follows the message of our
text, a word of forgiveness and reconciliation, sent by the
Lord as the herald and outrider of His own coming, to
bring gladness and hope ere He himself draws near.

Think of this message as a revelation *of love that is
stronger than death.*

The news of Christ's resurrection must have struck awe,
but not necessarily joy, into the disciples' hearts.   The
dearest ones suffer so solemn a change to our apprehensions when they pass into the grave, that to many a man
it would be maddening terror to meet those whom he
loved and still loves.   So there must have been a spasm
of fear even among Christ's friends when they heard of
Him as risen again, and much confusing doubt as to what
would be the amount of resemblance to His old self.
They probably dreaded to find Him far removed from
their familiar love, forgetful perhaps of much of the old
life, with other thoughts than before, with the atmosphere
of the other world round about Him, which glorified Him
indeed, but separated Him too from those whose grosser

lungs could live only in this thick air. These words of our text would go far to scatter all such fears. They link on the future to the past, as if His first thought when He rose had been to gather up again the dropped threads of their intercourse, and to carry on their ancient concord and companionship, as though no break had been at all. For all the disciples, and especially for him who is especially named, they confirm the identity of Christ's whole dispositions towards them now, with those which He had before. Death has not changed Him at all. Much has been done since He left them; the world's history has been changed, but nothing which has happened has had any effect on the reality of His love, and on the inmost reality of their companionship. In these respects they are where they were, and even Calvary and the tomb are but as a parenthesis. The old bonds are all re-knit, and the junction is all but imperceptible.

This is how we have to think of our Lord now, and for us. We, too, may have our share in that message, which came like morning twilight before He shone upon their darkness. To them it proclaimed a love which was stronger than death. To us it may foretell a love which is stronger than all change of circumstances. He is no more parted from us by the Throne than from them by the Cross. He descended into the lower parts of the earth, and His love lived on. So it does now, when He has ascended up far above all heavens. Love knows no difference of place, conditions, or functions. From out of the blazing heart of the Glory, the same tender face looks that bent over sick men's pallets, and that turned on Peter in the judgment-hall. The hand that holds the sceptre of the universe is the hand that was nailed to the Cross, and that was stretched out to that same Peter when he was ready to sink. The breast that is girt with the golden girdle of priestly sovereignty is the same tender home on which John's happy head rested in placid contentment. All the love that ever flowed from Christ flows from Him still. To Him, "whose nature and whose name are Love," it matters nothing whether He is in the house at Bethany, or in the upper room, or hanging on the Cross, or lying in the grave, or risen from the dead, or seated on the right hand of God. He is the same everywhere and always. " I have loved thee with an everlasting love."

Again, this message is the revelation of *a love that is not turned away by our sinful changes.*

Peter may have thought that he had, with his own words, broken the bond between him and his Lord. He had renounced his allegiance; was the renunciation to be accepted? He had said, "I am not one of them;" did Christ answer, "Be it so, one of them thou shalt no more be?" The message from the woman's lips settled the question, and let him feel that, though his grasp of Christ had relaxed, Christ's grasp of him had not. He might change, he might cease for a time to prize his Lord's love, he might cease either to be conscious of it or to wish for it; but that love could not change. It was unaffected by his unfaithfulness, even as it had not been originated by his fidelity. Repelled, it still lingered beside him. Disowned, it still asserted its property in him. Being reviled, it blessed; being persecuted, it endured; being defamed, it entreated; and, patient through all wrongs and changes, it loved on till it had won back the erring heart, and could fill it with the old blessedness again.

And is not that same miracle of long-enduring love presented before every one of us, as in Christ's heart for us? True, our sin interferes with our sense of it, and modifies the form in which it must deal with us; but, however real and disastrous may be the power of our evil in troubling the communion of love between us and our Lord, and in compelling Him to smite before He binds up, never forget that our sin is utterly impotent to turn away the tide, that sets to us from the heart of Christ. The earthborn vapours may hang about the low levels, and turn the gracious sun himself into a blood-red ball of lurid fire; but they reach only a little way up, and high above their region is the pure blue, and the blessed light pours down upon the upper surface of the white mist, and thins away its opaqueness, and dries up its clinging damp, and at last parts it into filmy fragments that float out of sight, and the dwellers on the green earth see the light, which was always there even when they could not behold it, and which, by shining on, has conquered all the obstructions that veiled its beams. Sin is mighty, but one thing sin cannot do, and that is to make Christ cease to love us. Sin is mighty, but one other thing sin cannot do, and that is to prevent Christ from manifesting His love to us sinners, that we may learn to love and so may cease to sin. Christ's love is

2ND SER. F

not at the beck and call of our fluctuating affections. It has its source deeper than in the springs in our hearts, in the depths of His own nature. It is not the echo or the answer to ours, but ours is the echo to His; and that being so, our changes do not reach to it, any more than earth's seasons affect the sun. For ever and ever He loves. Whilst we forget Him, He remembers us. Whilst we repay Him with neglect or with hate, He still loves. If we believe not, He still abides faithful to His merciful purpose, and, in spite of all that we can do, will not deny Himself, by ceasing to be the incarnate Patience, the perfect Love. He is Himself the great ensample of that "charity" which His Apostle painted; He is not easily provoked; he is not soon angry; He beareth all things; He hopeth all things. We cannot get away from the sweep of His love, wander we ever so far. The child may struggle in the mother's arms, and beat the breast that shelters it with its little hand; but it neither hurts nor angers that gentle bosom, and the firm but loving grasp holds it fast. He carries as a nurse does His wayward children, and, blessed be His name, His arm is too strong for us to shake it off, His love too divine for us to dam it back.

And still further, here we *see a love which sends a special message because of special sin.*

If one was to be singled out from the little company to receive by name the summons of the Lord to meet Him in Galilee, we might have expected it to have been that faithful friend who stood beneath the cross, till his Lord's own command sent him to his own home; or that

weeping mother whom he then led away with him ; or
one of the two who had been turned from secret disciples
into confessors by the might of their love, and had laid
His body with reverent care in the grave in the garden.
Strange reward for true love that they should be merged
in the general message, and strange recompense for
treason and cowardice that Peter's name should be thus
distinguished ! Is sin, then, a passport to His deeper
love ? Is the murmur true after all, " Thou never gavest
me a kid, but as soon as this thy son is come, which
hath devoured thy living with harlots, thou hast killed
for him the fatted calf ?" Yes, and no. No, inasmuch
as the unbroken fellowship hath in it calm and deep
joys which the returning prodigal does not know, and all
sin lays waste and impoverishes the soul. Yes, inasmuch
as He, who knows all our needs, knows that the denier
needs a special treatment to bring him back to peace,
and that the further a poor heart has strayed from Him,
the mightier must be the forthputting of manifested love,
if it is to be strong enough to travel across all the dreary
wastes, and draw back again, to its orbit among its sister
planets, the wandering star. The depth of our need
determines the strength of the restorative power put
forth. They who had not gone away would come at the
call addressed to them all, but he who had sundered
himself from them and from the Lord would remain in
his sad isolation, unless some special means were used to
bring him back. The more we have sinned, the less can
we believe in Christ's love ; and so the more we have
sinned, the more marvellous and convincing does He

make the testimony and operations of His love to us.   It
is ever to the poor bewildered sheep, lying panting in the
wilderness, that He comes.   Among His creatures, the
race which has sinned is that which receives the most
stupendous proof of the seeking Divine love.   Among
men, the publicans and the harlots, the denying Peters and
the persecuting Pauls, are they to whom the most persuasive entreaties of His love are sent, and on whom the
strongest powers of His grace are brought to bear.   Our
sin cannot check the flow of His love.   More marvellous
still, our sin occasions a mightier burst of the manifestation of His love, for eyes blinded by selfishness and carelessness, or by fear and despair, need to see a brightness
beyond the noonday sun, ere they can behold the
amazing truth of His love to them ; and what they need,
they get.   " Go, tell Peter."

Here, too, is the revelation of a love which *singles out
a sinful man by name.*

Christ does not deal with us in the mass, but soul by
soul.   Our finite minds have to lose the individual in
order to grasp the class.   Our eyes see the wood far off on
the mountain side, but not the single trees, nor each flut-
tering leaf. We think of "the race"—the twelve hundred
millions that live to-day, and the uncounted crowds that
have been, but the units in that inconceivable sum are
not separate in our view.   But He does not generalize so,
He has a clear individualizing knowledge of each ; each
separately has a place in His mind or heart.   To each
He says, " I know thee by name."   He loves the world,
because He loves every single soul with a distinct love

And His messages of blessing are as specific and individualizing as the love from which they come. He speaks to
each of us as truly as He singled out Peter here, as truly
as when His voice from heaven said, "Saul, Saul." English names are on His lips as really as Jewish ones. He
calls to *thee* by *thy* name—thou hast a share in His love.
To thee the call to trust Him is addressed, and to thee forgiveness, help, purity, life eternal are offered. Thou hast
sinned; that only infuses deeper tenderness into His be-
seeching tones. Thou hast gone further from Him than
some of thy fellows; that only makes His recovering
energy greater. Thou hast denied His name; that only
makes Him speak thine with more persuasive invitation.

Look, then, at this one instance of a love stronger
than death, mightier than sin, sending its special greeting
to the denier, and learn how deep the source, how
powerful the flow, how universal the sweep of that river
of the love of God, which streams to us through the
channel of Christ His Son!

II. Notice, secondly, *the secret meeting* between our Lord
and the Apostle. That is the second stage in the victorious
conflict of Divine love with man's sin. As I have said,
this interview took place on the day of the resurrection,
apparently before our Lord joined the two sorrowful
travellers to Emmaus, and certainly before He appeared
to the company gathered by night in the closed chamber.
The fact was well known, for it is referred to by Luke
and by Paul, but nothing beyond the fact seems to have
been known, or at all events is made public by them.
All this is very significant and very beautiful.

What tender consideration there is in meeting Peter alone, before seeing him in the companionship of the others ! How painful would have been the rush of the first emotions of shame awakened by Christ's presence, if their course had been checked by any eye but his own beholding them ! How impossible it would have then been to have poured out all the penitent confessions with which his heart must have been full, and how hard it would have been to have met for the first time, and not to have poured them out ! With most loving insight, then, into the painful embarrassment, and dread of unsympathizing standers-by, which must have troubled the contrite Apostle, the Lord is careful to give him the opportunity of weeping his fill on His own bosom, unrestrained by any thought of others, and will let him sob out his contrition to His own ear alone. Then the meeting in the upper chamber will be one of pure joy to Peter, as to all the rest. The emotions which he has in common with them find full play, in that hour when all are reunited to their Lord. The experience which belongs to himself alone has its solitary hour of unrecorded communion. The first to whom He, who is separate from sinners, appeared was Mary Magdalene, out of whom He had cast seven devils. The next were the women who bore this message of forgiveness ; and probably the next was the one among all the company who had sinned most grievously. So wondrous is the order of His preferences, coming ever nearest to those who need Him most.

And may we not regard this secret interview as representing for us what is needed on our part to make Christ's forgiving love our own? There must be the personal contact of my soul with the loving heart of Christ, the individual act of my own coming to Him, and, as the old Puritans used to say, "my transacting" with Him. Like the ocean of the atmosphere, His love encompasses me, and in it I live, and move, and have my being. But I must let it flow into my spirit, and stir the dormant music of my soul. I can shut it out, sealing my heart love-tight against it. I do shut it out, unless by my own conscious, personal act I yield myself to Him, unless by my own faith I come to Him, and meet Him, secretly and really as did the penitent Apostle, whom the message, that proclaimed the love of his Lord, emboldened to meet the Lord who loved, and by His own lips to be assured of forgiveness and friendship. It is possible to stumble at noontide, as in the dark. A man may starve, outside of barns filled with plenty, and his lips may be parched with thirst, though he is within sight of a broad river flowing in the sunshine. So a soul may stiffen into the death of self and sin, even though the voice, that wakes the dead to a life of love, be calling to it. Christ and His grace are yours if you will, but the invitations and beseechings of His mercy, the constant drawings of His love, the all-embracing offers of His forgiveness, may be all in vain, if you do not grasp them and hold them fast by the hand of faith.

That personal act must be preceded by the message of His mighty love. Ever He sends such messages as heralds of His coming, just as He prepared the way for His own approach to the Apostle, by the words of our text. Our faith must follow His word. Our love can only be called forth by the manifestation of His. But His message must be followed by that personal act, else His word is spoken in vain, and there is no real union between our need and His fulness, nor any cleansing contact of His grace with our foulness.

Mark, too, the intensely individual character of that act of faith by which a man accepts Christ's grace. Friends and companions may bring the tidings of the risen Lord's loving heart, but the actual closing with the Lord's mercy must be done by myself, alone with Him.

As if there were not another soul on earth, I and He must meet, and in solitude deep as that of death, each man for himself must yield to Incarnate Love, and receive eternal life. The flocks and herds, the wives and children have all to be sent away, and Jacob is left alone, before the mysterious Wrestler comes whose touch of fire lames the whole nature of sin and death, whose inbreathed power strengthens to hold Him fast till He speaks a blessing who desires to be overcome, and makes our yielding to Him our prevailing with Him. As one of the old mystics called prayer "the flight of the lonely man to the only God," so we may call the act of faith the meeting of the soul alone with Christ alone. Do you know anything of that personal communion ? Have you, your own very self, by your own penitence for your own sin, and your own thankful faith in the Love which thereby becomes truly yours, isolated yourself from all companionship, and joined yourself to

Christ? Then, through that narrow passage where we can only walk singly, you will come into a large place. The act of faith, which separates us from all men, unites us for the first time in real brotherhood, and they who, one by one, come to Jesus and meet Him alone, next find that they "are come to the city of God, to an innumerable company, to the festal choirs of angels, to the Church of the First-born, to the spirits of just men made perfect."

III. Notice, finally, the *gradual cure* of the pardoned Apostle.

He was restored to his office, as we read in the supplement to John's Gospel. In that wonderful conversation, full as it is of allusions to Peter's fall, Christ asks but one question, "Lovest thou Me?" That includes everything. Hast thou learned the lesson of My mercy? hast thou responded to My love? then thou art fit for My work, and beginning to be perfected. So the third stage in the triumph of Christ's love over man's sin is, when we, beholding that love flowing towards us, and accepting it by faith, respond to it with our own, and are able to say, "Thou knowest that I love Thee."

The all-embracing question is followed by an equally comprehensive command, "Follow thou Me," a two-worded compendium of all morals, a precept which naturally results from love, and certainly leads to absolute perfectness. With love to Christ for motive, and Christ Himself for pattern, and following Him for our one duty, all things are possible, and the utter defeat of sin in us is but a question of time.

And the certainty, as well as the gradual slowness of

that victory, are well set forth by the future history of the Apostle. We know how his fickleness passed away, and how his vehement character was calmed and conso- lidated into resolved persistency, and how his love of distinction and self-confidence were turned in a new direction, obeyed a divine impulse, and became powers. We read how he started to the front; how he guided the Church in the first stage of its development; how when- ever there was danger he was in the van, and whenever there was work his hand was first on the plough; how he bearded and braved rulers and councils; how—more difficult still for him—he lay quietly in prison sleeping like a child, between his guards, on the night before his execution; how—most difficult of all—he acquiesced in Paul's superiority; and, if he still needed to be with- stood and blamed, could recognize the wisdom of the rebuke, and in his calm old age could speak well of the rebuker as his "beloved brother Paul." Nor was the cure a change in the great lines of his character. These remain the same, the characteristic excellences possible to them are brought out, the defects are curbed and cast out. The new man is the old man with a new direction, obeying a new impulse, but retaining its in- dividuality. Weaknesses become strengths; the sancti- fied character is the old character sanctified; and the law of the change is, "Every man hath his proper gift of God, one after this manner, and another after that."

It is very instructive to observe how deeply the ex- periences of his fall, and of Christ's mercy then, had im- pressed themselves on his memory, and how constantly

they were present with him all through his after-life.
His Epistles are full of allusions which show this. For
instance, to go a step further back in his life, he remembered that the Lord had said to him, " Thou art Peter,"
and that his pride in that name had helped to his rash
confidence, and so to his sin. Therefore, when he is
cured of these, he takes pleasure in sharing his honour
with his brethren, and writes, " Ye also, as living stones,
are built up." He remembered the contempt for others
and the trust in himself with which he had said, " Though
all should forsake Thee, yet will not I ;" and, taught what
must come of that, he writes, " Be clothed with humility,
for God resisteth the proud, and giveth grace to the
humble." He remembers how hastily he had drawn his
sword and struck at Malchus, and he writes, " If when
ye do well and suffer for it, ye take it patiently, this
is acceptable with God." He remembers how he had
been surprised into denial by the questions of a sharp-
tongued servant-maid, and he writes, " Be ready always
to give an answer to every man that asketh you a reason
of the hope that is in you, with meekness." He remembers how the pardoning love of his Lord had
honoured him, unworthy, with the charge, " Feed My
sheep," and he writes, ranking himself as one of the
class to whom he speaks—" The elders I exhort, who
am also an elder . . . . feed the flock of God." He
remembers that last command, which sounded ever
in his spirit, " Follow thou Me," and discerning now,
through all the years that lay between, the presumptuous
folly and blind inversion of his own work and his

Master's which had lain in his earlier question, "Why cannot I follow Thee now? I will lay down my life for Thy sake"—he writes to all, "Christ also suffered for us, leaving us an example, that ye should follow His steps."

So well had he learned the lesson of his own sin, and of that immortal love which had beckoned him back, to peace at its side and purity from its hand. Let us learn how the love of Christ, received into the heart, triumphs gradually but surely over all sin, transforms character, turning even its weakness into strength, and so, from the depths of transgression and very gates of hell, raises men to God.

To us all this Divine message speaks. Christ's love is extended to us; no sin can stay it; no fall of ours can make Him despair. He will not give us up. He waits to be gracious. This same Peter once asked, "How oft shall my brother sin against me and I forgive him?" And the answer, which commanded unwearied brotherly forgiveness, revealed inexhaustible Divine pardon—"I say not unto thee until seven times, but until seventy times seven." The measure of the Divine mercy, which is the pattern of ours, is completeness ten times multiplied by itself; we know not the numbers thereof. "Let the wicked forsake his way . . . and let him return unto the Lord, for He will have mercy upon him; and to our God, for He will multiply to pardon."

TRANSFORMATION BY BEHOLDING.

2 COR. iii. 18.

We all, with open face beholding as in a glass the glory of the Lord, are changed into the same image.

THIS whole section of the Epistle in which our text occurs is a remarkable instance of the fervid richness of the Apostle's mind, which acquires force by motion, and like a chariot-wheel catches fire as it revolves. One of the most obvious peculiarities of his style is his habit of " going off at a word." Each thought is, as it were, barbed all round, and catches and draws into sight a multitude of others, but slightly related to the main purpose in hand. And this characteristic gives at first sight an appearance of confusion to his writings. But it is not confusion, it is richness. The luxuriant underwood which this fertile soil bears, as some tropical forest, does not choke the great trees, though it drapes them.

Paul's immediate purpose seems to be to illustrate the frank openness which ought to mark the ministry of Christianity. He does this by reference to the veil which Moses wore when he came forth from talking with God. There, he says in effect, we have a picture of the Old Dispensation—a partial revelation, gleaming through a veil, flashing through symbols, expressed here in a rite, there in a type, there again in an obscure prophecy, but never or scarcely ever fronting the world with an unveiled face and the light of God shining clear from it. Christianity is, and Christian teachers ought to be, the opposite of all this. It has, and they are to have, no esoteric doctrines, no hints where plain speech is possible, no reserve, no use of symbols and ceremonies to overlay truth, but an intelligible revelation in words and deeds, to men's understandings. It and they are plentifully to, " declare the thing as it is."

But he gets far beyond this point in his uses of his illustration. It opens out into a series of contrasts between the two revelations. The veiled Moses represents the clouded revelation of old. The vanishing gleam on his face recalls the fading glories of that which was abolished ; and then, by a quick turn of association, he thinks of the veiled readers in the synagogues, copies, as it were, of the lawgiver with the shrouded countenance ; only too significant images of the souls obscured by prejudice and obstinate unbelief, with which Israel trifles over the uncomprehended letter of the old law.

The contrast to all this lies in our text. Judaism had the one lawgiver who beheld God, while the people tarried below. Christianity leads *us all* to the mount of vision, and lets the lowliest pass through the fences, and go up where the blazing glory is seen. Moses veiled the face that shone with the irradiation of Deity. We with unveiled face are to shine among men. He had a momentary gleam, a transient brightness; we have a perpetual light. Moses' face shone, but the lustre was but skin deep. But the light that we have is inward, and works transformation into its own likeness.

So there is here set forth the very loftiest conception of the Christian life as direct vision, universal, manifest to men, permanent, transforming.

I. Note, then, first, *that the Christian life is a life of contemplating and reflecting Christ.*

It is a question whether the single word rendered in our version " beholding as in a glass," means that, or "reflecting as a glass does." The latter seems more in accordance with the requirements of the context, and with the truth of the matter in hand. Unless we bring in the notion of reflected lustre, we do not get any parallel with the case of Moses. Looking into a glass does not in the least correspond with the allusion which gave occasion to the whole section—to the glory of God smiting him on the face, till the reflected lustre with which it glowed became dazzling, and needed to be hid. And again, if Paul is here describing Christian vision of God as only indirect, as in a mirror, then that would be a point of inferiority in us as compared with Moses, who saw Him face to face. But the whole tone of the context prepares us to expect a setting forth of the particulars in which the Christian attitude towards the manifested God is above the Jewish. So, on the whole, it seems better to suppose that Paul meant "mirroring," than "seeing in a mirror."

But, whatever be the exact force of the word, the thing intended includes both acts. There is no reflection of the light without a previous reception of the light. In bodily sight, the eye is a mirror, and there is no sight without an image of the thing perceived formed in the perceiving eye. In spiritual sight, the soul which beholds is a mirror, and at once beholds and reflects. Thus, then, we may say that we have in our text the Christian life described as one of contemplation and manifestation of the light of God.

The great truth of a direct, unimpeded vision, as belonging to Christian men on earth, sounds strange to many of us. "That cannot be," you say; "does not Paul himself teach that we see through a glass darkly? Do we not walk by faith and not by sight? 'No man hath seen God at any time, nor can see Him;' and besides that absolute impossibility, have we not veils of flesh and sense, to say nothing of the covering of sin 'spread over the face of all nations,' which hide from us even so much of the eternal light as His servants above behold, who see His face and bear His name on their foreheads?"

But these apparent difficulties drop away when we take into account two things: first, the object of vision, and second, the real nature of the vision itself.

As to the former, who is the Lord, whose glory we receive on our unveiled faces? It is Jesus Christ. Here, as in the overwhelming majority of instances where that name occurs in the New Testament, it is the name of the manifested God, our brother. The glory which we behold and give back is not the incomprehensible, incommunicable lustre of the absolute Divine perfectness, but that glory which, as John says, we beheld in Him who tabernacled with us, full of grace and truth; the glory which was manifested in loving, pitying words, and loveliness of perfect deeds; the glory of the will resigned to God, and of God dwelling in and working through the will; the glory of faultless and complete manhood, and therein of the express image of God.

And as for the vision itself, that seeing which is denied to be possible is the bodily perception and the full comprehension of the Infinite God; that seeing which is affirmed to be possible, and actually bestowed in Christ, is the beholding of Him with the soul by faith; the immediate direct consciousness of His presence, the perception of Him in His truth by the mind, the sense of Him in His love by the heart, the contact with His gracious energy in our recipient and opening spirits. Faith is made the antithesis of sight. It is so, in certain respects. But faith is also paralleled with and exalted above the mere bodily perception. He who believing grasps the living Lord, has a contact with Him as immediate and as real as that of light with the eyeball, and knows Him with a certitude as reliable as that which sight gives. "Seeing is believing," says sense; "Believing is seeing," says the spirit which clings to the Lord, "whom having not seen" it loves. A bridge of perishable flesh, which is not myself but my tool, connects me with the outward world. *It* never touches myself at all, and I

2ND SER. G

know it only by trust in my senses. But nothing inter venes between my Lord and me, when I love and trust Then Spirit is joined to spirit, and of His presence I have the witness in myself. He is the light, which proves its own existence by revealing itself, which strikes with quick ening impulse on the eye of the spirit that beholds by faith. Believing we see, and, seeing, we have that light in our souls to be "the master light of all our seeing." We need not think that to know by the consciousness of our trusting souls is less than to know by the vision of our fallible eyes; and though flesh hides from us the spiritual world in which we float, yet the only veil which really dims God to us—the veil of sin, the one separating prin ciple—is done away in Christ, for all who love Him; so as that he who has not seen and yet has believed, has but the perfecting of his present vision to expect, when flesh drops away and the apocalypse of the heaven comes. True, in one view, "we see through a glass darkly;" but also true, "we all, with unveiled face, behold and reflect the glory of the Lord."

Then note still further Paul's emphasis on the *univer-sality* of this prerogative: "We *all*." This vision does not belong to any select handful : the spiritual aristocracy of God's Church is not the distinction of the lawgiver, the priest, or the prophet; does not depend upon special powers or gifts, which in the nature of things can only belong to a few. There is none of us so weak, so low, so ignorant, so compassed about with sin, but that upon our happy faces that light may rest, and into our darkened hearts that sunshine may steal.

In that Old Dispensation, the light that broke through clouds was but that of the rising morning. It touched the mountain tops of the loftiest spirits: a Moses, a David, an Elijah caught the early gleams; while all the valleys slept in the pale shadow, and the mist clung in white folds to the plains. But the moon has come, and, from its steadfast throne in the very zenith, the sun which never sets pours down its rays into the deep recesses of the narrowest gorge, and every little daisy and hidden flower catches its brightness, and there is nothing hid from the heat thereof. We have no privileged class or caste now; no fences to keep out the mob from the place of vision, while lawgiver and priest gaze upon God. Christ reveals Himself to all His servants in the measure of their desire after Him. Whatsoever special gifts may belong to a few in His Church, the greatest gift belongs to all. The servants and the handmaidens have the Spirit, the children prophesy, the youths see visions, the old men dream dreams. "The mob," "the masses," "the plebs," or whatever other contemptuous name the heathen aristocratic spirit has for the bulk of men, makes good its standing within the Church, as possessor of Christ's chiefest gifts. Redeemed by Him, it can behold His face and be glorified into His likeness. Not as Judaism with its ignorant mass, and its enlightened and inspired few: we *all* behold the glory of the Lord.

Again, this *contemplation involves reflection*, or giving forth the light which we behold.

They who behold Christ have Christ formed in them,

as will appear in my subsequent remarks. But apart from such considerations, which belong rather to the next part of this sermon, I touch on this thought here for one purpose—to bring out this idea—that what we *see* we shall certainly *show*. That will be the inevitable result of all true possession of the glory of Christ. The necessary accompaniment of vision is reflecting the thing beheld. Why, if you look closely enough into a man's eye, you will see in it little pictures of what he beholds at the moment; and if our hearts are beholding Christ, Christ will be mirrored and manifested on our hearts. Our characters will show what we are looking at, and ought, in the case of Christian people, to bear His image so plainly, that men cannot but take knowledge of us that we have been with Jesus.

This ought to lead all of us who say that we have seen the Lord, to serious self-questioning. Do beholding and reflecting go together in our cases? Are our characters like those transparent clocks, where you can see not only the figures and hands, but the wheels and works? Remember that, consciously and unconsciously, by direct efforts and by insensible influences on our lives, the true secret of our being ought to come, and will come forth to light. The convictions which we hold, the emotions that are dominant in our hearts, will mould and shape our being. If we have any deep living perception of Christ, bystanders, looking into our faces, will be able to tell what it is that up yonder is making them like the faces of the angels—even the vision of the opened heavens and of the exalted Lord. These two things are inseparable : the one describes the attitude and action of the Christian man towards Christ; the other the very same attitude and action in relation to men. And you may be quite sure that, if little light comes from a Christian character, little light comes into it; and if it be swathed in thick veils from men, there will be no less thick veils between it and God.

Nor is it only that our fellowship with Christ will, as a matter of course, show itself in our characters, and beauty born of that communion "shall pass into our face," but we are also called on, as Paul puts it here, to make direct conscious efforts for the communication of the light which we behold. As the context has it, God hath shined in our hearts, that we might give the light of the knowledge of the glory of God in the face of Christ Jesus. Away with all veils ! No reserve, no fear of the consequences of plain speaking, no diplomatic prudence regulating our frank utterance, no secret doctrines for the initiated ! We are to "renounce the hidden things of dishonesty." Our power and our duty lies in the full exhibition of the truth. We are only clear from the blood of men when we, for our parts, make sure that if any of it be hid, it is hid not by reason of obscurity or silence on our parts, but only by reason of the blind eyes, before which the full-orbed radiance gleams in vain. All this is as true for every one possessing that universal prerogative of seeing the glory of Christ, as it is for an Apostle. The business of all such is to make known the name of Jesus, and if from idleness, or carelessness, or selfishness, they shirk that plain duty, they are counteracting God's very purpose in shining on their hearts, and going far to quench the light which they darken.

Take this, then, Christian men and women, as a plain practical lesson from this text. You are bound to manifest what you believe, and to make the secret of your lives, in so far as possible, an open secret. Not that you are to drag into light before men the sacred depths of your own soul's experience. Let these lie hid. The world will be none the better for your confessions, but it needs your Lord. Show Him forth, not your own emotions about Him. What does the Apostle say close by my text? "We preach not ourselves, but Christ Jesus the Lord." Self-respect and reverence for the sanctities of our deepest emotions forbid our proclaiming these from the house-tops. Let these be curtained, if you will, from all eyes but God's, but let no folds hang before the picture of your Saviour that is drawn on your heart. See to it that you have the unveiled face turned towards Christ to be irradiated by His brightness, and the unveiled face turned towards men, from which shall shine every beam of the light which you have caught from your Lord. "Arise! shine, for thy light is come, and the glory of the Lord is risen upon thee!"

II. Notice, secondly, that this *life of contemplation is therefore a life of gradual transformation.*

The brightness on the face of Moses was only skin-deep. It faded away, and left no trace. It effaced none of the marks of sorrow and care, and changed none of the lines of that strong, stern face. But, says Paul, the glory which we behold sinks inward, and changes us, as we look, into its own image. Thus the superficial lustre, that had neither permanence nor transforming power, becomes an illustration of the powerlessness of law to change the moral character into the likeness of the fair ideal which it sets forth. And, in opposition to its weakness, the Apostle proclaims the great principle of Christian progress, that the beholding of Christ leads to the assimilation to Him.

The metaphor of a mirror does not wholly serve us here. When the sunbeams fall upon it, it flashes in the light, just because they do not enter its cold surface. It is a mirror, because it does not drink them up, but flings them back. The contrary is the case with these sentient mirrors of our spirits. In them, the light must first sink in before it can ray out. They must first be filled with the glory, before the glory can stream forth. They are not so much like a reflecting surface as like a bar of iron, which needs to be heated right down to its obstinate black core, before its outer skin glow with the whiteness of a heat that is too hot to sparkle. The sunshine must fall on us, not as it does on some lonely hill-side, lighting up the grey stones with a passing gleam that changes nothing, and fades away, leaving the solitude to its sadness; but as it does on some cloud cradled near its setting, which it drenches and saturates with fire till its cold heart burns, and all its wreaths of vapour are brightness palpable, glorified by the light which lives amidst its mists. So must we have the glory sink into us before it can be reflected from us. In deep inward beholding we must have Christ in our hearts, that He may shine forth from our lives.

And this contemplation will be gradual transformation. There is the great principle of Christian morals. "We all beholding . . . are changed." The power to which is committed the perfecting of our characters lies in looking upon Jesus. It is not the mere beholding, but the gaze of love and trust that moulds us by silent sympathy into the likeness of His wondrous beauty, who is fairer than the children of men. It was a deep true thought which the old painters had, when they drew John as likest to his Lord. Love makes us like. We learn *that* even in our earthly relationships, where habitual familiarity with parents and dear ones stamps some tone of voice or look, or little peculiarity of gesture, on a whole house. And when the infinite reverence and aspiration which the Christian soul cherishes to its Lord are superadded, the transforming power of loving contemplation of Him becomes mighty beyond all analogies in human friendship, though one in principle with these. What a marvellous thing that a block of rude sandstone, laid down before a perfect marble, shall become a copy of its serene loveliness just by lying there! Lay your hearts down before Christ. Contemplate Him. Love Him. Think about Him. Let that pure face shine upon heart and spirit, and as the sun photographs itself on the sensitive plate exposed to its light, and you get a likeness of the sun by simply laying the thing in the sun, so He will "be formed in you." Iron near a magnet becomes magnetic. Spirits that dwell with Christ become Christ-like.

The Roman Catholic legends put this truth in a coarse way, when they tell of saints who have gazed on some ghastly crucifix till they have received, in their tortured flesh, the copy of the wounds of Jesus, and have thus borne in their body the marks of the Lord. The story is hideous and gross, the idea beneath is ever true. Set your faces towards the Cross with loving reverent gaze, and you will "be conformed unto His death," that in due time you may "be also in the likeness of His resurrection."

Dear friends, surely this message—"behold and be like"—ought to be very joyful and enlightening to many of us, who are wearied with painful struggles after isolated pieces of goodness, that elude our grasp. You have been trying and trying and trying half your lifetime to cure faults, and make yourselves better and stronger. Try this other plan. Let love draw you, instead of duty driving you. Let fellowship with Christ elevate you, instead of seeking to struggle up the steeps on hands and knees. Live in sight of your Lord, and catch His spirit. The man that travels with his face northwards has it grey and cold. Let him turn to the warm south, where the midday sun dwells, and his face will glow with the brightness that he sees. "Looking unto Jesus" is the sovereign cure for all our ills and sins. It is the one condition of running with patience "the race that is set before us." Efforts after self-improvement which do not rest on it will not go deep enough, nor end in victory. But from that gaze will flow into our lives a power which will at once reveal the true goal, and brace every sinew for the struggle to reach it. Therefore, let us cease from self, and fix our eyes on our Saviour till His image imprints itself on our whole nature.

Such transformation, it must be remembered, comes gradually. The language of the text regards it as a life-long process. "We *are* changed;" that is a continuous operation. "From glory to glory;" that is a course which has well-marked transitions and degrees. Be not impatient if it be slow. It will take a lifetime. Do not fancy that it is finished with you. Life is not long enough for it. Do not be complacent over the partial transformation which you have felt. There is but a fragment of the great image yet reproduced in your soul, a faint outline dimly traced, with many a feature wrongly drawn, with many a line still needed, before it can be called even approximately complete. See to it that you neither turn away your gaze, nor relax your efforts till all that you have beheld in Him is repeated in you.

Likeness to Christ is the aim of all religion. To it conversion is introductory; doctrines, devout emotion, worship and ceremonies, churches and organizations are valuable as auxiliary. Let that wondrous issue of God's mercy be the purpose of our lives, and the end as well as the test of all the things which we call our Christianity. Prize and use them as helps towards it, and remember that they are helps only in proportion as they show us that Saviour, the image of whom is our perfectness, the beholding of whom is our transformation.

III. Notice, lastly, *that the life of contemplation finally becomes a life of complete assimilation.*

'Changed into the same image, from glory to glory."

The lustrous light which falls upon Christian hearts from the face of their Lord is permanent, and it is progressive. The likeness extends, becomes deeper, truer, every way perfecter, comprehends more and more of the faculties of the man; soaks into him, if I may say so, until he is saturated with the glory: and in all the extent of his being, and in all the depth possible to each part of that whole extent, is like his Lord. That is the hope for heaven, towards which we may indefinitely approximate here, and at which we shall absolutely arrive there. There we expect changes which are impossible here, while compassed with this body of sinful flesh. We look for the merciful exercise of His mighty working to "change the body of our lowliness, that it may be fashioned like unto the body of His glory;" and that physical change in the resurrection of the just rightly bulks very large in good men's expectations. But we are somewhat apt to think of the perfect likeness of Christ, too much in connection with that transformation that begins only after death, and to forget that the main transformation must begin here. The glorious, corporeal life like our Lord's, which is promised for heaven, is great and wonderful, but it is only the issue and last result of the far greater change in the spiritual nature, which by faith and love begins here. It is good to be clothed with the immortal vesture of the resurrection, and in that to be like Christ. It is better to be like Him in our hearts. His true image is that we should feel as He does, should think as He does, should will as He does; that we should have the same sympathies, the same loves, the same attitude towards God, and the same attitude towards men. It is that His heart and ours should beat in full accord, as with one pulse, and possessing one life. Wherever there is the beginning of that oneness and likeness of spirit, all the rest will come in due time. As the spirit, so the body. The whole nature must be transformed and made like Christ's, and the process will not stop till that be accomplished in all who love Him. But the beginning here is the main thing, which draws all the rest after it as of course. "If the spirit of Him that raised up Jesus from the dead dwell in you, He that raised up Christ from the dead shall also quicken your mortal bodies, by His spirit that dwelleth in you."

And, while this complete assimilation in body and spirit to our Lord is the end of the process which begins here by love and faith, my text, carefully considered, adds a further very remarkable idea. "We are all changed," says Paul, "into the *same* image." Same as what? Possibly the same as we behold; but more probably the phrase, especially "image" in the singular, is employed to convey the thought of the blessed likeness of all who become perfectly like Him. As if he had said, "Various as we are in disposition and character, unlike in the histories of our lives, and all the influences that these have had upon us, differing in everything but the common relation to Jesus Christ, we are all growing like the same image, and we shall come to be perfectly like it, and yet each retain his own distinct individuality." "We being many are one, for we are all partakers of one."

Perhaps, too, we may connect with this another idea, which occurs more than once in Paul's Epistles. In that to the Ephesians, for instance, he says that the Christian ministry is to continue, till a certain point of progress has been reached, which he describes as our *all* coming to " *a* perfect *man.*" The whole of us together make a perfect man : the whole make one image. That is to say, perhaps the Apostle's idea is, that it takes the aggregated perfectness of the whole Catholic Church, one throughout all ages, and containing a multitude that no man can number, to set worthily forth anything like a complete image of the fulness of Christ. No one man, even raised to the highest pitch of perfection, and though his nature be widened out to perfect development, can be the full image of that infinite sum of all beauty; but the whole of us taken together, with all the diversities of natural character retained and consecrated, being collectively His body which He vitalizes, may, on the whole, be not a wholly inadequate representation of our perfect Lord. Just as we set round a central light sparkling prisms, each of which catches the glow at its own angle, and flashes it back of its own colour, while the sovereign completeness of the perfect white radiance comes from the blending of all their separate rays, so they who stand round about the starry throne receive each the light in his own measure and manner, and give forth each a true and perfect, and altogether a complete image of Him that enlightens them all, and is above them all.

And whilst thus all bear the same image, there is no monotony ; and while there is endless diversity, there is no discord. Like the serene choirs of angels in the old monk's pictures, each one with the same tongue of fire on the brow, with the same robe flowing in the same folds to the feet, with the same golden hair, yet each a separate self, with his own gladness, and a different instrument for praise in his hand, and his own part in that "undisturbed song of pure concent," we shall all be changed into the same image, and yet each heart grow great with its own blessedness, and each spirit bright with its own proper lustre of individual and characteristic perfection.

The law of the transformation is the same for earth and for heaven. Here we see Him in part, and beholding grow like. There we shall see Him as He is, and the likeness will be complete. That Transfiguration of our Lord (which is described by the same word as occurs in this text) may become for us the symbol and the prophecy of what we look for. As with Him, so with us; the indwelling glory shall come to the surface, and the countenance shall shine as the light, and the garments shall be "white as no fuller on earth can white them." Nor shall that be a fading splendour, nor shall we fear as we enter into the cloud, nor, looking on Him, shall flesh bend beneath the burden, and the eyes become drowsy, but we shall be as the Lawgiver and the Prophet who stood by Him in the lambent lustre, and shone with a brightness above that which had once been veiled on Sinai. We shall never vanish from His side, but dwell with Him in the abiding temple which He has built, and there, looking upon Him for ever, our happy souls shall change as they gaze, and behold Him more perfectly as they change, for "we know that when He shall appear we shall be like Him, for we shall see Him as He is."

DAVID'S CRY FOR PARDON.

PSALM li. 1, 2.

Blot out my transgressions. Wash me throughly from mine iniquity, and cleanse me from my sin.

A WHOLE year had elapsed between David's crime and David's penitence. It had been a year of guilty satisfaction not worth the having; of sullen hardening of heart against God and all His appeals. The thirty-second Psalm tells us how *happy* David had been during that twelvemonth, of which he says, " My bones waxed old through my roaring all the day long. For day and night Thy hand was heavy on me." Then came Nathan with his apologue, and with that dark threatening that the sword should never depart from his house, the fulfilment of which became a well-head of sorrow to the king for the rest of his days, and gave a yet deeper poignancy of anguish to the crime of his spoiled favourite Absalom. The stern words have their effect. The frost that had bound his soul melted all away, and he confessed his sin, and was forgiven then and there. " I have sinned against the Lord," is the confession as recorded in the historical books; and, says Nathan, "The Lord hath made to pass from thee the iniquity of thy sin." Immediately, as would appear from the narrative, that very same day, the child of Bathsheba and David was smitten with fatal disease, and died in a week. And it is *after* all these events—the threatening, the penitence, the pardon, the punishment—that he comes to God, who had so freely forgiven, and likewise so sorely smitten him, and wails out these prayers : "Blot out my transgressions, wash me from mine iniquity, cleanse me from my sin."

One almost shrinks from taking as the text of a sermon words like these, in which a broken and contrite spirit groans for deliverance, and which are, besides, hallowed by the thought of the thousands who have since found them the best expression of their sacredest emotions. But I would fain try not to lose the feeling that breathes through the words, while seeking for the thoughts which are in them, and hope that the light which they throw upon the solemn subjects of guilt and forgiveness, may not be for any of us a mere cold light.

I. Looking then at this triad of petitions, they teach us first *how David thought of his sin.*

You will observe the reiteration of the same earnest cry in all these clauses. And if you glance over the remainder of this psalm, you will find that he asks for the gifts of God's Spirit, with a similar threefold repetition. Now this characteristic of the whole psalm is worth notice in the outset. It is not a mere piece of Hebrew parallelism. The requirements of poetical form but partially explain it. It is much more the earnestness of a soul that cannot be content with once asking for the blessings and then passing on, but dwells upon them with repeated supplication, not because it thinks that it shall be heard for its much speaking, but because it longs for them so eagerly.

And besides that, though the three clauses do express the same general idea, they express it under various modifications, and must be all taken together before we get the whole of the Psalmist's thought of sin.

Notice again that he speaks of his evil as transgressions and as sin, first using the plural and then the singular. He regards it first as being broken up into a multitude of isolated acts, and then as being all gathered together into one knot, as it were, so that it is one thing. In one aspect it is " my transgressions "—" that thing that I did about Uriah, that thing that I did about Bath-sheba, those other things that these dragged after them." One by one the acts of wrong-doing pass before him. But he does not stop there. They are not merely a number of deeds, but they have, deep down below, a common root from which they all came—a centre in which they all inhere. And so he says, not only " Blot out my *transgressions*," but "Wash me from mine *iniquity*." He does not merely generalize, but he sees and he feels what you and I have to feel, if we judge rightly of our evil actions, that we cannot take them only in their plurality as so many separate deeds, but that we must recognize them as coming from a common source, and

2ND SER   **H**

we must lament before God not only our sins but our sin—not only the outward acts of transgression, but that alienation of heart from which they all come ; not only sin in its manifold manifestations as it comes out in the life, but in its inward roots as it coils round our hearts. You are not to confess acts alone, but let your contrition embrace the principle from which they come.

Further, in all the petitions we see that the idea of his own single responsibility for the whole thing is upper-most in David's mind. It is *my* transgression, it is *mine* iniquity, and *my* sin. He has not learned to say with Adam of old, and with some so-called wise thinkers to-day : " I was tempted, and I could not help it." He does not talk about " circumstances," and say that they share the blame with him. He takes it all to himself. " It was *I* did it. True, I was tempted, but it was my soul that made the occasion a temptation. True, the circumstances led me astray, but they would not have led me astray if I had been right, and *where* as well as *what* I ought to be." It is a solemn moment when that thought first rises in its revealing power to throw light into the dark places of our souls. But it is likewise a blessed moment, and without it we are scarcely aware of ourselves. Conscience quickens consciousness. The sense of transgression is the first thing that gives to many a man the full sense of his own individuality. There is nothing that makes us feel how awful and incom-municable is that mysterious personality by which every one of us lives alone after all companionship, so much as the contemplation of our relations to God's law.

"Every man shall bear his own burden." "Circum-stances," yes; "bodily organization," yes; "tempera-ment," yes; "the maxims of society," "the conven-tionalities of the time," yes. All these things have something to do with shaping our single deeds and with influencing our character; but after we have made all allowances for these influences which affect *me*, let us ask the philosophers who bring them forward as diminish-ing or perhaps annihilating responsibility, "And what about that *me* which these things influence?" After all, let me remember that the deed is *mine*, and that every one of us shall, as Paul puts it, give account of *himself* before God.

Passing from that, let me point for one moment to another set of ideas that are involved in these petitions. The three words which the Psalmist employs for sin give prominence to different aspects of it. Transgression is not the same as iniquity, and iniquity is not the same as sin. They are not aimless, useless synonyms, but they have each a separate thought in them. The word rendered "transgression" literally means rebellion, a breaking away from and setting oneself against lawful authority. That translated "iniquity" literally means that which is twisted, bent. The word in the original for "sin" literally means missing a mark, an aim. And this threefold view of sin is no discovery of David's, but is the lesson which the whole Old Testament system had laboured to print deep on the national consciousness. That lesson, taught by law and ceremonial, by denuncia-tion and remonstrance, by chastisement and deliverance,

the penitent king has learned.   To all men's wrong-
doings these descriptions apply, but most of all to his.
Sin is ever, and his sin especially is, rebellion, the deflec-
tion of the life from the straight line which God's law
draws so clearly and firmly, and hence a missing the
aim.

Think how profound and living is the consciousness of
sin which lies in calling it *rebellion*. It is not merely,
then, that we go against some abstract propriety, or
break some impersonal law of nature when we do wrong,
but that we rebel against a rightful Sovereign.   In a
special sense this was true of the Jew, whose nation
stood under the government of a Divine King, so that
sin was treason, and breaches of the law acts of rebellion against God.   But it is as true of us all.   Our
theory of morals will be miserably defective, and our
practice will be still more defective, unless we have
learned that morality is but the garment of religion,
that the definition of virtue is obedience to God, and
that the true sin in sin is not the yielding to impulses
that belong to our nature, but the assertion in the act
of yielding, of our independence of God and of our
opposition to His will.   And all this has application to
David's sin.   He was God's viceroy and representative,
and he sets to his people the example of revolt, and lifts
the standard of rebellion.   It is as if the ruler of a
province declared war against the central authority of
which he was the creature, and used against it the very
magazines and weapons with which it had entrusted him.
He had rebelled, and in an eminent degree, as Nathan

said to him, given to the enemies of God occasion to blaspheme.

Not less profound and suggestive is that other name for sin, that which is twisted, or bent, mine "iniquity." It is the same metaphor which lies in our own word "wrong," that which is wrung or warped from the straight line of right. To that line, drawn by God's law, our lives should run parallel, bending neither to the right hand nor to the left. But instead of the firm directness of such a line, our lives show wavering deformity, and are like the tremulous strokes in a child's copy-book. David had the pattern before him, and by its side his unsteady purpose, his passionate lust had traced this wretched scrawl. The path on which he should have trodden was a straight course to God, unbending like one of these conquering Roman roads, that will turn aside for neither mountain nor ravine, nor stream nor bog. If it had been thus straight, it would have reached its goal. Journeying on that way of holiness, he would have found, and we shall find, that on it no ravenous beast shall meet us, but with songs and everlasting joy upon their lips the happy pilgrims draw ever nearer to God, obtaining joy and gladness in all the march, until at last sorrow and sighing shall flee away. But instead of this he had made for himself a crooked path, and had lost his road and his peace in the mazes of wandering ways. "The labour of the foolish wearieth every one of them, because he knoweth not how to come to the city."

Another very solemn and terrible thought of what

sin is, lies in that final word for it, which means "missing an aim." How strikingly that puts a truth which syren voices are constantly trying to sing us out of believing! Every sin is a blunder as well as a crime. And that for two reasons, because, first, God has made us for Himself, and to take anything besides for our life's end or our heart's portion is to divert ourselves from our true destiny; and because, second, that being so, every attempt to win satisfaction or delight by such a course is and must be a failure. Sin misses the aim if we think of our proper destination. Sin misses its own aim of happiness. A man never gets what he hoped for by doing wrong, or, if he seem to do so, he gets something more that spoils it all. He pursues after the fleeing form that seems so fair, and when he reaches her side, and lifts her veil, eager to embrace the tempter, a hideous skeleton grins and gibbers at him. The syren voices sing to you from the smiling island, and their white arms and golden harps and the flowery grass draw you from the wet boat and the weary oar; but when a man lands he sees the fair form end in a slimy fish, and she slays him and gnaws his bones. "He knows not that the dead are there, and that her guests are in the depths of hell." Yes! every sin is a mistake, and the epitaph for the sinner is "Thou fool."

II. These petitions also show us, in the second place, *How he thinks of forgiveness.* As the words for sin expressed a threefold view of the burden from which the Psalmist seeks deliverance, so the triple prayer, in like manner, sets forth that blessing under three aspects. I is not merely pardon for which he asks. He is making no sharp dogmatic distinction between forgiveness and cleansing.

The two things run into each other in his prayer, as they do, thank God, in our own experience, the one being inseparable, in fact, from the other. It is absolute deliverance from the power of sin, in all forms of that power, whether as guilt or as habit, for which he cries so piteously; and his accumulative petitions are so exhaustive, not because he is coldly examining his sin, but because he is intensely feeling the manifold burden of his great evil.

That first petition conceives of the Divine dealing with sin as being the erasure of a writing, perhaps of an indictment. There is a special significance in the use of the word here, because it is also employed in the description of the Levitical ceremonial of the ordeal, where a curse was written on a scroll and blotted out by the priest. But apart from that the metaphor is a natural and suggestive one. Our sin stands written against us. The long gloomy indictment has been penned by our own hands. Our past is a blurred manuscript, full of false things and bad things. We have to spread the writing before God, and ask Him to remove the stained characters from its surface, that once was fair and unsoiled.

Ah! brethren, some people tell us that the past is irrevocable, that the thing once done can never be undone, that the life's diary written by our own hands can never be cancelled. The melancholy theory of some thinkers and teachers is summed up in the words, infinitely sad and despairing when so used, "What I have written I have written." Thank God, we know better than that. We know who blots out the handwriting "that is against us, nailing it to His cross." We know that of God's great mercy our future may "copy fair our past," and the past may be all obliterated and removed. And as sometimes you will find in an old monkish library the fair vellum that once bore lascivious stories of ancient heathens and pagan deities turned into the manuscript in which a saint has penned his Contemplations, an Augustine his Confessions, or a Jerome his Translations, so our souls may become palimpsests. The old wicked heathen characters that we have traced there may be blotted out, and covered over by the writing of that Divine Spirit who has said, "I will put my laws into their minds, and write them in their hearts." As you run your pen through the finished pages of your last year's diaries, as you seal them up and pack them away, and begin a new page in a clean book on the first of January, so it is possible for every one of us to do with our lives. Notwithstanding all the influence of habit, notwithstanding all the obstinacy of long-indulged modes of thought and action, notwithstanding all the depressing effect of frequent attempts and frequent failures, we may break ourselves off from all that is sinful in our past lives, and begin afresh, saying, "God helping me, I will write another sort of biography for myself for the days that are to come." We cannot erase these sad records from our past. The ink is indelible ; and besides all that we have visibly written in

these terrible autobiographies of ours, there is much that
has sunk into the page, there is many a "secret fault,"
the record of which will need the fire of that last day to
make it legible. Alas for those who learn the black
story of their own lives for the first time then! Learn it
now, my brother, and learn likewise that Christ can wipe
it all clean off the page, clean out of your nature, clean
out of God's book. Cry to Him, with the Psalmist,
"Blot out my transgressions!" and He will calm and
bless you with the ancient answer, "I have blotted out
as a thick cloud thy transgressions, and as a cloud thy
sins."

Then there is another idea in the second of these
prayers for forgiveness: "*Wash me throughly* from
mine iniquity." That phrase does not need any explanation, except that the word expresses the antique
way of cleansing garments by treading and beating.
David, then, here uses the familiar symbol of a robe,
to express the "habit" of the soul, or, as we say, the
character. That robe is all splashed and stained. He
cries to God to make it a robe of righteousness and a
garment of purity.

And mark that he thinks the method by which this
will be accomplished is a protracted and probably a
painful one. He is not praying for a mere declaration
of pardon, he is not asking only for the one complete,
instantaneous act of forgiveness, but he is asking for a
process of purifying which will be long and hard. "I
am ready," says he, "in effect, to submit to any sort of
discipline, if only I may be clean. Wash me, beat me,

tread me down, hammer me with mallets, dash me against stones, rub me with smarting soap and caustic nitre—do anything, anything with me, if only those foul spots melt away from the texture of my soul."

A solemn prayer, my brethren, if we pray it aright, which will be answered by many a sharp application of God's Spirit, by many a sorrow, by much very painful work, both within our own souls and in our outward lives, but which will be fulfilled at last in our being clothed like our Lord, in garments which shine as the light.

We know, dear brethren, who has said, "I counsel thee to buy of Me white raiment, that the shame of thy nakedness may not appear." And we know well who were the great company before the throne of God, that had washed their robes and made them white in the blood of the Lamb. "Though your sins be as scarlet, they shall be as white as snow; though they be red like crimson, they shall be as wool." "Wash me throughly from mine iniquity."

The deliverance from sin is still further expressed by that third supplication, "Cleanse me from my sin." That is the technical word for the priestly act of declaring ceremonial cleanness—the cessation of ceremonial pollution, and for the other priestly act of making, as well as declaring, clean from the stains of leprosy.

And with reference to both of these uses, the Psalmist employs it here. That is to say, he thinks of his guilt not only as a blotted past record which he has written, not only as a garment spotted by the flesh which his spirit wears, but he thinks of it too as inhering in himself, as a leprosy and disease of his own personal nature. He thinks of it as being, like that, incurable, fatal, twin sister to and precursor of death; and he thinks of it as capable of being cleansed only by a sacerdotal act, only by the great High Priest and by His finger being laid upon it. And we know who it was that—when the leper, whom no man in Israel was allowed to touch on pain of uncleanness, came to His feet—put out His hand in triumphant consciousness of power, and touched him, and said, "I *will:* be thou clean." Let this be thy prayer, "Cleanse me from my sin;" and Christ will answer, "Thy leprosy hath departed from thee."

III. These petitions likewise show us *whence the Psalmist draws his confidence for such a prayer.* "According to the multitude of Thy tender mercies, blot out my transgressions." His whole hope rests upon God's own character, as revealed in the endless continuance of His acts of love. He knows the number and the greatness of his sins, and the very depth of his consciousness of sin helps him to a corresponding greatness in his apprehension of God's mercy. As he says in another of his Psalms, "Innumerable evils have compassed me about; they are more than the hairs of my head. . . . Many, O Lord my God, are Thy wonderful works. . . . They are more than can be numbered." This is the blessedness of all true penitence, that the more profoundly it feels our own sore need and great sinfulness, in that very proportion does it recognize the yet greater mercy and all-sufficient grace of our loving God, and from the lowest depths beholds the stars in the sky, which they who dwell amid the surface-brightness of the noonday cannot discern.

God's own revealed character, His faithfulness and persistency, notwithstanding all our sins, in that mode of dealing with men which has blessed all generations with His tender mercies—these were David's pleas. And for us who have the perfect love of God perfectly expressed in His Son, that same plea is incalculably strengthened, for we can say, "According to Thy tender mercy in Thy dear Son, for the sake of Christ, blot out my transgressions." Is the depth of our desire, and is the firmness of our confidence, proportioned to the increased clearness of our knowledge of the love of our God? Does the cross of Christ lead us to as trustful a penitence as David had, to whom meditation on God's providences and the shadows of the ancient covenant were chiefest teachers of the multitude of His tender mercies?

Remember further that a comparison of the narrative in the historical books seems to show, as I said, that this Psalm followed Nathan's declaration of the Divine forgiveness, and that therefore these petitions of our text are the echo and response to that declaration.

Thus we see that the revelation of God's love precedes, and is the cause of, the truest penitence; that our prayer for forgiveness is properly the appropriation, or the effort to appropriate, the Divine promise of forgiveness; and that the assurance of pardon, so far from making a man think lightly of his sin, is the thing that drives it home to his conscience, and first of all teaches him what it really is. As long as you are tortured with thoughts of a possible hell because of guilt, as long as you are troubled by the contemplation of consequences affecting your happiness as ensuing upon your wrongdoing, so long there is a foreign and disturbing element in even your deepest and truest penitence. But when you know that God has forgiven—when you come to see the "multitude of Thy tender mercies," when the fear of punishment has passed out of your apprehensions, then you are left with a heart at leisure from dread, to look the fact and not the consequences in the face, and to think of the moral nature and not of the personal results of your sin. And so one of the old prophets, with profound truth, says, "Thou shalt be ashamed and confounded, and never open thy mouth any more because of thy sin, when I am pacified towards thee for all thou hast done."

Dear friends, the wheels of God's great mill may grind us small, without our coming to know or to hate our sin. About His chastisements, about the revelation of His wrath, that old saying is true to a great extent: "If you bray a fool in a mortar, his folly will not depart from him." You may smite a man down, crush him, make his bones to creep with the preaching of vengeance and of hell, and the result of it will often be, if it be anything at all, what it was in the case of that poor wretched Judas, who, because he only saw wrath, flung *himself* into despair, and was lost, not because he had betrayed

Christ, but because he believed that there was no forgiveness for the man that had betrayed.

But Love comes, and "Love is Lord of all." God's
assurance, "I have forgiven," the assurance that we do
not need to plead with Him, to bribe Him, to buy
pardon by tears and amendment, but that it is already
provided for us—the blessed vision of an all-mighty love
treasured in a dying Saviour, the proclamation "God
was in Christ, reconciling the world unto Himself, not
imputing their trespasses unto them"—oh these are the
powers that break, or rather that melt our hearts; these
are the keen weapons that wound to heal our hearts;
these are the teachers that teach a godly sorrow that
needeth not to be repented of. Think of all the
patient, pitying mercy of our Father, with which He
has lingered about our lives, and softly knocked at the
door of our hearts! Think of that unspeakable gift in
which are wrapped up all His tender mercies—the gift
of Christ who died for us all! Let it smite upon your
heart with a rebuke mightier than all the thunders of
law or terrors of judgment. Let it unveil for you not
only the depths of the love of God, but the darkness of
your own selfish rebellion from Him. Measure your
crooked lives by the perfect rightness of Christ's. Learn
how you have missed the aim which He reached, who
could say, "I delight to do Thy will, O my God." And
et that same infinite love that teaches sin announce
frank forgiveness and prophesy perfect purity. Then,
with heart fixed upon Christ's cross, let your cry for
pardon be the echo of the most sure promise of pardon

which sounds from His dying lips; and as you gaze on Him who died that we might be freed from all iniquity, ask Him to blot out your transgressions, to wash you throughly from your iniquity, and to cleanse you from your sins. Ask, for you cannot ask in vain; ask earnestly, for you need it sorely; ask confidently, for He has promised before you ask; but ask, for unless you do, you will not receive. Ask, and the answer is sent already—"The blood of Jesus Christ cleanseth from all sin."

DAVID'S CRY FOR PURITY.

PSALM li. 10—12.

Renew a right spirit within me . . . and take not Thy Holy Spirit
from me . . . and uphold me with Thy free Spirit.

WE ought to be very thankful that the Bible never
conceals the faults of its noblest men. David
stands high among the highest of these. His words have
been for ages the chosen expression for the devotions of
the holiest souls ; and whoever has wished to speak
longings after purity, lowly trust in God, the aspirations
of love, or the raptures of devotion, has found no words
of his own more natural than those of the poet-
king of Israel. And this man sins , black, grievous
sin. Self-indulgent, he stays at home while his army
is in the field. His moral nature, relaxed by this
shrinking from duty, is tempted, and easily conquered.
The sensitive poet nature, to which all delights of eye
and sense appeal so strongly, is for a time too strong for
the devout soul. One sin drags on another. As self-
indulgence opened the door for lust, so lust, which
dwells hard by hate, draws after it murder. The king is

a traitor to his subjects, the soldier untrue to the chivalry of arms, the friend the betrayer of the friend. Nothing can be blacker than the whole story, and the Bible tells the shameful history in all its naked ugliness.

Many a precious lesson is contained in it. For instance, It is not innocence which makes men good. "This is your man after God's own heart, is it?" runs the common shallow sneer. Yes; not that God thought little of his foul sin, nor that "saints" make up for adultery and murder by making or singing psalms; not that "righteousness" as a standard of conduct is lower than "morality;" but that, having fallen, he learned to abhor his sin, and with deepened trust in God's mercy, and many tears, struggled out of the mire, and with unconquered resolve and strength, drawn from a Divine source, sought still to press towards the mark. It is not the attainment of purity, not the absence of sin, but the presence and operation, though it be partial, of an energy which is at war with all impurity, that makes a man righteous. That is a lesson worth learning.

Again, David was not a hypocrite because of this fall of his. All sin is inconsistent with a religious character. But it is not for us to say what sin is incompatible with a religious character.

Again, the worst sin is not some outburst of gross transgression, forming an exception to the ordinary tenor of a life, bad and dismal as such a sin is; but the worst and most fatal are the small continuous vices, which root under ground and honeycomb the soul. Many a man who thinks himself a Christian, is in more danger from the daily commission, for example, of small pieces of sharp practice in his business, than ever was David at his worst.   White ants pick a carcase clean sooner than a lion will.

Most precious of all, the lesson as to the possibility of all sin being effaced, and of the high hopes which even a man sunk in transgression has a right to cherish, as to the purity and beauty of character to which he may come. What a prayer these clauses contain to be offered by one who has so sinned !   What a marvellous faith in God's pardoning love, and what a boldness of hope in his own future, they disclose !   They set forth a profound ideal of a noble character; they make of that ideal a prayer; they are the prayer of a great transgressor, who is also a true penitent.   In all these aspects they are very remarkable, and lead to valuable lessons.   Let us look at them from these points of view successively.

I. Observe that *here is a remarkable outline of a holy character.*

It is to be observed that these three gifts—a right spirit, Thy Holy Spirit, a free spirit—the central one alone is in the original spoken of as God's ; the "Thy" of the last clause of the English Bible being an unnecessary supplement.   And I suppose that this central petition stands in the middle, because the gift which it asks is the essential and fundamental one, from which there flow, and, as it were, diverge on the right hand and on the left, the other two.   God's Holy Spirit given to a man makes the human spirit holy, and then makes it "right" and "free." Look then at the petitions, not in the order in which they stand in the text, but in the order which the text indicates as the natural one.

Now as to that fundamental petition, "Take not Thy Holy Spirit from me," one thing to notice is that David regards himself as possessing that Spirit. We are not to read into this Psalm the fully-developed New Testament teaching of a personal Paraclete, the Spirit whom Christ reveals and sends. To do that would be a gross anachronism. But we are to remember that it is an anointed king who speaks, on whose head there has been poured the oil that designated him to his office, and, in its gentle flow and sweet fragrance, symbolised from of old the inspiration of a Divine influence that accompanied every Divine call. We are to remember, too, how it had fared with David's predecessor. Saul had been chosen by God; had been for a while guided and upheld by God. But he fell into sin, and—not because he fell into it, but because he continued in it; not because he did wrong, but because he did not repent—the solemn words are recorded concerning him, that the Spirit of the Lord departed from Saul, and an evil spirit from the Lord troubled him. The Divine influence which came on the towering head of the son of Kish, through the anointing oil that Samuel poured upon his raven hair, left him, and he stood God-forsaken because he stood God-forsaking. And so David looks back from the horrible pit and miry clay into which he had fallen, where, stained with blood and lust, he lies, to that sad gigantic figure, remembered so well and loved by him so truly—the great king who sinned away his soul, and bled out his life on the heights of Gilboa. He sees in that blasted pine-tree, towering above the forest but dead at the top, and barked and scathed all down the sides by the lightning scars of passion, the picture of what he himself will come to, if the blessing that was laid upon his ruddy locks and his young head by the aged Samuel's anointing should pass from him too as it had done from his predecessor. God had departed from Saul, because Saul had refused His counsel and departed from Him ; and Saul's successor, trembling as he remembers the fate of the founder of the monarchy, and of his vanished dynasty, prays with peculiar emphasis of meaning, "Take not Thy Holy Spirit from *me*."

That Holy Spirit, the Spirit of God, had descended upon him when he was anointed king, but it was no mere official consecration which he had thereby received. He had been fitted for regal functions by personal cleansing and spiritual gifts. And it is the man as well as the king, the sinful man much rather than the faulty king, that here wrestles with God, and stays the heavenly Visitant whom his sin has made to seem as if He would depart. What he desires most earnestly, next to that pardon which he has already sought and found, is that his spirit should be made holy by God's Spirit. That is, as I have said, the central petition of his three-fold prayer, from which the others come as natural consequences.

And what is this "holiness" which David so earnestly desires? Without attempting any lengthened analysis of the various shades of meaning in the word, our purpose will be served if I point out that in all probability the primary idea in it is that of separation. God is holy— that is, separated by all the glory of His perfect nature from His creatures. Things are holy—that is, separated from common uses, and appropriated to God's service. Whatever He laid His hand on and claimed in any especial manner for His, became thereby holy, whether it were a ceremony, or a place, or a tool. Men are holy, when they are set apart for God's service, whether they be officially consecrated for certain offices, or have yielded themselves by an inward devotion based on love to be His.

The ethical signification which is predominant in our use of the word and has made it little more than a synonym for moral purity is certainly not the original meaning, as is sufficiently clear from the fact that the word is applied to material things which could have no moral qualities, and sometimes to persons who were not pure, but who were in some sense or other set apart for God's service.

But gradually that meaning becomes more and more completely attached to the word, and "holiness" is not only separation for God, but separation from sin. That is what David longs for in this prayer ; and the connection of these two meanings of the word is worth pointing out in a sermon, for the sake of the great truth which it suggests, that the basis of all right- ness and righteousness in a human spirit is its conscious and glad devotion to God's service and uses. A re- ference to God must underlie all that is good in men,

and, on the other hand, that consecration to God is a
delusion or a deception which does not issue in separation from evil. "Holiness" is a loftier and a truer
word than "morality," "virtue," or the like ; it differs
from these in that it proclaims that surrender to God is
the very essence of all good, while they seek to construct
a standard for human conduct, and to lay a foundation
for human goodness, without regard to Him. Hence,
irreligious moralists dislike the very word, and fall back
upon pale, colourless phrases rather than employ it. But
they are inadequate for the purpose. Man's duties can
never be summed up in any expression which omits
man's relation to God. How do I stand to Him? Do
I belong to Him by joyous yielding of myself to be His
instrument ? That, my friends, is the question, the
answer to which determines everything about me.
Rightly answered, there will come all fruits of grace
and beauty in the character as a natural consequence ;
"whatsoever things are lovely and of good report," every
virtue and every praise grow from the root of consecration to God. Wrongly answered, there will come only
fruits of selfishness and evil, which may simulate virtue,
but the blossom shall go up in dust, and the root in
stubble. Do you seek purity, nobleness, strength, and
beauty of soul? Learn that all these inhere and flow
from the one act of giving up yourself to God, and in
their truest perfection are found only in the spirit that is
His. Holiness considered as moral excellence is the
result of holiness considered as devotion to God. And
learn too that holiness in both aspects comes from the

operation and indwelling in our spirits of a Divine Spirit, which draws away our love from self to fix it on Him, which changes our blindness into light, and makes us by degrees like itself, "holy, harmless, undefiled, separate from sinners." The Spirit of the Lord is the energy which produces all righteousness and purity in human spirits.

Therefore, all our desires after what is good and true should shape themselves into the desire for that Spirit. Our prayer should be, " Make me separate from evil, and that I may be so, claim and keep me for Thine own. As Thou hast done with the Sabbath amongst the days, with the bare summit of the hill of the Lord's house among the mountains, with Israel amidst the nations, so do with me; lay Thine hand upon me for Thine own. Let my spirit, O God, know its destination for Thee, its union with Thee. Then being Thine, it will be clean. Dwell in me, that I may know myself Thine. Seal me with that gracious influence which is the proof that Thou possessest me, and the pledge that I possess Thee. 'Take not Thy Holy Spirit from me.'"

So much for the chief of these petitions, which gives the ideal character in its deepest relations. There follow two other elements in the character, which on either side flow from the central source. The *holy* spirit in a man will be a *right* spirit and a *free* spirit. Consider these further thoughts in turn.

"A right spirit." You will observe that our translators have given an alternative rendering in the margin, and, as is not seldom the case, it is a better one than that adopted in the text. "A constant or firm spirit" is the Psalmist's meaning. He sees that a spirit which is conscious of its relation to God, and set free from the perturbations of sin, will be a spirit firm and settled, established and immoveable in its obedience and its faith. For Him, the root of all steadfastness is in con-secration to God.

And so this collocation of ideas opens the way for us to important considerations bearing upon the practical ordering of our natures and of our lives. For instance —There is no stability and settled persistency of righteous purpose possible for us, unless we are made strong because we lay hold on God's strength, and stand firm because we are rooted in Him. Without that hold-fast, we shall be swept away by storms of calamity or by gusts of passion. Without that to steady us, our own boiling lusts and desires will make every fibre of our being quiver and tremble. Without that armour, there will not be solidity enough in our character to bear with-out breaking the steady pressure of the world's weight, still less the fierce hammering of special temptation. To stand erect, and in that sense to have a right spirit— one that is upright and unbent,—we must have sure footing in God, and have His energy infused into our shrinking limbs. If we are to be stable amidst earth-quakes and storms, we must be built on the Rock, and build rock-like upon it. Build thy strength upon God. Let His Holy Spirit be the foundation of thy life, and then thy tremulous and vagrant soul shall be braced and fixed. The building will become like the foundation, and will grow into "a tower of strength that stands four-square to every wind." Rooted in God, thou shalt be unmoved by "the loud winds when they call;" or if still the tremulous leaves are huddled together before the blast, and the swaying branches creak and groan, the bole will stand firm and the gnarled roots will not part from their anchorage, though the storm-giant drag at them with a hundred hands. The spirit of holiness will be a firm spirit.

But there is another phase of connection between these two points of the ideal character—if my spirit is to be holy and to preserve its holiness, it must be firm. That is to say, you can only get and keep purity by resistance. A man who has not learned to say "no"— who is not resolved that he *will* take God's way in spite of every dog that can bay or bark at him, in spite of every silvery voice that woos him aside—will be a weak and a wretched man till he dies. In such a world as this, with such hearts as ours, weakness *is* wickedness in the long run. Whoever lets himself be shaped and guided by anything lower than an inflexible will, fixed in obedience to God, will in the end be shaped into a deformity and guided to wreck and ruin. Dreams however rapturous, contemplations however devout, emotions however deep and sacred, make no man pure and good without hard effort, and that to a large extent in the direction of resistance. Righteousness is not a mere negative idea, and Scripture morality is something much deeper than prohibitions. But there is no law for us without prohibitions, and no righteousness without casting out evil that is strong in us, and fighting against evil that is attractive around us. Therefore we need firmness to guard holiness, to be the hard shell in which the rich fruit matures. We need a wholesome obstinacy in the right that will neither be bribed nor coaxed nor bullied, nor anyhow persuaded out of the road in which we know that we should walk. "Add to your faith manly vigour." Learn that an indispensable requisite of holiness is prescribed in that command, "Whom resist, steadfast in the faith." And remember that the ground of all successful resistance and the need for it are alike taught in that series of petitions, which makes a holy spirit the foundation of a constant spirit, and a constant spirit the guard of a holy spirit.

Then consider, for a moment, the third element in the character which David longs to possess—a *free* spirit. He who is holy because full of God's Spirit, and constant in his holiness, will likewise be free. That is the same word which is in other places translated "willing"—and the scope of the Psalmist's desire is, "Let my spirit be emancipated from sin by *willing* obedience." This goes very deep into the heart of all true godliness. The only obedience which God accepts is that which gladly, and almost as by an instinctive inward impulse, harmonizes the human will with the Divine. "Lo, I come: in the volume of the book it is written of me, I delight to do Thy will, and Thy law is within my heart." That is a blessed thought, that we may come to do Him service not because we must, but because we like; not as serfs, but as sons; not thinking of His law as a slave-driver that cracks his whip over our heads, but as a friend that lets us know how we may please Him whom it is our delight to obey. And so the Psalmist prays, " Let my obedience be so willing that I had rather do what Thou wilt than anything besides."

" *Then*," he thinks, " I shall be free." Of course—for the correlative of freedom is lawful authority, and the definition of freedom is willing submission. If for us duty is joy, and all our soul's desires flow with an equable motion parallel to the will of God, then there is no sense of restraint in keeping within the limits beyond which we do not seek to go. The willing spirit sets us free, free from the "ancient solitary reign" of the despot Self, free from the mob rule of Passions and Appetites, free from the incubus of evil habits, free from the authority of men's voices and example. Obedience is freedom to them that have learned to love the lips that command. We are set free that we may serve : " O Lord, truly I am Thy servant ; Thou hast loosed my bonds." We are set free in serving : " I will walk at liberty, for I keep Thy precepts." Let a willing, free spirit uphold me.

II. Observe, too, that *Desires for holiness should become Prayers.*

David does not merely long for certain spiritual excellences ; he goes to God for them. And his reasons for doing so are plain. If you will look at the former verses of this Psalm, you will see that he had found out two things about his sin, both of which make him sure that he can only be what he should be by God's help.

He had learned what his crimes were in relation to God, and he had further learned what they indicated about himself. The teaching of his bitter experience as to the former of these two matters lies in that saying which some people have thought strange: "Against *Thee only* have I sinned." What! Had he not committed a crime against human law? had he not harmed Uriah and Bathsheba? were not his deeds an offence to his whole kingdom? Yes, he knew all that; but he felt that over and above all that was black in his deed, considered in its bearing upon men, it was still blacker when it was referred to God; and a sadder word than "crime" or "fault" had to be used about it. I have done wrong as against my fellows, but, worse than that, I have *sinned* against God. The notion of *sin* implies the notion of God. Sin is wilful transgression of the law of *God*. An atheist can have no conception of sin. But bring in God into human affairs, and men's faults immediately assume the darker tint, and become men's sins. Therefore the need of prayer if these evils are to be blotted out. If I had done crime against man only, I should not need to ask God for pardon or cleansing; but I have sinned against Him, and done this evil in His sight, therefore my desires for deliverance address themselves to Him, and my longings for purity must needs break into the cry of intreaty to that God with whom is forgiveness, and redemption from all iniquity.

And still further, looking at the one deed he sees in it something more than an isolated act. It leads him

down to its motive; that motive carries him to the
state of mind in which it could have power; that state
of mind, in which the motive could have power, carries
him still deeper to the bias of his nature as he had
received it from his parents. And, thinking of how he
had fallen, how upon his terraced palace roof there the
eye had inflamed the heart, and the heart had yielded
so quickly to the temptations of the eye, he finds no
profounder explanation of the disastrous eclipse of goodness than this: "Behold, I was shapen in iniquity."

Is that a confession or a palliation, do you think?
Is he trying to shuffle off guilt from his own shoulders?
By no means, for these words are the motive for
the prayer, "Purge me, and I shall be clean." That
is to say, he has learned that isolated acts of sin
inhere in a common root, and that root a disposition
inherited from generation to generation to which evil
is familiar and easy, to which good, alas! is but too
alien and unwelcome. None the less is the evil done
his deed. None the less has he to wail in full consciousness of his individual responsibility: "Against
Thee have *I* sinned." But the effect of this second
discovery, that sin has become so intertwisted with his
being that he cannot shake off the venomous beast
into the fire and feel no harm, is the same as that of
the former—to drive him to God, who alone can heal
the nature and separate the poison from his blood.

Dear friends, there are some of you that are wasting
your lives in paroxysms of fierce struggle with the
evil that you have partially discovered in yourselves,

alternating with long languor fits of collapse and apathy, and who make no solid advance, just because you will not lay to heart these two convictions—your sin has to do with God, and your sins come from a sinful nature. Because of the one fact, you must go to God for pardon; because of the other, you must go to God for cleansing. There, in your heart, like some black well-head in a dismal bog, is the source of all the swampy corruption that fills your life. You cannot stanch it, you cannot drain it, you cannot sweeten it. Ask Him, who is above your nature and without it, to change it by His own new life infused into your spirit. He will heal the bitter waters. He alone can. Sin is against God; sin comes from an evil heart; therefore, if your longings for that ideal perfectness are ever to be fulfilled, you must make prayers of them, and cry to Him who hears, "Create in me a clean heart, O God; take not Thy Holy Spirit from me."

III. Finally, observe that *Prayers for perfect cleansing are permitted to the lips of the greatest sinners.*

Such longings as these might seem audacious, when the atrocity of the crime is remembered, and by man's standard they are so. Let the criminal be thankful for escape, and go hide himself, say men's pardons. But here is a man, with the evil savour of his debauchery still tainting him, daring to ask for no mere impunity, but for God's choicest gifts. Think of his crime, think of its aggravations from God's mercies to him, from his official position, from his past devotion. Remember that this cruel voluptuary is the sweet singer of Israel, who had taught men songs of purer piety and subtler emotion than the ruder harps of older singers had ever flung from their wires. And this man, so placed, so gifted, set up on high to be the guiding light of the nation, has plunged into the filth of these sins, and quenched all his light there. When he comes back penitent, what will he dare to ask? Everything that God can give to bless and gladden a soul. He asks for God's Spirit, for His presence, for the joy of His salvation; to be made once again, as he had been, the instrument that shall show forth His praise, and teach transgressors God's ways. Ought he to have had more humble desires? Does this great boldness show that he is leaping very lightly over his sin? Is he presumptuous in such prayers? God be thanked—no! But, knowing all his guilt, and broken and contrite in heart (crushed and ground to powder, as the words mean), utterly loathing himself, aware of all the darkness of his deserts, he yet cherishes unconquerable confidence in the pitying love of God, and believes that in spite of all his sin, he may yet be pure as the angels of heaven—ly, even holy as God is holy.

Thank God we have such an example for our heartening. Lay it to heart, brethren! You cannot believe too much in God's mercy. You cannot expect too much at His hands. He is "able to do exceeding abundantly above all that we ask or think." No sin is so great but that, coming straight from it, a repentant sinner may hope and believe that all God's love will be lavished upon him, and the richest of God's gifts granted to his desires.

Even if our transgression is aggravated by a previous life of godliness, and have given the enemies great occasion to blaspheme, as David did, yet David's penitence may in our souls lead on to David's hope, and the answer will not fail us. Let no sin, however dark, however repeated, drive us to despair of ourselves, because it hides from us our loving Saviour. Though beaten back again and again by the surge of our passions and sins, like some poor shipwrecked sailor sucked back with every retreating wave and tossed about in the angry surf, yet keep your face towards the beach where there is safety, and you will struggle through it all, and, though it were but on some floating boards and broken pieces of the ship, will come safe to land. He will uphold you with His Spirit, and take away the weight of sin that would sink you, by His forgiving mercy, and bring you out of all the weltering waste of waters to the solid shore.

So whatever thy evil behaviour, come with it all, and cast thyself before Him, with whom is plenteous redemption. Embrace in one act the two truths, thine own sin, and God's infinite mercy in Jesus Christ. Let not the one blind you to the other ; let not the one lead you to a morbid despondency, which is blind to Christ, nor the other to a superficial estimate of the deadliness of sin, which is blind to thine own self. Let the cross teach thee what sin is, and let the dark background of thy sin bring into clear prominence the cross that bringeth salvation. Know that thou art utterly black and sinful. Believe that God is eternally, utterly, inconceivably, merciful. **Learn** both, in Him who is the standard by which we can estimate our sin, and the proof and medium of God's mercy. Trust thyself and all thy foulness to Jesus Christ; and, so doing, look up from whatsoever horrible pit and miry clay thou mayest have fallen into, with this prayer, " Create in me a clean heart, O God, and renew a right spirit within me—take not Thy Holy Spirit from me, and uphold me with Thy free Spirit." Then the answer shall come to you from Him who ever puts the best robe upon His returning prodigals, and gives His highest gifts to sinners that repent—" From all your filthiness will I cleanse you, a new heart also will I give you, and a new spirit will I put within you, and I will put My Spirit within you, and cause you to walk in My statutes."

2ND SER

JOSEPH'S FAITH.

GENESIS l. 25.

Joseph took an oath of the children of Israel, saying, God will surely visit you, and ye shall carry up my bones from hence.

THIS is the one act of Joseph's life which the author of the Epistle to the Hebrews selects as the sign that he too lived by faith. "By faith Joseph, when he died, made mention of the departing of the children of Israel; and gave commandment concerning his bones."

It was at once a proof of how entirely he believed God's promise, and of how earnestly he longed for its fulfilment. It was a sign too of how little he felt himself at home in Egypt, though to outward appearance he had become completely one of its people. The ancestral spirit was in him true and strong, though he was "separate from his brethren." He bore an Egyptian name, a swelling title, he married an Egyptian woman, he had an Egyptian priest for father-in-law, but he was an Israelite in heart; and in the midst of official cares and a surfeit of honours, his desires turned away from them all towards the land promised by God to his fathers.

And when he lay dying, he could not bear to think that his bones should moulder in the country where his life had been spent. " I know that this is not our land after all; swear to me that when the promise that has tarried so long comes at last, you will take me, all that is left of me, and carry it up, and lay it in some corner of the blessed soil, that I too may somehow share in the inheritance of His people. God shall surely visit you. Carry my bones up hence."

Perhaps there is in this wish a trace of something besides faith in God's promises. Of course, there is a natural sentiment which no clearness of knowledge of a future state wholly dispels. We all feel as if somehow our bodies remain a part of ourselves even after death and we have wishes where they shall lie. But perhaps Joseph had a more definite belief on the matter than that. What theory of another life does an Egyptian mummy express? Why all that sedulous care to preserve the poor relics? Was it not a consequence of the belief that somehow or other there could be no life without a body, and that in some mysterious way the preservation of that contributed to the continuance of this? And so Joseph, who was himself going to be embalmed and put into a mummy-case, may have caught something of the tone of thought prevalent around him, and have believed that to carry his bones to the land of promise was, in some obscure manner, to carry *him* thither. Be that as it may, whether the wish came from a mistake about the relation of flesh and spirit, or only from the natural desire which we too possess, that our graves may not be among

K 2

strangers, but beside our father's and our mother's—that
is not the main thing in this fact. The main thing is
that this dying man believed God's promise, and claimed
his share in it.

And on this the writer of the Epistle to the Hebrews,
whoever he was, fastens. Neglecting the differences in
knowledge between Joseph and the Christians whom he
addresses, and pointing back to the strong confidence
in God and longing for participation in the promises
which brightened the glazing eye and gave *him* "hope
in his death," he declares that the principle of action
which guided this man in the dim twilight of early revelation, is that same faith which ought to guide us who
live in the full light of the unsetting sun.

Taking, then, this incident, with the New Testament
commentary upon it, it leads us to a truth which we
often lose sight of, but which is indispensable if we
would understand the relations of the earlier and later
days.

I. *Faith is always the same, though knowledge varies.*—
There is a vast difference between a man's creed and a
man's faith. The one may vary, does vary within very
wide limits; the other remains the same. The things
believed have been growing from the beginning—the
attitude of mind and will by which they have been
grasped has been the same from the beginning, and will
be the same to the end. And not only so, but it will be
substantially the same in heaven as it is on earth. For
there is but one bond which unites men to God; and
that emotion of loving trust is one and the same in the

dim twilight of the world's morning, and amid the blaze of the noonday of heaven. The contents of faith, that on which it relies, the treasure it grasps, changes; the essence of faith, the act of reliance, the grasp which holds the treasure, does not change.

It is difficult to decide how much Joseph's gospel contained. From our point of view it was very imperfect. The spiritual life was nourished in him and in the rest of "the world's grey fathers" on what looks to us but like seven basketsful of fragments. They had promises, indeed, in which we, looking at them with the light of fulfilment blazing upon them, can see the broad outlines of the latest revelation, and can trace the future flower all folded together and pale in the swelling bud. But we shall err greatly if we suppose, as we are apt to do, that these promises were to them anything like what they are to us. It requires a very vigorous exercise of very rare gifts to throw ourselves back to their position, and to gain any vivid and approximately accurate notion of the theology of these ancient lovers of God.

This, at any rate, we may, perhaps, say: they had a sure and clear knowledge of the living God, who had talked with them as with a friend; they knew His inspiring, guiding presence; they knew the forgiveness of sins; they knew, though they very dimly understood, the promise, "In thy seed shall all the families of the earth be blessed." How far they looked across the gulf of death and beheld anything—even cloudland—on the other side, is a question very hard to answer, and about

which confident dogmatism, either affirmative or negative, is unwarranted.   But it is to be remembered that,
whether they had any notion of a future state or no,
they had a promise which fulfilled for them substantially
the same office as that does for us.   The promise of the
land of Canaan gleaming before them through the mists,
bare and "earthly" as it seems to us when compared
with our hope of an inheritance incorruptible in the
heavens, is, by the author of the Epistle to the Hebrews,
identified with that hope of ours, for he expressly says
that whilst they were looking for an earthly Canaan
they were "desiring a better country, that is an
heavenly."   So that, whether they definitely expected a
life after death or not, the anticipation of the land promised to them and to their fathers held the same place
in their creed, and as a moral agent in their lives, which
the rest that remains for the people of God ought to
do in ours.

   And it is to be taken into account also that fellowship with God has in it the germ of the assurance of
immortality.   It seems almost impossible to suppose a
state of mind in which a man living in actual communion with God shall believe that death is to end it
all.   Christ's proof that immortal life was revealed in the
Pentateuch, was the fact that God there called Himself
the God of Abraham and of Isaac and of Jacob; by
which our Lord meant us to learn that men who are
brought into personal relations with God can never die,
that it is impossible that a soul which has looked up
to the face of the unseen Father with filial love should

be left in the grave, or that those who are separated to be His, as He is theirs, should see corruption. The relation once established is eternal, and some more or less definite expectation of that eternity seems inseparable from the consciousness of the relation.

But be that as it may, and even taking the widest possible view of the contents of the patriarchal creed, what a rude outline it looks beside ours! Can there be anything in common between us? Can they be in any way a pattern for us? Yes; as I said, faith is one thing, creed is another. Joseph and his ancestors were joined to God by the very same bond which unites us to Him. There has never been but one path of life: "They *trusted* God and were lightened, and their faces were not ashamed." In that old Covenant the one thing needful was trust in the living Jehovah. In the new, the one thing needful is the very same emotion, directed to the very same Lord, manifested now and incarnate in the Divine Son, our Saviour. In this exercise of loving confidence, in which reason and will and affection blend in the highest energy and holiest action, Joseph and we are one. Across the gulf of centuries we clasp hands; and in despite of all superficial differences of culture and civilization, and all deeper differences in knowledge of God and His loving will, Pharaoh's prime minister, and the English workman, and the Hindoo ryot, may be alike in what is deepest—the faith which grasps God. How all that mysterious Egyptian life fades away as we think of the fundamental identity of religious emotion then and now! It disguises our brother from us, as it did from the wandering Arabs who came to buy corn, and could not recognise in the swarthy imperious Egyptian, with strange head-dress and unknown emblems hanging by chains of gold about his neck, the fair boy whom they had sold to the merchants. But beneath it all is the brother's heart, fed by the same life-blood which feeds ours. He trusts in God, he expects a future because God has promised it, and, therefore, he is separated from those among whom he dwells, and knit to us in this far-off island of the sea, who so many centuries after are partakers of like precious faith.

And incomplete as his creed was, Joseph may have been a better Christian than some of us, and was so, if what he knew nourished his spiritual life more than what we know nourishes ours, and if his heart and will twined more tenaciously round the fragments of revelation which he possessed, and drew from them more support and strength than we do from the complete Gospel which we have.

Brethren, what makes a Christian is not the theology you have in your heads, but the faith and love you have in your hearts. We must, indeed, have a clear statement of truth in orderly propositions,—that is, a system of dogmas,—to have anything to trust to at all. There can be no saving faith in an unseen Person, except through the medium of thoughts concerning Him, which thoughts put into words are a creed. The antithesis which is often eagerly urged upon us—not doctrines, but Christ—is a very incomplete and misleading one. "Christ" is a mere name, empty of all significance till it be filled with definite statements of who and what Christ is. But whilst I, for my part, believe that we must have doctrines to make Christ a reality, and an object of faith to grasp at all, I would urge all the more earnestly, because I thus believe, that, when we have these doctrines, it is not the creed that saves, but the faith. We are united to Christ, not by the doctrine of His nature and work, needful as that is, but by trusting in Him as that which the doctrine declares Him to be—Redeemer, Friend, Sacrifice, Divine Lover of our souls. Let us always remember that it is not the amount of religious knowledge which I have got, but the amount which I use, that determines my religious position and character. Most of us have in our creeds principles that have no influence upon our moral and active life ; and, if so, it matters not one whit how pure, how accurate, how comprehensive, how consistent, how scriptural my conceptions of the Gospel may be. If they be not powers in my soul, they only increase my responsibility and my liability to condemnation. The dry light of the understanding is of no use to anybody. You must turn your creed into a faith before it has power to bless and save.

There are hosts of so-called Christians who get no more good out of the most solemn articles of their orthodox belief than if they were heathens. What is the use of your saying that you believe in God the Father Almighty, when there is no child's love and happy confidence in your heart ? What the better are you for believing in Jesus Christ, His Divine nature,

His death and glory, when you have no reliance on Him, nor any least flutter of trembling love towards Him? Is your belief in the Holy Ghost of the smallest consequence, if you do not yield to His hallowing power? What does it matter that you believe in the forgiveness of sins, so long as you do not care a rush whether yours are pardoned or no? And is it anything to you or to God that you believe in the life everlasting, if all your work, and hopes, and longings are confined to "this bank and shoal of time?" Are you any more a Christian because of all that intellectual assent to these solemn verities? Is not your life like some secularized monastic chamber, with holy texts carved on the walls, and saintly images looking down from glowing windows on revellers and hucksters who defile its floor? Your faith, not your creed, determines your religion. Many a "true believer" is a real "infidel."

Thank God that the soul may be wedded to Christ, even while a very partial conception of Christ is in the understanding. The more complete and adequate the creed, indeed, the mightier and more fruitful in blessing will the faith naturally be; and every portion of the full orb of the Sun of Righteousness which is eclipsed by the shadow of our intellectual misconceptions, will diminish the light and warmth which falls upon our souls. It is no part of our duty to pronounce what is the minimum of a creed which Faith needs for its object. For myself, I confess that I do not understand how the spiritual life can be sustained in its freshness and fervour, in its fulness and reality, without a belief in the Divinity and saving work of Jesus Christ. But with that belief for the centre which faith grasps, the rest may vary indefinitely. All who stand around that centre, some nearer, some further off, some mazed in errors which others have cast behind them, some of them seeing and understanding more, and some less of Him and of His work —are His. He loves them, and will save them all. Knowledge varies. The faith which unites to God remains the same.

II. We may gather from this incident another consideration, namely, that *Faith has its noblest office in detaching from the present.*

All his life long, from the day of his captivity, Joseph was an Egyptian in outward seeming. He filled his place at Pharaoh's court, but his dying words open a window into his soul, and betray how little he had felt that he belonged to the order of things in the midst of which he had been content to live. This man, too, surrounded by an ancient civilization, and dwelling among granite temples and solid pyramids, and firm based sphinxes, the very emblems of eternity, confessed that here he had no continuing city, but sought one to come. As truly as his ancestors who dwelt in tabernacles; like Abraham journeying with his camels and herds, and pitching his tent outside the walls of Hebron; like Isaac in the grassy plains of the South country; like Jacob keeping himself apart from the families of the land, their descendant, an heir with them of the same promise, showed that he too regarded himself as a "stranger and a sojourner." Dying, he said, "Carry my bones up from hence." Therefore we may be sure that, living, the hope of the inheritance must have burned in his heart as a hidden light, and made him an alien everywhere but on its blessed soil.

And faith will always produce just such effects. In exact proportion to its strength, that living trust in God will direct our thoughts and desires to the "King in His beauty, and the land that is very far off." In proportion as our thoughts and desires are thus directed, they will be averted from what is round about us; and the more longingly our eyes are fixed on the furthest horizon, the less shall we see flowers at our feet. To behold God pales the otherwise dazzling lustre of created brightness. They whose souls are fed with heavenly manna, and who have learned that it is their necessary food, will scent no dainties in the fleshpots of Egypt, for all their rank garlic and leeks. It is simply a question as to which of two classes of ideas occupy the thoughts, and which of two sets of affections engage the heart. If vulgar brawling and rude merrymakers fill the inn, there will be no room for the pilgrim thoughts which bear the Christ in their bosom, and have angels for their guard; and if these holy wayfarers enter, their serene presence will drive forth the noisy crowd, and turn the place into a temple. Nothing but Christian faith gives to the furthest future the solidity and definiteness which it must have if it is to be a breakwater for us against the fluctuating sea of present cares and thoughts.

If the unseen is ever to rule in men's lives, it must be through their thoughts. It must become intelligible, clear, real. It must be brought out of the flickering moonlight of fancy and surmises, into the sunlight of certitude and knowledge. Dreams, and hopes, and peradventures are too unsubstantial stuff to be a bulwark against the very real, undeniable present. And such certitude is given through faith which grasps the promises of God, and twines the soul round the risen Saviour so closely that it sits with Him in heavenly places. Such certitude is given by faith alone.

If the unseen is ever to rule in men's lives, it must become not only an object for certain knowledge, but also for ardent wishes. The vague sense of possible evils lurking in its mysteries must be taken out of the soul, and there must come somehow an assurance that all it wraps in its folds is joy and peace. It must cease to be doubtful, and must seem infinitely desirable. Does anything but Christian faith engage the heart to love, and all the longing wishes to set towards, the things that are unseen and eternal? Where besides then can there be found a counterpoise weighty enough to heave up the souls that are laden with the material, and cleaving to the dust? Nowhere. The only possible deliverance from the tyrannous pressure of the trifles amidst which we live is in having the thoughts familiarized with Christ in heaven, which will dwarf all that is on earth, and in having the affections fixed on Him, which will emancipate them from the pains and sorrows that ever wait upon love of the mutable and finite creatures.

Let us remember that such deliverance from the present is the condition of all noble, joyous, pure life. It needs Christianity to effect it indeed, but it does not need Christianity to see how desirable it is, and how closely connected with whatever is lovely and of good report is this detachment from the near and the visible. A man that is living for remote objects is, in so far, a better man than one who is living for the present. He will become thereby the subject of a mental and moral discipline that will do him good. And, on the other hand, a life which has no far-off light for its guiding star, has none of the unity, of the self-restraint, of the tension, of the conscious power which makes our days noble and strong. Whether he accomplish them or fail, whether they be high or low, the man who lets future objects rule present action is in advance of the other. "To scorn delights and live laborious days," which is the prerogative of the man with a future, is always the best. He is rather a beast than a man who floats lazily on the warm sunny wavelets as they lift him in their roll, and does not raise his head high enough above them to see and steer for the solid shore where they break. But only he has found the full, con trolling, blessing, quickening power that lies in the thought of the future, and in life directed by it, to whom that future is all summed in the name of his Saviour. Whatever makes a man live in the past and in the future raises him ; but high above all others stand those to whom the past is an apocalypse of God, with Calvary for its centre, and all the future is fellow-ship with Christ, and joy in the heavens. Having these hopes, it will be our own faults if we are not pure and gentle, calm in changes and sorrows, armed against frowning dangers, and proof against smiling temptations. They are our armour,—"Put on the breastplate of faith . . . . and for an helmet the hope of salvation."

A very sharp test for us all lies in these thoughts. This change of the centre of interest from earth to heaven is the uniform effect of faith. What, then, of us? On Sundays we profess to seek for a city; but what about the week, from Monday morning to Saturday night? What difference does our faith make in the current of our lives? How far are they unlike—I do not mean externally and in occupations, but in principle — the lives of men who "have no hope?" Are you living for other objects? Are you nurturing other hopes in your hearts as a man may guard a little spark of fire with both his hands, to light him amid the darkness and the howling storm? Do you care to detach yourself from the world? or are you really "men of this world, which have their portion in this life," even while Christians by profession? A question which I have no right to ask, and no power to answer but for myself; a question which it concerns your souls to ask and to answer very definitely for yourselves. There is no need to preach an exaggerated and impossible abstinence from work and enjoyment in the world where God has put us, or to set up a standard "too high for mortal life beneath the sky." Whatever need there may have sometimes been to protest against a false asceticism, and withdrawing from active life for the sake of one's personal salvation, times are changed now. What we want to-day is, "Come ye out and be ye separate, and touch not the unclean thing." In my conscience I believe that multitudes are having the very heart of the Christian life eaten out by absorption in earthly pursuits and loves, and by the effacing of all distinction in outward life, in occupation, in recreation, in tastes and habits between people who call themselves Christians, and people who do not care at all whether there is another world or not. There can be but little strength in our faith if it does not compel us to separation. If it has any power to do anything at all, it will certainly do that. If we are naturalised as citizens there, we cannot help being aliens here. "Abraham," says the New Testament, "dwelt in tabernacles, *for* he looked for a city." Just so! The tent life will always be the natural one for those who feel that their mother country is beyond the stars. We should be like the wandering Swiss, who hear in a strange land the rude old melody that used to echo among the Alpine pastures. The sweet sad tones kindle home sickness that will not let them rest: no matter where they are, or what they are doing, no matter what honour they have carved out for themselves with their swords, they throw off the livery of the alien king which they have worn, and turning their backs upon pomp and courts, seek the free air of the mountains, and find home better than a place by a foreign throne. Let us esteem the reproach of Christ greater riches than the treasures of Egypt, and go forth to Him without the camp, for here have we no continuing city.

III. Again, we have here an instance that *Faith makes men energetic in the duties of the present.*

The remarks which I have been making must be completed by that consideration, or they become hurtful and one-sided. You know that common sarcasm, that Christianity degrades this present life by making it merely the portal to a better, and teaches men to think of it as only evil, to be scrambled through anyhow. I confess that I wish the sneer were a less striking contrast to what Christian people really think. But it is almost as gross a caricature of the teaching of Christianity as it is of the practice of Christians.

Take this story of Joseph as giving us a truer view of the effect on present action of faith in, and longing for, God's future. He was, as I said, a true Hebrew all his days. But that did not make him run away from Pharaoh's service. He lived by hope, and that made him the better worker in the passing moment, and kept him tugging away all his life at the oar, administering the affairs of a kingdom.

Of course it is so. The one thing which saves this life from being contemptible is the thought of another. The more profoundly we feel the reality of the great eternity whither we are being drawn, the greater do all things here become. They are made less in their power to absorb or trouble, but they are made infinitely greater in importance as preparations for what is beyond. When they are first they are small, when they are second they

2ND SER. L

are great. When the mist lifts, and shows the snowy summits of the "mountains of God," the nearer lower ranges which we thought the highest dwindle indeed, but gain in sublimity and meaning by the loftier peaks to which they lead up. Unless men and women live for eternity, they *are* "merely players," and all their busy days "like a tale told by an idiot, full of sound and fury, *signifying nothing.*" How absurd, how monotonous, how trivial it all is, all this fret and fume, all these dying joys and only less fleeting pains, all this mill-horse round of work which we pace, unless we are, mill-horse-like, driving a shaft that goes *through the wall*, and grinds something that falls into "bags that wax not old" on the other side. The true Christian faith teaches us that this is the workshop where God makes men, and the next the palace where He shows them. All here is apprenticeship and training. It is of no more value than the attitudes into which gymnasts throw themselves, but as a discipline most precious. The end makes the means important; and if we believe that God is preparing us for immortal life with Him by all our work, then we shall do it with a will : otherwise we may well be languid as we go on for thirty or forty years, some of us doing the same trivial things, and getting nothing out of them but food, occupation of time, and a mechanical aptitude for what is not worth doing.

It is the horizon that gives dignity to the foreground. A picture without sky has no glory. This present, unless we see gleaming beyond it the eternal calm of the heavens, above the tossing tree-tops with withering leaves, and the smoky chimneys, is a poor thing for our eyes to gaze at, or our hearts to love, or our hands to toil on. But when we see that all paths lead to heaven, and that our eternity is affected by our acts in time, then it is blessed to gaze, it is possible to love the earthly shadows of the uncreated beauty, it is worth while to work.

Remember, too, that faith will energize us for any sort of work, seeing that it raises all to one level and brings all under one sanction, and shows all as co-operating to one end. Look at that muster-roll of heroes of faith in the Epistle to the Hebrews, and mark the variety of grades of human life represented there,—statesmen, soldiers, prophets, shepherds, widow women, martyrs,— all fitted for their tasks and delivered from the snare that was in their calling by that faith which raised them above the world, and therefore fitted them to come down on the world with stronger strokes of duty. This is the secret of doing with our might whatsoever our hand finds to do—to trust Christ, to live *with* Him, and *by* the hope of the inheritance.

Then, brethren, let us see that our clearer revelation bears fruit in a faith in the great Divine promises as calm and firm as this dying patriarch had. Then the same power will work not only the same detachment and energy in life, but the same calmness and solemn light of hope in death. It is very beautiful to notice how Joseph dying almost overleaps the thought of death as a very small matter. His brethren who stood by his bedside might well fear what might be the consequences to their people when the powerful protector, the prime minister of the kingdom, was gone. But the dying man has firm hold of God's promises, and he knows that these will be fulfilled, whether he live or no. "I die," says he, "but God shall surely visit you. *He* is not going to die; and though I stand no more before Pharaoh, you will be safe."

Thus we may contemplate our own going away, or the departure of the dearest from our homes, and of the most powerful for good in human affairs, and in the faith of God's true promises may feel that no man is indispensable to our well-being or to the world's good. God's chariot is self-moving. One after another, who lays his hand upon the ropes and hauls for a little space, drops out of the ranks. But it will go on, and in His majesty He will ride prosperously.

And for himself, too, the dying man felt that death was a very small matter. "Whether I live or die I shall have a share in the promise. Living, perhaps my feet would stand upon its soil; dying, my bones will rest there." And we, who know a resurrection, have in it that which makes Joseph's fond fancy a reality, and reduces the importance of that last enemy to nothing. Some will be alive and remain till the coming of the Lord, some will be laid in the grave till His voice call them forth, and carry their bones up from hence to the land of the inheritance. But whether we be of generations that fell on sleep looking for the promise of His coming, or whether of the generation that go forth to meet Him when He comes, it matters not. All who have lived by faith will there be gathered at last. The brightest hopes of the present will be forgotten then when we, too, shall stand in the latter day, wearing the likeness of His glory; when, extricated wholly from the bondage of corruption and the dust of death, we, perfected in body, soul, and spirit, shall enter the calm home, where we shall change the solitude of the desert, and the transitoriness of the tent, and the dangers of the journey, for the society, and the stability, and the security of the city which hath foundations, whose builder and maker is God.

THE SEVEN STARS AND THE SEVEN CANDLESTICKS.

REVELATION ii. 1.

He that holdeth the seven stars in His right hand, who walketh
in the midst of the seven golden candlesticks.

IT is one of the obligations which we owe to hostile
criticism that we have been forced to recognise with
great clearness the wide difference between the representation of Christ in John's Gospel and that in the
Apocalypse. That there is such a contrast is unquestionable. The Prince of all the kings of the earth,
going forth conquering and to conquer, strikes one at
once as being unlike the Christ whom the Evangelist
painted weeping at the grave of Lazarus. We can afford
to recognise the fact, though we demur to the inference
that both representations cannot have proceeded from
one pen. Surely that is not a necessary conclusion unless
the two pictures are contradictory. Does the variety
amount to discordance? Unless it do, the variety casts
no shadow of suspicion on the common authorship. I
for my part, see no inconsistency in them, and thankfully
accept both as completing each other.

This grand vision, which forms the introduction to the whole Book of the Apocalypse, gives us indeed the Lord Jesus clothed with majesty and wielding supreme power, but it also shows us the old love and tenderness. It was the old voice which fell on John's ear, in words heard from Him before, "Fear not." It was the same hand as he had often clasped that was lovingly laid upon him to strengthen him. The assurance which He gives His Apostle declares at once the change in the circumstances of His Being, and in the functions which He discharges, and the substantial identity of His Being through all the changes: "I am the first and the last. . . . I am the living, who was dead, and behold I am alive for evermore." This vision and the whole book call to us, "Behold the Lion of the Tribe of Judah;" and when we look, "Lo, in the midst of the throne, stands a Lamb as it had been slain"—the well-known meek and patient Jesus, the suffering Redeemer—"the Lamb of God which taketh away the sins of the world."

Still further, this vision is the natural introduction to all that follows, and indeed defines the main purpose of the whole book, inasmuch as it shows us Christ sustaining, directing, dwelling, in His Churches. We are thus led to expect that the remainder of the prophecy shall have the Church of Christ for its chief subject, and that the politics of the world, and the mutations of nations, shall come into view mainly in their bearing upon that.

The words of our text, then, which resumes the principal emblem of the preceding vision, are meant to set forth

permanent truths in regard to Christ's Churches, His relation to them, and theirs to the world, which I desire to
bring to your thoughts now.   They speak to us of the
Churches and their servants, of the Churches and their
work, of the Churches and their Lord.

I. We have in the symbol important truths concerning
the Churches and their servants.

The seven stars are the angels of the seven Churches.
Now I need not spend time in enumerating all the strange
and mystical interpretations which have been given to
these angels of the Churches.   I see no need for taking
them to have been anything but men; the recognised
heads and representatives of the respective communities.
The word "angel" means messenger.   Those superhuman beings, who are usually designated by it, are so
called, not to describe their nature, but their function.
They are "God's messengers," and their name means
only that.   Then the word is certainly used, both in its
Hebrew and Greek forms, in reference to men.   It is
applied to priests, and even in one passage, as it would
appear, to an officer of the synagogue.   If here we find
that each Church had its angel, who had a letter addressed
to him, who is spoken to in words of rebuke and exhortation, who could sin and repent, who could be
persecuted and die, who could fall into heresies and be
perfected by suffering, it seems to me a violent and
unnecessary hypothesis that a superhuman being is in
question.   And the name by which he is called need not
imply more than his function,—that of being the messenger and representative of the Church.

Believing this as the more probable meaning of the phrase, I see in the relations between these men and the little communities to which they belonged, an example of what should be found existing between all congregations of faithful men and the officers whom they have chosen, be the form of their polity what it may. There are certain broad principles which must underlie all Christian organizations, and are incomparably more important than the details of Church government.

Note then, first, that *the messengers are rulers.* They are described in a double manner—by a name which expresses subordination, and by a figure which expresses authority. I need not do more than remind you that throughout Scripture, from the time when Balaam beheld from afar the *star* that should come out of Jacob and the sceptre that should rise out of Israel, that has been the symbol for rulers. It is so notably in this Book of Revelation. Whatever other ideas, then, are connected with its use here, this leading one of authority must not be lost sight of.

But this double representation of these persons as being in one aspect servants and in another rulers, perfectly embodies the very essential characteristic of all office and power in Christ's Church. It is a repetition in pictorial form of the great principle, so sadly forgotten, which He gave when He said, "He that is greatest among you, let him be your servant." The higher are exalted that they may serve the lower. Dignity and authority mean liberty for more and more self-forgetting work. Power binds its possessor to toil. Wisdom is stored in one, that from him it may flow to the foolish; strength is given that by its holder feeble hands may be stayed. *Noblesse oblige.* The King himself has obeyed the law. "Jesus, knowing the Father had given all things into His hands, took a towel, and girded Himself." We are redeemed because He came to minister, and to give His life a ransom for many. He is among us "as He tha serveth." God Himself has obeyed the law. He is above all that He may bless all. He, the highest, stoops the most deeply. His dominion is built on love, and stands in giving. And that law which makes the throne of God the refuge of all the weak, and the treasury of all the poor, is given for our guidance in our humble measure. Wheresoever Christian men think more of themselves and of their dignity than of their brethren and their work; wheresoever gifts are hoarded selfishly or selfishly squandered; wheresoever the accidents of authority, its baubles and signature, its worldly consequences, and its pride of place, bulk larger in its possessors' eyes than its solemn obligations;—there the law is broken, and the heathen devilish notion of rule lays waste the Church of God.

The true idea is not certain to be held, nor its tempting counterfeit to be avoided, by any specific form of organization. Wherever there are offices, there will be danger of officialism. Where there are none, that will not drive out selfishness. Quakerism and Episcopacy, with every form of Church government that lies between, are in danger from the same source—our forgetfulness that, in Christ's kingdom, to rule is to serve. All Churches have shown that their messengers could become "lords over God's heritage." The true spirit of Christ's servants is not secured by any theory about the appointment or the duties of the servants, but only by fellowship and sympathy with the Master who helps us all, and cares nothing for any glory which He cannot share with His disciples.

But to be servant of all does not mean to do the bidding of all. The service which imitates Christ is helpfulness, not subjection. Neither the Church is to lord it over the messenger, nor the messenger over the Church. The true bond is broken by official claims of dominion; it is broken just as much by popular claims to control. All alike are to stand free from all men—in independence of will, thought, and action; shaping their lives and moulding their beliefs, according to Christ's will and Christ's word; and repelling all coercion, from whatsoever quarter it comes. All alike are by love to serve one another; counting every possession, material, intellectual, and spiritual, as given for the general good. The one guiding principle is, "He that is chiefest among you, let him be your servant," and the other, which guards this from misconstruction and abuse from either side, "One is your Master, even Christ, and all ye are brethren."

Another point to be observed in this symbol is, that the *messengers and the Churches have at bottom the same work to do.*

Stars shine, so do lamps. Light comes from both, in different fashion indeed, and of a different quality, but still both are lights. These are in the Saviour's hands those are by His side; but each is meant to stream ou rays of brightness over a dark night. So, essentially, all Christian men have the same work to do. The ways of doing it differ, but the thing done is one. Whatever be the difference between those who hold offices in God's Church and the bulk of their brethren, there is no difference here. The loftiest gifts, the most conspicuous position, the closest approach to the central un, have no other purpose than that which the lowliest powers, in the obscurest corner, are meant to subserve. The one distributing Spirit divides to each man severally as He will; and whether He endows him with starlike gifts, which soar above and blaze over half the world with lustre that lives through the centuries, or whether he set him in some cottage-window to send out a tiny cone of light, that pierces a little way into the night for an hour or two, and then is quenched—it is all one. The manifestation of the Spirit is given to every man for the same purpose,—to do good with. And we have all one office and function to be discharged by each in his own fashion—namely, to give the light of the knowledge of the glory of God in the face of Christ Jesus.

Again, observe, *the Churches and their messengers are alike in their religious condition and character.* The successive letters treat his strength or weakness, his fervour or coldness, his sin or victory over evil, as being theirs. He represents them completely. And that representative character seems to me to be the only reason worth considering for supposing that these angels are super human beings, inasmuch as it seems that the identification is almost too entire to be applicable to the relation of any man to the community. But, perhaps, if we think of the facts which every day's experience shows us, we may see even in this solemn paralleling of the spiritual state of the Churches and of their servants, a strong reason for holding to our interpretation, as well as a very serious piece of warning and exhortation for us all.

For is it not true that the religious condition of a Church, and that of its leaders, teachers, pastors, ever tend to be the same, as that of the level of water in two connected vessels? There is such a constant interaction and reciprocal influence that uniformity results. Either a living teacher will, by God's grace, quicken a languid Church, or a languid Church will, with the devil's help, stifle the life of the teacher. Take two balls of iron, one red hot, and one cold, and put them down beside each other. How many degrees of difference between them, after half an hour, will your thermometer show? Thank God for the many instances in which one glowing soul, all aflame with love of God, has sufficed to kindle a whole heap of dead matter, and send it leaping skyward in ruddy brightness! Alas! for the many instances in which the wet green wood has been too strong for the little spark, and has not only obstinately resisted, but has ignominiously quenched its ineffectual fire! Thank God, that when His Church lives on a high level of devotion, it has never wanted for single souls who have towered even above that height, and have been elevated by it, as the snowy Alps spring not from the flats of Holland, but from the high central plateau of Europe. Alas! for the leaders who have rayed out formalism, and have chilled down the Church to their own coldness, and stiffened it to their own deadness!

Let us, then, not bandy reproaches from pulpit to pew, and from pew to pulpit; but remembering that the spiritual character of each helps to determine the condition of the whole and the general condition of the body determines the vigour of each part, let us go together to God with acknowledgments of common faithlessness, and of our individual share in it, and let us ask Him to quicken His Church, that it may yield messengers who in their turn shall be the helpers of His people and the glory of God.

II. The text brings before us, *the Churches and their work.*

Of course, you understand that what the Apostle saw was not seven candlesticks, which are a modern piece of furniture, but seven lamps. There is a distinct reference in this, as in all the symbols of the Apocalypse, to the Old Testament. We know that in the Jewish Temple there stood, as an emblem of Israel's work in the world, the great seven-branched candlestick burning for ever before the veil and beyond the altar. The difference between the two symbols is as obvious as their resemblance. The ancient lamp had all the seven bowls springing from a single stem. It was a formal unity. The New Testament seer saw not one lamp with seven arms rising from one pillar, but seven distinct lamps—the emblems of a unity which was not formal, but real. They were one in their perfect manifoldness, because of Him who walked in the midst. In which difference lies a representation of one great element in the superiority of the Church over Israel, that for the hard material oneness of the separated nation there has come the true spiritual oneness of the Churches of the saints, one not because of any external connection, but by reason that Christ is in them. The seven-branched lamp lies at the bottom of the Tiber. There let it lie. We have a better thing, in these mani fold lights, which stand before the Throne of ne New Temple, and blend into one, because lighted from one Source, fed by one Spirit, tended and watched by one Lord.

But looking a little more closely at this symbol, it suggests to us some needful thoughts as to the position and work of the Church, which is set forth as being *light, derived light, clustered light.*

The Church is to be light. That familiar image, which applies, as we have seen, to stars and lamps alike, lends itself naturally to point many an important lesson as to what we have to do, and how we ought to do it. Think, for instance, how spontaneously light streams forth. "Light is light, which circulates." The substance which is lit cannot but shine; and if we have any real possession of the truth, we cannot but impart it; and if we have any real illumination from the Lord, who is the light, we cannot but give it forth. There is much good done in the world by direct conscious effort. There is perhaps more done by spontaneous unconscious shining, by the involuntary influence of character, than by the lip or the pen. We need not balance the one form of usefulness against the other. We need both. But,

Christian men and women, do you remember that from you a holy impression revealing Jesus ought to flow as constantly, as spontaneously, as light from the sun! Our lives should be like the costly box of fragrant ointment which that penitent, loving woman lavished on her Lord, the sweet, penetrating, subtle odour of which stole through all the air till the house was filled. So His name, the revelation of His love, the resemblance to His character, should breathe forth from our whole being; and whether we think of it or no, we should be unto God a sweet savour of Christ.

Then think again how *silent* and gentle, though so mighty, is the action of the light. Morning by morning God's great mercy of sunrise steals upon a darkened world in still, slow, self-impartation; and the light which has a force that has carried it across gulfs of space that the imagination staggers in trying to conceive, yet falls so gently that it does not move the petals of the sleeping flowers, nor hurt the lids of an infant's eyes, nor displace a grain of dust. Its work is mighty, and done without "speech or language." Its force is gigantic, but, like its Author, its gentleness makes its dependents great. So should we live and work, clothing all our power in tenderness, doing our work in quietness, disturbing nothing but the darkness, and with silent increase of beneficent power filling and flooding the dark earth with healing beams.

Then think again that heaven's light is self *invisible*, and, revealing all things, reveals not itself. The source you can see, but not the beams. So we are to shine, not showing ourselves but our Master—not coveting fame or conspicuousness—glad if, like one to whom He bore testimony that he was a light, it be said of us to all that ask who we are, " He was not that light, but was sent to bear witness of that light," and rejoicing without stint or reservation that for us, as for John the Baptist, the necessity is, that we must decrease and Christ must increase.

We may gather from this emblem in the text the further lesson that *the Church's light is derived light.* Two things are needed for the burning of a lamp : that it should be lit, and that it should be fed. In both respects the light with which we shine is derived. We are not suns, we are moons ; reflected, not self-originated, is all our radiance. That is true in all senses of the figure : it is truest in the highest. It is true about all in every man which is of the nature of light. Christ is the true light which lighteth every man that cometh into the world. Whatsoever beam of wisdom, whatsoever ray of purity, whatsoever sunshine of gladness has ever been in any human spirit, from Him it came, who is the Light and Life of men : from Him it came, who brings to us in form fitted for our eyes, that otherwise inaccessible light of God in which alone we see light. And as for the more special work of the Church (which chiefly concerns us now) the testimony of Christ to John which I have just quoted in another connection gives us the principle which is true about all. " He was not that light," the Evangelist said of John, denying that in him was original and native radiance. " He was a lamp burning "—where

the idea is possibly rather "lighted" or made to burn—
and therefore shining, and in whose light men could rejoice for a little while. A derived and transient light is
all that any man can be. In ourselves we are darkness,
and only as we hold fellowship with Him do we become
capable of giving forth any rays of light. The condition
of all our brightness is that Christ shall give us light.
He is the source, we are but reservoirs. He the fountain, we only cisterns. He must walk amidst the candlesticks, or they will never shine. He must hold the stars
in his hand, or they will drop from their places and
dwindle into darkness. Therefore our power for service
lies in reception ; and if we are to live *for* Christ, we
must live *in* Christ.

But there is still another requisite for the shining of
the light. The prophet Zechariah once saw in vision the
great Temple lamp, and by its side two olive-trees from
which golden oil flowed through golden pipes to the
central light. And when he expressed his ignorance of
the meaning of the vision, this was the interpretation by
the angel who talked with him : "Not by might, nor by
power, but by My Spirit, saith the Lord of Hosts." The
lamp that burns must be kept fed with oil. Throughout
the Old Testament the soft gracious influences of God's
Spirit are symbolized by oil, with which therefore
prophets, priests, and kings were designated to their
office. Hence the Messiah in prophecy says, " The
Spirit of the Lord is upon me, because He hath anointed
me." Thus the lamp too must be fed, the soul which is
to give forth the light of Christ must first of all have

been kindled by Him, and then must constantly be supplied with the grace and gift of His Divine Spirit. Solemn lessons, my friends, gather round that thought. What became of those who had lamps without oil? Their lamps had gone out, and their end was darkness. Oh! let us beware lest by any sloth and sin, we choke the golden pipes, through which there steals into our tiny lamps the soft flow of that Divine oil which alone can keep up the flame. The wick, untrimmed and unfed, may burn for a little while, but it soon chars, and smokes, and goes out at last in foul savour offensive to God and man. Take care lest you resist the Holy Spirit of God. Let your loins be girt and your lamps burning; and that they may be, give heed that the light caught from Jesus be fed by the pure oil which alone can save it from extinction.

Again, the text sets before us the *Church's light as blended or clustered light.*

Each of these little communities is represented by one lamp. And that one light is composed of the united brightness of all the individuals who constitute the community. They are to have a character, an influence, a work as a society, not merely as individuals. There is to be co-operation in service, there is to be mingling of powers, there is to be subordination of individuals to the whole, and each separate man and his work is to be gladly merged in the radiance that issues from the community. A Church is not to be merely a multitude of separate points of brilliancy, but the separate points are to coalesce into one great orbed brightness. You know

M 2

these lights which we use now in public places, where
you have a ring pierced with a hundred tiny holes, from
each of which bursts a separate flame ; but when all are
lit, they run into one brilliant circle, and lose their
separateness in the rounded completeness of the blended
blaze.   That is like what Christ's Church ought to be.
We each by our own personal contact with Him, by our
individual communion with our Saviour, become light in
the Lord, and yet we joyfully blend with our brethren,
and, fused into one, give forth our mingled light.   We
unite our voices to theirs, knowing that all are needed to
send out the Church's choral witness and to hymn the
Church's full-toned praise.   The lips of the multitude
thunder out harmony, before which the melody of the
richest and sweetest single voice is thin and poor.

Union of heart, union of effort is commended to us
by this symbol of our text.   The great law is, work
together if you would work with strength.   To separate
ourselves from our brethren is to lose power.   Why,
half-dead brands heaped close will kindle one another,
and flame will sparkle beneath the film of white ashes
on their edges.   Fling them apart and they go out.
Rake them together and they glow.   Let us try not to
be little feeble tapers, stuck in separate sockets, and
each twinkling struggling rays over some inch or so of
space ; but draw near to our brethren, and be workers
together with them, that there may rise a glorious flame
from our summed and collective brightness which shall
be a guide and hospitable call to many a wandering and
weary spirit.

III. Finally, the text shows us *the Churches and their Lord*.

He it is who holds the stars in His right hand, and walks among the candlesticks. That strong grasp of that mighty hand—for the word in the original conveys more than "holds," it implies a tight and powerful grip —sustains and guards His servants, whose tasks need special grace, and whose position exposes them to special dangers. They may be of good cheer, for none shall pluck them out of His hand. That strengthening and watchful presence moves among His Churches, and is active on their behalf. The symbols are but the pictorial equivalent of His own parting promise, "Lo, I am with you always!"

That presence is a plain literal fact, however feebly we lay hold of it. It is not to be watered down into a strong expression for the abiding influence of Christ's teaching or example, nor even to mean the constant benefits which flow to us from His work, nor the presence of His loving thoughts with us. All these things are true and blessed, but none of them, nor all of them taken together, reach to the height of this great promise. He is absent in body, He is present in person. Talk of a "real presence!" This is *the* real presence : "I will not leave you orphans, I will come unto you." Through all the ages, in every land wheresoever two or three are gathered in His name, there is He in the midst of them. The presence of Christ with His Church is analogous to the Divine presence in the material universe. As in it, the presence of God is the condition of all life; and if He were not here, there were no beings and no "here:" so in the Church, Christ's presence constitutes and sustains it, and without Him it would cease.   So St. Augustine says, "Where Christ, there the Church."

I know what wild absurdities these statements appear, to many men who have no faith in the true Divinity of our Lord.   Of course, the belief of His perpetual presence with His people implies the belief that He possesses Divine attributes.   This mysterious Person, who lived among men the exemplar of all humility, departing, leaves a promise which is either the very acme of insane arrogance, or comes from the consciousness of indwelling Divinity.   He declares that, from generation to generation, He will in very deed be with all who in every place call upon His name.   Who does He thereby claim to be?

For what purpose is He there with His Churches? The text assures us that it is to hold up and to bless. His unwearied hand sustains, His unceasing activity moves among them.   But beyond these purposes, or rather included in them, the vision of which the text is the interpretation brings into great prominence the thought that He is with us to observe, to judge, and, if need be, to punish.   Mark how almost all the attributes of that majestic figure suggest such thoughts.   The eyes like a flame of fire, the feet glowing as if in a furnace, hot to burn, heavy to tread down all evil where He walks, from the lips a two-edged sword to smite, and thank God to heal, the countenance as the sun shineth

in his strength—this is the Lord of the Churches
Yes, and this is the same loving and forbearing Lord
whom the Apostle had learned to trust on earth, and
found again revealed from heaven.

Brethren! He dwells with us; He guards and pro-
tects His Churches to the end, else they perish. He
rules all the commotions of earth, all the errors of His
people, all the delusions of lies, and overrules them all
for the strengthening and purifying of His Church. But
He dwells with us likewise as the watchful observer
out of these eyes of flame, of all our faults, as the merciful destroyer with the sword of His mouth, of every
error and every sin. Thank God for the chastising
presence of Christ. He loves us too well not to smite
us when we need it. He will not be so cruelly kind,
so foolishly fond, as in anywise to suffer sin upon us.
Better the eye of fire than the averted face. Better the
sharp sword than His holding His peace as He did with
Caiaphas and Herod. Better the Judge in our midst,
though we should have to fall at His feet as dead,
than that He should say, "I will go and return to My
place." Pray Him not to depart, and submit to the
merciful rebukes and effectual chastisement which prove
that, for all our unworthiness, He loves us still, and has
not cast us away from His presence.

Nor let us forget how much of hope and encouragement lies in the examples, which these seven Churches
afford, of His long-suffering patience. That presence
was granted to them all, the best and the worst,—the
decaying love of Ephesus, the licentious heresies of

Pergamos and Thyatira, the all but total deadness of Sardis, and the self-satisfied indifference of Laodicea, concerning which even He could say nothing that was good. All had Him with them as really as the faithful Smyrna and the steadfast Philadelphia. We have no right to say with how much of theoretical error and practical sin the lingering presence of that patient pitying Lord may consist. For others our duty is the widest charity,—for ourselves the most careful watchfulness.

For these seven Churches teach us another lesson— the possibility of quenched lamps and ruined shrines. Ephesus and her sister communities, planted by Paul, taught by John, loved and upheld by the Lord, warned and scourged by Him,—where are they now? Broken columns and roofless walls remain ; and where Christ's name was praised, now the minaret rises by the side of the mosque, and daily echoes the Christless proclamation, " There is no God but God, and Mahomet is His prophet." The grace of God," says Luther somewhere, " is like a flying summer shower." It has fallen upon more than one land, and passed on. Judæa had it, and lies barren and dry. These Asiatic coasts had it, and flung it away. Let us receive it, and hold it fast, lest our greater light should bring greater condemnation, and here, too, the candlestick should be removed out of its place.

Remember that solemn strange legend which tells us that, on the night before Jerusalem fell, the guard of the Temple heard through the darkness a voice mighty and sad, saying, " Let us depart," and were aware as of the

sound of many wings passing from out of the Holy
Place ; and on the morrow the iron heels of the Roman
legionaries trod the marble pavement of the innermost
shrine, and heathen eyes gazed upon the empty place
where the glory of the God of Israel should have dwelt,
and a torch, flung by an unknown hand, burned with fire
the holy and beautiful house where He had promised
to put His name for ever.   And let us learn the lesson,
and hold fast by that Lord whose blood has purchased,
and whose presence preserves through all the unworthiness and the lapses of men, that Church against which
the gates of hell shall not prevail.

MANHOOD CROWNED IN JESUS.

HEBREWS ii. 8, 9.

We see not yet all things put under Him, but we see Jesus.

ONE of our celebrated astronomers is said to have taught himself the rudiments of his starry science when lying on the hill-side, keeping his father's sheep. Perhaps the grand Psalm to which these words refer had a similar origin, and may have come from the early days of the shepherd king, when, like those others of a later day, he abode in the field of Bethlehem, keeping watch over his flock by night. The magnificence of the Eastern heavens, with their " larger constellations burning," filled his soul with two opposite thoughts—man's smallness and man's greatness. I suppose that in a mind apt to pensive reflections, alive to moral truths, and responsive to the impressions of God's great universe, the unscientific contemplation of any of the grander forms of nature produces that double effect. And certainly the grandest of them all, which is spread over our heads, little as we dwellers in cities can see the heavens for daily smoke and nightly lamps, forces both these thoughts upon us. They seem so far above us, they swim into their stations night after night, and look down with cold unchanging beauty on sorrow, and hot strife, and shrieks, and groans, and death. They are so calm, so pure, so remote, so eternal. Thus David felt man's littleness. And yet— and yet, bigness is not greatness, and duration is not life, and the creature that knows God is highest. So the consciousness of man's separation from, and superiority to, these silent stars, springs up strong and victorious over the other thought. Remember that, in David's time, the nations near, who were believed to be the very centre of wisdom, had not got beyond the power of these impressions, but on Chaldean plains worshipped the host of heaven. The psalm then is a protest against the most fascinating, and to David's age the most familiar, form of idolatry. These great lights are not rulers, but servants ; we are more than they, because we have spirits which link us with God.

Then, kindling as he contemplates man as God meant him to be, the poet bursts into rapturous celebration of man's greatness in these respects—that he is visited by God, capable of Divine communion, and a special object of Divine care ; that he is only lower than the loftiest, and that but in small degree and in one specific respect, because they, in their immortal strength, are not entangled in flesh as we ; that over all others of God's creatures on earth he is king.

"Very fine words," may be fairly said ; " but do they correspond to facts ? What manhood are you talking about?   Where is this being, so close to God, so lowly before Him, so firmly lord of all besides?"   That is the question which the writer of the Epistle to the Hebrews deals with in our text.   He has quoted the psalm as an illustration of his thesis that Christ, and we in Christ, are exalted above angels, and then he proceeds to admit that, as a matter of fact, men are not what David describes them as being.   But the psalm is not, therefore, an exaggeration, nor a dream, nor a mere ideal of the imagination.   True, as a matter of fact, men are not all this.   But, as a matter of fact, Jesus Christ is, and in His possession of all that the psalm painted, our possession is commenced and certified.   It *is* an ideal picture, but it is realized in Jesus, and, having been so in Him, we have ground to believe that it will be so in us.   We see not yet all things put under man—alas no, but—we see Jesus crowned with glory and honour; and as He tasted death for every man, so in His exaltation He is prophecy and pledge that the grand old words shall one day be fulfilled in all their height and depth.

The text, then, brings before us a threefold sight.   It bids us *look around*, and if that sadden us, it bids us *look up*, and thence it bids us draw confidence to *look forward*.   There is an estimate of present facts, there is a perception by faith of the unseen fact of Christ's glory, and there follows from that the calm prospect for the future for ourselves and for our brethren.   Let us deal with these considerations in order.

1. *Look at the sight around us.*

" We see not yet all things put under man."   Where

are the men of whom any portion of the Psalmist's words is true? Look at them—are these the men of whom he sings? Visited by God! crowned with glory and honour! having dominion over the works of His hands! Is this irony or fact?

Let consciousness speak. Look at ourselves. **If** that psalm be God's thought of man, the plan that He hangs up for us His workmen to build by, what a wretched thing my copy of it has turned out to be! Is this a picture of me? How seldom I am conscious of the visits of God; how full I am of weaknesses and imperfections—the solemn voice within me tells me at intervals when I listen to its tones. On my brow there gleams no diadem; from my life, alas! there shines at the best but a fitful splendour of purity, all striped with solid masses of blackness. And as for dominion over creatures, how superficial my rule over them, how real their rule over me! I can tame animals or slay them; I can use the forces of nature for my purposes; I can make machinery, and bid the lightning do my errands, and carry messages, the burden of which is mostly money, or power, or sorrow. But all these, and the whole set of things like them, are not ruling over God's creation. That consists in using all for God, and for our own growth in wisdom, strength, and goodness; and he only is master of all things who is servant of God. "All are yours, and ye are Christ's." If so, what are most of us but servants, not lords, of earth and its goods? We fasten our very lives on them, we tremble at the bare thought of losing them, we give our best efforts to get them—we say to the fine gold, "Thou art my confidence." We do not possess them, they possess us: and so, though materially we may have conquered the earth (and wonderfully proud of it we are now), spiritually, which is the same as to say *really*, the earth has conquered us.

The same impression of human incompleteness is made by all the records of human lives which we possess. Go into a library, and take down volume after volume— the biographies and autobiographies of the foremost men, the saints and sages whom we all reverence.   Is there one on whose monument the old psalm could truthfully be written? Are not the honest autobiographies what one of the noblest of them is called, "Confessions?" Are not the memoirs the stories of flawed excellence, stained purity, limited wisdom? There are no perfect men in them—no men after the pattern of David's words.   Or if some enthusiastic admirer has drawn a picture without shadows, we feel that it is without life or likeness ; and we look for faults and limitations that we may be sure of brotherhood.

And if we take a wider range, and listen to the sad voice of history chronicling the past, where in all her tragic story of bright hopes brought to nothing, of powers built up by force and rotted down by pride and selfishness, of war and wrong, of good painfully sought, and partially possessed, and churlishly treasured, and quickly lost—where on all her blotted pages, stained with tears, and sweat, and blood, do we find a record that verifies the singer's rapture, and shows us men like this?

Or let observation speak. Bring before your minds, by an exercise of imagination vivifying and uniting into one impression, the facts which we all know of the social and moral condition—to say nothing now of the religious state—of any country upon earth. Think of the men in all lands who are helpless, hopeless, full of animal sins and lusts, full of stupid ignorance. Take our psalm and read it in some gaol, or in a lunatic asylum, or at the door of some gin-palace, or at the mouth of a court in the back streets of any city in England, and ask yourselves, "Are these people, with narrow foreheads and villanous scowls, with sodden cheeks and foul hands, the fulfilment or the contradiction of its rapturous words?" Or think of naked savages, who look up to bears and lions as their masters, who are stunted by cold or enervated by heat, out of whose souls have died all memories beyond yesterday's hunger, and all hopes greater than a full meal to-morrow —and say if these are God's men. So little are they like it that some of us are ready to say that they are not men at all.

What then? Are we to abandon in despair our hopes for our fellows, and to smile with quiet incredulity at the rhapsodies of sanguine theorists like David? If we are to confine our view to earth—yes. But there is more to see than the sad sights around us. All these men—these imperfect, degraded, half brutified men—have their share in our psalm. They have gone out, and wasted their substance in riotous living; but from the swine-trough and the rags they may come to the best robe and the feast in the father's house. The veriest barbarian, with

scarcely a spark of reason or a flickering beam of conscience, sunken in animal delights, and vibrating between
animal hopes and animal fears—to him may belong the
wondrous attributes : to be visited by God, crowned
with glory and honour, higher than all stars, and lord
of all creatures.

It sounds like a wild contradiction, I know : and I do
not in the least wonder that people pressed by a sense
of all the misery that is done under the sun, and faintly
realizing for themselves Christ's power to heal their own
misery and cleanse their own sins, should fling away their
Bibles, and refuse to believe that "God hath made of
one blood all nations of men," and that Christ has a
message for the world. I venture to believe both the
one and the other. I believe that though angels weep,
and we should be smitten with shame, at the sight of
what man has made of man, and we of ourselves, yet
that God shall be true though every man fail Him, and
will fulfil unto the children the mercy which He has
promised to the fathers. "All the promises of God in
Christ are yea." And so against all the theories of the
desperate school, and against all our own despondent
thoughts, we have to oppose the sunny hopes which
come from such words as those of our text. Looking
around us, we have indeed to acknowledge with plaintive
emphasis, "we see not yet all things put under Him"—
but, looking up, we have to add with triumphant confidence that we speak of a fact which has a real bearing
on our hopes for men—" we see Jesus."

II. So, secondly, *Look upwards to Jesus.*

Christ in glory appears to the author of this epistle to be the full realization of the Psalmist's ideal. Our text deals only with the exalted dignity and present majesty of the ascended Lord; but before touching upon that, we may venture, for a moment, to dwell upon the past of Christ's life as being also the carrying out of David's vision of true manhood. We have to look backward as well as upward, if we would have a firm hope for men. The ascended Christ upon the throne, and the historical Christ upon the earth, teach us what man may be, the one in regard of dignity, the other in regard of goodness.

Here *is* a fact. Such a life was verily once lived on earth; a life of true manhood, whatever more it was. In it we may see two things: first, we may see from His perfect purity what it is possible for man to become; and second, we may see from His experience who said, "The Father hath not left Me alone, because I do always the things which please Him," how close a fellowship is possible between the human spirit that lives for and by obedience, and the Father of us all. The man Christ Jesus was visited by God, yea, God dwelt with Him ever; whatever more He was,—and He was infinitely more,—He was also our example of communion, as He was our example of righteousness.

And that life is to be our standard. I refuse to take other men, the highest, as specimens of what we may become. I refuse to take other men, the lowest, as instances of what we are condemned to be. Here in Jesus Christ is the type; and, albeit it is alone in its beauty, yet it is more truly a specimen of manhood than

2ND SER.   N

the fragmentary, distorted, incomplete men are who are found everywhere besides. Christ is the power to conform us to Himself, as well as the pattern of what we may be. He and none lower, He and none beside, is the pattern man. Not the great conqueror, nor the great statesman, nor the great thinker, but the great Lover, the perfectly good—is the man as God meant him to be. As it has been said, with pardonable extravagance, "Aristotle was but the rubbish of an Adam," so in sober truth we may affirm that the noblest and fairest characters, approximating as they may to the picture in the psalm, and giving us some reason to hope that more is possible for us than we sometimes think, are after all but fragments of precious stones as compared with that one entire and perfect chrysolite, whose unflawed beauty and completeness drinks in, and flashes forth, the whole light of God. He is not ashamed to call us brethren. Therefore, if we would know what a man is, and what a man may become, let us not only look inward to our own faults, nor around us at these broken bits of goodness, but let us look back to Christ, and be of good cheer. We hear and see more than enough of men's folly, stupidity, godlessness, and sin. Nevertheless—we see Jesus. Let us have hope.

But turn now to the consideration of what is more directly intended by our text, namely, the contemplation of Christ in the heavens, "crowned with glory and honour," as the true type of man. What does Scripture teach us to see in the exalted Lord?

It sets before us, first, a *perpetual* manhood. The

whole force of the words before us depends on the assumption that, in all His glory and dominion, Jesus Christ remains what He was on earth, truly and properly man. There is a strong tendency in many minds to think of Christ's incarnation and humanity as transitory. I do not mean that such a conception is thrown into articulate form as a conscious article of belief, but it haunts people none the less, and gives a feeling of unreality and remoteness to what the Scripture says of our Lord's present life. Many believers in the eternal existence and divinity of our Lord think of His incarnation much after the fashion in which heathendom conceived that the gods came down in the likeness of men—as if it were a mere transitory appearance, the wearing of a garb of human nature but for a moment. Whereas the Biblical representation is that for evermore, by an indissoluble union, the Human is assumed into the Divine, and that "to-day and for ever" He remains the man Christ Jesus. Nor is a firm grasp of that truth of small importance, nor is the truth itself a theological subtlety, without bearing upon human interests and practical life. Rather it is the very hinge on which turn our loftiest hopes. Without it, that mighty work which He ever carries on, of succouring them that are tempted, and having compassion with us, were impossible. Without that permanent manhood, His mighty work of preparing a place for us, and making heaven a home for men because a man is its Lord, were at an end. Without it He in His glory would be no prophecy of man's dominion, nor would He have entered for us into the holy place.   Grasp firmly the essential, perpetual manhood of Jesus Christ, and then to see Him crowned with glory and honour gives the triumphant answer to the despairing question that rises often to the lips of every one who knows the facts of life, " Wherefore hast Thou made all men in vain ? "

Again, we see in Jesus, exalted in the heavens, *a corporeal manhood.*   That thought touches upon very dark subjects, concerning which Scripture says little, and no other voice says anything at all.   The resurrection and ascension of Jesus Christ are our great reasons for believing that man, in his perfect condition, has body as well as spirit.   And that belief is one chief means of giving definiteness and reality to our anticipations of a future life.   Without the belief of a corporeal manhood, the unseen world becomes vague and shapeless, is taken out of the range of our faculties altogether, and soon becomes powerless to hold its own against the pressure of palpable present realities.   But we see Jesus—ascended up on high in man's body.   Therefore He is somewhere now.   Heaven is a place as well as a state ; and however, for the present, the souls that sleep in Jesus may have to " wait for the adoption, to wit, the redemption of the body," and, being unclothed, may be wrapped about with Him, and rest in His bosom, yet the perfect men who shall one day stand before the Lord, shall have body, and soul, and spirit—like Him who is a man for ever, and for ever wears a human frame.

Further, we see in Jesus *transfigured manhood.*

Once when He was on earth, as some hidden light breaks through all veils, the pent-up glory of the great " God with us " seemed to stream through His flesh, and tinge with splendour even the skirts of His garments. " He was transfigured before them," not as it would appear by light reflected from above, but by radiance up-bursting from within. And besides all its other lessons, that solemn hour on the Mount of Transfiguration gave some small hint and prelude of the possibilities of glory that lay hidden in Christ's material body, which possibilities become realities after (though not, in His case, *by*) death ; when He ascended up on high, beautiful and changed, being clothed with " the body of His glory." For Him, as for us, flesh here means weakness and dishonour. Fo: us, though not for Him, flesh means corruption and death. For Him, as for us, that natural body, which was adequate to the needs and adapted to the material constitution of this earth, must be changed into the spiritual body correspondent to the conditions of that kingdom of God which flesh and blood cannot enter. For us, through Him, the body of humiliation shall be changed into likeness of the body of His glory. We see Jesus, and in Him manhood transfigured and perfected.

Finally, we see in Jesus *sovereign manhood.* The Psalmist thought of man as crowned with glory and honour, as having dominion over the works of God's hands. And here is his thought embodied in far higher manner than ever he imagined possible. Here is a man exalted to absolute, universal dominion. The sovereignty of Jesus Christ is not a metaphor, nor a rhetorical hyperbole. It is, if we believe the New Testament writers, a literal prose fact. He directs the history of the world, and presides among the nations. He is the prince of all the kings of the earth. He wields the forces of nature, He directs the march of providence, He is Lord of the unseen worlds, and holds the keys of death and the grave. "The government is upon His shoulders," and upon Him hangs "all the glory of His Father's house." Angels served Him in His lowliness, and strengthened Him in His agony; they watched His grave, and when He ascended on high, the multitudes of the heavenly hosts, even thousands of angels, were the chariot of the conquering Lord. Angels are His servants now, and all do worship Him. He holdeth the stars in His right hand, and all creatures gather obedient round His throne. His voice is law, His will is power. He says to this one "Go," and he goeth; He rebukes winds and seas, diseases and devils, and they obey; to all He says, "Do this," and they do it. He speaks, and it is done. "On His head are many crowns." Thou art the King of Glory, O Christ—and, seeing Jesus, we see man crowned with glory and honour.

III. Finally, then, *look forward.*

Though it be only too true that the vision seems to tarry, and that weary centuries roll on, and bring us but so little nearer its accomplishment; though the fair promise, at which the morning stars sang together, and all the sons of God shouted for joy, seems to have faded away; though the hope of the Psalmist is unfulfilled yet; though the strain of a yet higher mood, proclaiming peace on earth, which later shepherds of Bethlehem heard from amid the silent stars, has died away, and the war shout lives on; still, in the strength which flows from seeing Jesus exalted, we can look for a certain future, wherein men shall be all that God proposed, and all that their Saviour is. Rolling clouds hide the full view, but through them gleams the lustrous walls of the city which hath the foundations. We look forward, and we see men sharing in Christ's glory, and gathered together round His throne.

Christ is the measure of man's capacities. He is the true pattern of human nature. Christ is the prophecy and pledge of man's dominion. From Christ comes the power by which the prophecy is fulfilled, and the pattern reproduced in all who love Him. Whosoever is joined to Him receives into his soul that spirit of life in Christ which unfolds and grows according to its own law, and has for its issue and last result the entire conformity between the believing soul and the Saviour by whom it lives. It were a poor consolation to point to Christ and say, "Look what man has become, and may become," unless we could also say, "A real and living oneness exists between Him and all who cleave to Him, so that their characters are changed, their natures cleansed, their future altered, their immortal beauty secured." He is more than pattern, He is power; more than specimen, He is source; more than example, He is redeemer. He has been made in the likeness of sinful flesh, that we may be in the likeness of His body of glory. He has been made "sin for us, that we might be made the righteousness of God in Him." His exaltation, if it were ever so much a fact, and ever so firmly believed, yields no basis for hope as to any beyond Himself, but on one supposition. To see man exalted and his glory ensured in Christ's, the glory of Christ must be connected, as is done in our text, with His tasting death for every man. When I know that He has died for me, and for all my brethren who sit in darkness, and hear each other groan as the poison shoots through their veins, then I can feel that, as He has been in the likeness of our death, we shall also be in the likeness of His resurrection. Brethren, the Cross, and the Cross alone, certifies our participation in the Crown. Unless Jesus Christ have and exercise that wondrous power of delivering from sin and self, and of quickening to a new life, which He exercises only as Sacrifice and Saviour, there were nothing which were more irrelevant to the hopes of man's future han the story of His purity and of His dominion. What were all that to men writhing with evil? What hope for single souls or for the world in the knowledge that He was good, or in the belief that He had gone up on high? If that were all, what would it all matter? The lack-lustre eyes that have grown wan with waiting will have no light of hope kindled in them by such a gospel as that. But bid them look, languid and weary as they are, to Him who is lifted up, that whosoever believeth on Him should not perish—that vision will give to the still loftier sight of Christ on the throne its true meaning, as not a barren triumph for Himself alone, but as victory for us—yea, our victory in Him. If we can say, "God, who is rich in

mercy for His great love wherewith He loved us, even
when we were dead in sins, hath quickened us together,"
then we can add, "and hath raised us up together, and
made us sit together in heavenly places in Jesus Christ."

And what wonderful hopes, dimly discerned indeed,
but firmly founded, we have a right to cherish, if what
we see in Jesus we may predict for His brethren! We
shall be like Him in all these points to which we have
already referred. We, too, shall have a corporeal manhood transfigured and glorified. We, too, shall have
perfect union and communion with the Father. We, too,
shall be invested with all the unknown prerogatives
which are summed up in that last promise of His, beyond
which nothing more glorious can be conceived, "To him
that overcometh will I grant to sit with Me on My
throne." Then the ancient word will be fulfilled in
manner beyond our dreams, "Thou hast put all things
under his feet." Who can tell what accessions of power,
what new faculties, what new relations to an external
universe, what new capacity of impressing a holy will
upon all things, what new capability of receiving from all
things their most secret messages concerning God their
Maker, may be involved in such words? We see darkly.
The hopes for the future lie around us as flowers in some
fair garden where we walk in the night, their petals closed
and their leaves asleep, but here and there a whiter
bloom gleams out, and sweet faint odours from unseen
sources steal through the dewy darkness. We can understand but little of what this majestic promise of sovereign
manhood may mean. But the fragrance, if not the sight,

of that gorgeous blossom is wafted to us. We know that
" the upright shall have dominion in the morning." We
know that to His servants authority over ten cities will
be given. We know that we shall be "kings and priests
to God." The fact we know, the contents of the fact we
wait to prove. "It doth not yet appear what we shall be."
Enough that we shall reign with Him, and that in the
kingdom of the heavens dominion means service, and
the least is the greatest.

We, too, shall be exalted above all creatures—far above
all principality and power, even as Christ is Lord of
angels. What that may include, we can but dimly sur-
mise. Nearness to God, knowledge of His heart and
will, likeness to Christ, determine superiority among
pure and spiritual beings. And Scripture, in many a
hint and half-veiled promise, bids us believe that men
who have been redeemed from their sins by the blood
of Christ, and have made experience of departure and
restoration, are set to be the exponents of a deeper
knowledge of God to powers in heavenly places, and,
standing nearest the throne, become the chorus leaders
of new praises from lofty beings who have ever praised
Him on immortal harps. They who know sin, who
remember sorrow, who learned God by the Cross
of Christ, and have proved His forgiving and sanctifying grace, must needs have a more wondrous knowledge, and be knit to Him by a tenderer bond than
the elder brethren who never transgressed His commandments. The youngest brother of the king is
nearer to him than the oldest servant who stands

before his face. Our brother is Lord of all, and His dominion is ours.

But we can speak little, definitely, about such matters. It is enough for the servant that he be as his Lord. This confidence, which may be certain, though it be not accurate, should satisfy our minds without curious detail, and should quiet our hearts however they be tempted to cast it away. Many enemies whisper to us doubts. The devil tempted first to sin by insinuating the question, "Shall ye surely die?" The devil often tempts now to sin by insinuating exactly the opposite doubt, "Can it be that you will live?" It seems to us often incredible that such hopes of immortal life should be true about such poor creatures, such wretched failures, as we feel ourselves to be. It seems often incredible that they should have any connection with men such as we see them on the average to be. We are tempted, too, in these days, to think that our psalm belongs to an exploded school of thought, to a simple astronomy which made the earth the centre of the universe, and conceived of moon and stars as tiny spangles on the hem of light's garment. We are told that science lights us to other conclusions as to man's place in creation than such as David cherished. No doubt it does as to man physically considered. But the answer to my own evil conscience, to the sad inferences from man's past and present, to the conclusions which are illegitimately sought to be extended from man's material place in a material universe to man's spiritual place as an immortal and moral being, lies in that twofold sight which we have been regarding—Christ on the cross the measure of man's worth in the eyes of God, and of man's place in the creation; Christ on the throne the prophecy of man's dignity, and of his most sure dominion.

When bordering on despair at the sight of so much going wrong, so much ignorance, sorrow, and vice, so many darkened understandings, and broken hearts, such wide tracts of savagery and godlessness, I can look up to Jesus, and can see far, far away—the furthest thing on the horizon—like some nebula, faint, it is true, and low down, but flickering with true starry light—the wondrous vision of many souls brought into glory, even a world redeemed.

When conscious of personal imperfection and much sin, no thought will bring peace nor kindle hope but this, that Christ has died to bring me to God, and lives to bring me to glory. Then, dear brethren, "behold the Lamb of God which taketh away the sin of the world." Behold Jesus entered within the veil for us. Look away from the imperfect men, the partial teachers, the incomplete saints, the powerless helpers around you, to Him, the righteous, the wise, the strong. Look at no man any more, as the hope for yourself, as the pattern for your life, save Jesus only. The gaze will feed your triumphant hope, and will make that hope a partial reality. Here you will be visited by God, here you will in some degree have all things for yours, if you are Christ's. Here, from far beneath, look up through the heavens to Him who is "made higher than" them all.

And hereafter, from the supreme height and pinnacle of the throne of Christ, we shall look down on sun, moon, and stars that once shone so far above us; and, conscious that His grace has raised us up on high, and put all things under our feet, shall exclaim with yet deeper thankfulness and more reverent wonder, "What is man, that Thou art mindful of him, and the son of man, that Thou visitest him?"

PERPETUAL YOUTH.

MARK xvi. 5.

And entering into the sepulchre, they saw a young man sitting on
the right side, clothed in a long white garment.

MANY great truths concerning Christ's death, and
its worth to all higher orders of being, are taught
by the presence of that angel form, clad in the whiteness
of his own God-given purity, sitting in restful contemplation in the dark house where the body of Jesus had lain.
"Which things the angels desire to look into." Many
precious lessons of consolation and hope, too, lie in the
wonderful words which he spake from his Lord and
theirs to the weeping waiting women. But to touch
upon these ever so slightly would lead us too far from
our more immediate purpose.

It strikes one as very remarkable that this superhuman being should be described as a "*young* man."
Immortal youth, with all of buoyant energy and fresh
power which that attribute suggests, belongs to those
beings whom Scripture faintly shows as our elder

brethren. No waste decays their strength, no change robs them of forces which have ceased to increase. For them there never comes a period when memory is more than hope. Age cannot wither them. As one of our modern mystics has said, hiding imaginative spiritualism under a crust of hard, dry matter-of-fact, " In heaven the oldest angels are the youngest."

What is true of them is true of God's children, who are "accounted worthy to obtain that world and the resurrection from the dead ;" "they are equal unto the angels." For believing and loving souls, death too is a birth. All who pass through it to God, shall, in deeper meaning than lay in the words at first, "return unto the days of their youth ;" and when the end comes, and they are clothed with their house from heaven, they shall stand by the throne, like him who sat in the sepulchre, clothed with lustrous light and radiant with unchanging youth.

Such a conception of the condition of the dead in Christ may be followed out in detail into many very elevating and strengthening thoughts. Let me attempt to set forth some of these now.

The life of the faithful dead is eternal progress towards infinite perfection.

For body and for spirit the life of earth is a definite whole, with distinct stages, which succeed each other in a well-marked order. There is youth, and maturity, and decay—the slow climbing to the narrow summit, a brief moment there in the streaming sunshine, and then a sure and gradual descent into the shadows beneath.

The same equable and constant motion urges the orb of our lives from morning to noon, and from noon to evening. The glory of the dawning day, with its golden clouds and its dewy freshness, its new awakened hopes and its unworn vigour, climbs by silent inevitable stages to the hot noon. But its ardours flame but for a moment; but for a moment does the sun poise itself on the meridian line, and the short shadow point to the pole. The inexorable revolution goes on, and in due time come the mists and dying purples of evening and the blackness of night. The same progress which brings April's perfumes burns them in the censer of the hot summer, and buries summer beneath the falling leaves, and covers the grave with winter's snow.

> " Everything that grows
> Holds in perfection but a little moment."

So the life of man, being under the law of growth, is, in all its parts, subject to the consequent necessity of decline. And very swiftly does the direction change from ascending to descending. At first, and for a little while, the motion of the dancing stream, which broadens as it runs, and bears us past fields each brighter and more enamelled with flowers than the one before it, is joyous ; but the slow current becomes awful as we are swept along when we would fain moor and land—and to some of us it comes to be tragic and dreadful at last, as we sit helpless, and see the shore rush past and hear the roar of the falls in our ears, like some poor wretch caught in the glassy smoothness above Niagara, who has flung down the oars, and, clutching the gunwale with idle hands, sits effortless and breathless till the plunge comes. Many a despairing voice has prayed as the sands run out, and joys fled, "Sun, stand thou still on Gibeon; and thou, Moon, in the valley of Ajalon." But in vain. Once the wish was answered; but, for all other fighters, the twelve hours of the day must suffice for victory and for joy. Time devours his own children. The morning hours come to us with full hands and give, the evening hours come with empty hands and take; so that at the last "naked shall he return to go as he came." Our earthly life runs through its successive stages, and for it, in body and mind, old age is the child of youth.

But the perfect life of the dead in Christ has but one phase, youth. It is growth without a limit and without decline. To say that they are ever young is the same thing as to say that their being never reaches its climax, that it is ever but entering on its glory. That is, as we have said, the true conception of their life is that of eternal progress towards infinite perfection.

For what is the goal to which they tend? The likeness of God in Christ—all His wisdom, His love, His holiness. He is all theirs, and all that He is to be transfused into their growing greatness. "He is made unto them of God, wisdom, and righteousness, and salvation and redemption," nor can they cease to grow till they have outgrown Jesus and exhausted God. On the one hand is infinite perfection, destined to be imparted to the redeemed spirit. On the other hand is a capability of indefinite assimilation to, by reception

2ND SER.   O

of, that infinite perfection. We have no reason to set bounds to the possible expansion of the human spirit. If only there be fitting circumstances and an adequate impulse, it may have an endless growth. Such circumstances and such impulse are given in the loving presence of Christ in glory. Therefore we look for an eternal life which shall never reach a point, beyond which no advance is possible. The path of the just in that higher state shineth more and more, and never touches the zenith. Here we float upon a land-locked lake, and on every side soon reach the bounding land; but there we are on a shoreless ocean, and never hear any voice that says, " Hitherto shalt thou come, and no farther." Christ will be ever before us, the yet unattained end of our desires; Christ will be ever above us, fairer, wiser, holier, than we ; after unsummed eternities of advance there will yet stretch before us a shining way that leads to Him. The language, which was often breathed by us on earth in tones of plaintive confession, will be spoken in heaven in gladness, " Not as though I had attained, either were perfect, but I follow after." The promise that was spoken by Him in regard of our mortality will be repeated by Him in respect of our celestial being, " I am come that they might have life, and that they might have it *more abundantly.*" And as this advance has no natural limit, either in regard of our Pattern or of ourselves, there will be no reverse direction to ensue. Here the one process has its two opposite parts ; the same impulse carries up to the summit and forces down from it. But not so then. The growth will never merge into decay, nor exacting Hours come to recall the gifts, which their free-handed sisters gave.

They who live in Christ, beyond the grave, begin with a relative perfection. They are thereby rendered capable of more complete Christ-likeness. The eye by gazing into the day becomes more recipient of more light; the spirit cleaves closer to a Christ, more fully apprehended and more deeply loved; the whole being, like a plant reaching up to the sunlight, grows by its yearning towards the light, and by the light towards which it strains—lifts a stronger stem and spreads a broader leaf, and opens into immortal flowers tinted by the sunlight with its own colours. This blessed and eternal growth towards Him whom we hold, to begin with, and never can exhaust, is the perpetual youth of God's redeemed.

We ought not to think of those whom we have loved and lost as if they had gone, carrying with them declining powers, and still bearing the marks of this inevitable law of stagnation, and then of decay, under which they groaned here. Think of them rather as having, if they sleep in Jesus, reversed all this, as having carried with them, indeed, all the gifts of matured experience and ripened wisdom which the slow years brings but likewise as having left behind all the weariness of accomplished aims, the monotony of a formed character, the rigidity of limbs that have ceased to grow. Think of them as receiving again from the hands of Christ much of which they were robbed by the lapse of years. Think of them as then crowned with loving-kindness and satisfied with good, so that their youth is renewed like the eagle's. Think of them as again joyous, with the joy of beginning a career, which has no term but the sum of all perfection in the likeness of the infinite God. They rise like the song-bird, aspiring to the heavens, circling round, and ever higher, which "singing still doth soar, and soaring ever singeth"—up and up through the steadfast blue to the sun! "Even the youths shall faint and be weary, and the young men shall utterly fall; but they that wait upon the Lord shall renew their strength." They shall lose the marks of age as they grow in eternity, and they who have stood before the throne the longest shall be likest him, who sat in the sepulchre young with immortal strength, radiant with unwithering beauty.

II. *The life of the faithful dead recovers and retains the best characteristics of youth.*

Each stage of our earthly course has its own peculiar characteristics, as each zone of the world has its own vegetation and animal life. And, for the most part, these characteristics cannot be anticipated in the preceding stage, nor prolonged into the succeeding. To some small extent they will bear transplanting, and he is nearest a perfect man, who carries into each period of his life some trace of the special beauty of that which went before, making "the child the father of the man," and carrying deep into old age the simple self-forgetfulness of the child and the energy of the youth. But this can only be partially done by any effort; and even those whose happily-constituted temperaments make it comparatively easy for them, do often carry the weaknesses rather than the strength of the earlier into the later epochs. It is easier to be always childish than to be always childlike. The immaturity and heedlessness of youth bear carriage better than the more precious vintages of that sunny land—its freshness of eye and heart, its openness of mind, its energy of hand. Even when these are in any measure retained—beautiful as they are in old age—they are but too apt to be associated with an absence of the excellences more proper to the later stages of life, and to involve a want of patient judgment, of sagacious discrimination, of rooted affections, of prudent persistent action. Beautiful indeed it is when the grace of the children and the strength of the young men live on in the fathers, and the last of life encloses all that was good, in all that went before. But miserable it is, and quite as frequent a case when grey hairs cover a childish brain, and an aged heart throbs with the feverish passion of youthful blood. So for this life it is difficult, and often not well, that youth should be prolonged into manhood and old age.

But the thought is none the less true, that the perfection of our being requires the reappearance and the continuance of all that was good in each successive stage of it in the past. The brightest aspects of youth will return to all who live in Jesus, beyond the grave, and will be theirs for ever. Such a consideration branches out into many happy anticipations, which we can but very cursorily touch on here.

For instance—Youth is the time *for hope.* The world

lies all before us, fair and untried. We have not learnt
our own weakness by many failures, nor the dread possibilities that lie in every future. The past is too brief to
occupy us long, and its furthest point too near to be
clothed in the airy purple, which draws the eye and stirs
the heart. We are conscious of increasing powers which
crave for occupation. It seems impossible but that
success and joy shall be ours. So we live for a little
while in a golden haze; we look down from our peak
upon the virgin forests of a new world, that roll away to
the shining waters in the west, and then we plunge into
their mazes to hew out a path for ourselves, to slay the
wild beasts, and to find and conquer rich lands. But
soon we discover what hard work the march is, and
what monsters lurk in the leafy coverts, and diseases
hover among the marshes, and how short a distance
ahead we can see, and how far off it is to the treasure-
cities we dreamed of; and if at last we gain some
cleared spot whence we can look forward, our weary
eyes are searching at most for a place to rest, and all
our hopes have dwindled to hopes of safety and repose.
The day brings too much toil to leave us leisure for
much anticipation. The journey has had too many
failures, too many wounds, too many of our comrades
left to die in the forest glades, to allow of our expecting
much. We plod on, sometimes ready to faint, sometimes with lighter hearts, but not any more winged by
hope as in the golden prime,—unless indeed for those
of us who have fixed our hopes on God, and so get
through the march better, because, be it rough or smooth,

long or short, He moves before us to guide, and all our ways lead to Him. But even for these, there comes, before very long, a time when they are weary of hoping for much more here, and when that light of youth fades into common day. Be it so! They will get the faculty and the use of it back again in far nobler fashion, when death has taken them away from all transient, and faith has through death given for their possession and their expectation, the certitudes of eternity. It will be worth while to look forward again, when we are again standing at the beginning of a life. It will be possible once more to hope, when disappointments are all past. A boundless future stretching before us, of which we know that it is all blessed, and that we shall reach all its blessedness, will give back to hearts that have long ceased to drink of the delusive cup which earthly hope offered to their lips, the joy of living in a present, made bright by the certain anticipation of a yet brighter future. Losing nothing by our constant progress, and gaining all which we foresee, we shall remember and be glad, we shall hope and be confident. With "the past unsighed for, and the future sure," we shall have that magic gift, which earth's disappointments dulled, quickened by the sure mercies of the heavens.

Again, youth has mostly a certain *keenness of relish* for life which vanishes only too soon. There are plenty of our young men and women too, of this day, no doubt, who are as *blasé* and wearied before they are out of their teens as if they were fifty. So much the sadder for them, so much the worse for the social state which

breeds such monsters. For monsters they are: there
ought to be in youth a sense of fresh wonder undimmed
by familiarity, the absence of satiety, a joy in joyful
things because they are new as well as gladsome. The
poignancy of these early delights cannot long survive.
Custom stales them all, and wraps everything in its robe
of ashen grey. We get used to what was once so fresh
and wonderful, and do not care very much about anything any more. We smile pitying smiles—sadder than
any tears—at "boyish enthusiasm," and sometimes plume
ourselves on having come to "years which bring the
philosophic mind;" and all the while we know that we
have lost a great gift, which can never come back any
more, here.

But what if that eager freshness of delight may yet
be ours once again? What if the eternal youth of the
heavens means, amongst other things, that *there* are
pleasures which always satisfy but never cloy? What
if, in perpetual advance, we find and keep for ever that
ever new gladness, which here we vainly seek in perpetual distraction? What if constant new influxes of
Divine blessedness, and constant new visions of God,
keep in constant exercise that sense of wonder, which
makes so great a part of the power of youth? What if,
after all that we have learned and all that we have
received, we still have to say, "It doth not yet appear
what we shall be." Then, I think, in very profound and
blessed sense, heaven would be perpetual youth.

I need not pause to speak of other characteristics of
that period of life—such as its enthusiasm, its life by

impulse rather than by reason, its buoyant energy and delight in action. All these gifts, so little cared for when possessed, so often misused, so irrevocably gone with a few brief years, so bitterly bewailed, will surely be found again, where God keeps all the treasures He gives and we let fall. For transient enthusiasm, heaven will give us back a fervour of love like that of the seraphs, that have burned before His throne unconsumed and undecaying for unknown ages. For a life of instinctive impulse, we shall then receive a life in which impulse is ever parallel with the highest law, and, doing only what we would, we shall do only what we ought. For energy which wanes as the years wax, and delight in action which is soon worn down into mechanical routine of toil, there is bestowed strength akin to His who fainteth not, neither is weary. All that maturity and old age robbed us of is given back in nobler form. All the limitation and weakness which they brought, the coldness, the monotony, the torpor, the weariness—all shall drop away. But we shall keep all the precious things which they brought us. None of the calm wisdom, the ripened knowledge, the full-summed experience, the powers of service acquired in life's long apprenticeship, will be taken from us.

All will be changed indeed. All will be cleansed of the impurity which attaches to all. All will be accepted and crowned, not by reason of its goodness, but by reason of Christ's sacrifice, which is the channel of God's mercy. But though in themselves unworthy, and having nothing fit for the heavens, yet the souls tha' trust in Jesus, the Lord of Life, shall bear into their glory the characters which by His grace they wrought out here on earth, transfigured and perfected, but still the same. And to make up that full-summed completeness, will be given to them at once the perfection of all the various stages through which they passed on earth. The perfect man in the heavens will include the graces of childhood, the energies of youth, the steadfastness of manhood, the calmness of old age ; as on some tropical trees, blooming in more fertile soil and quickened by a nearer sun than ours, you may see at once bud, blossom, and fruit—the expectancy of spring, and the maturing promise of summer, and the fulfilled fruition of autumn—hanging together on the unexhausted bough.

III. *The faithful dead shall live in a body that cannot grow old.*

Scripture assures us, I believe, that the dead in Christ are now in full, conscious enjoyment of His presence, and of all the blessedness that to dwell in Christ can bring to a spirit. All, then, which we have been saying applies to the present condition of those who sleep in Jesus. As concerning toil and trouble they take rest in sleep, as concerning contact with an outer world they slumber untroubled by its noise ; but as concerning their communion with their Lord they, like us, "whether we wake or sleep, live together with Him." But we know too, from Scripture, that the dead in Christ wait for the resurrection of the body, without which they cannot be perfected, nor restored to full activity of outward life in connection with an external creation.

The lesson which we venture to draw from this text enforces the familiar teaching of Scripture as to that body of glory—that it cannot decay, nor grow old. In this respect, too, eternal youth may be ours. Here we have a bodily organization which, like all other living bodies, goes through its appointed series of changes, wastes in effort, and so needs reparation by food and rest, dies in growing, and finally waxes old and dissolves. In such a house, a man cannot be ever young. The dim eye and shaking hand, the wrinkled face and thin grey hairs cannot but age the spirit, since they weaken its instruments.

If the redeemed of the Lord are to be always young in spirit, they must have a body which knows no weariness, which needs no repose, which has no necessity of dying impressed upon it. And such a body Scripture plainly tells us shall belong to those who are Christ's, at His coming. Our present acquaintance with the conditions of life makes that great promise seem impossible to many learned men amongst us. And I know not that anything but acquaintance with the sure word of God and with a risen Lord will make that seeming impossibility again a great promise for us. If we believe it at all, I think we must believe it because the resurrection of Jesus Christ says so, and because the Scriptures put it into articulate words as the promise of His resurrection. "Ye do err," said Christ long ago, to those who denied a resurrection, "not knowing the Scriptures nor the power of God." Then knowledge of the Scriptures leads to belief in the resurrection of the dead,

and our ignorance of the power of God disposes of all
the doubts, which are raised on the supposition that His
present works are the pattern of His future, or the limits
of His unexhausted energy.

We are content then to fall back on Scripture words,
and to believe in the resurrection of the dead simply
because it is, as we believe, told us from God.

For all who accept the message, this hope shines clear,
of a *building* of God imperishable and solid, when contrasted with the *tent* in which we dwell here—of a body
"raised in corruption," "clothed with immortality," and so,
as in many another phrase, declared to be exempt from
decay, and therefore vigorous with unchanging youth.
How that comes we cannot tell. Whether because that
body of glory has no proclivity to mutation and decay,
or whether the perpetual volition and power of God
connteract such tendency, giving, as the Book of Revelation says, "to eat of the tree of life which is in the midst
of the paradise of God"—matters not at all. The truth
of the promise remains, though we have no means of
knowing more than the fact, that we shall receive a body,
fashioned like His who dieth no more. There shall be
no weariness nor consequent need for repose—"they
rest not day nor night." There shall be no faintness
nor consequent craving for sustenance—"they shall
hunger no more, neither thirst any more." There shall
be no disease—"the inhabitant thereof shall no more
say, I am sick," "neither can they die any more, for they
are equal unto the angels."

And if all this be true, that glorious and undecaying

body shall then be the equal and fit instrument of the perfected spirit, not, as it is now, the adequate instrument only of the natural life.

The deepest emotions then will be capable of expression—nor, as now, like some rushing tide, choke the floodgates through whose narrow aperture they try to press, and be all tossed into foam in the attempt. We shall then seem what we are, as we shall also be what we ought. All outward things shall then be fully and clearly communicated to the spirit; that glorious body will be a perfect instrument of knowledge. All that we desire to do we shall then do, nor be longer tortured with tremulous hands that can never draw the perfect circle we plan, and stammering lips that will not obey the heart, and throbbing brain that *will* ache when we would have it clear. The young spirit shall have for true yokefellow a body that cannot tire, nor grow old, nor die.

The aged saints of God shall rise then in youthful beauty. More than the long-vanished comeliness shall on that day rest on faces that were here haggard with anxiety, and pinched with penury and years. No more palsied hands, no more scattered grey hairs, no more dim and horny eyes, no more stiffened muscles and slow throbbing hearts. "It is sown in weakness, it is raised in power." It is sown in decaying old age, it is raised in immortal youth. His servants shall stand in that day among "the young-eyed cherubim," and be like them for ever. So we may think of the dead in Christ. But do not forget that Christian faith may largely do for us

here what God's grace and power will do for us in
heaven, and that even now we may possess much of this
great gift of perpetual youth.   If we live for Christ by
faith in Him, then may we carry with us all our days the
energy, the hope, the joy of the morning tide, and be
children in evil while men in understanding.   With
unworn and fresh heart we may bring forth fruit in old
age, and have the crocus in the autumnal fields as well as
in the spring-time of our lives.   So blessed, we may
pass to a peaceful end, because we hold His hand who
makes the path smooth and the heart quiet.   Trust
yourselves, my brethren, to the immortal love and
perfect work of the Divine Saviour, and by His dear
might your days will advance by peaceful stages, whereof
each gathers up and carries forward the blessings of all
that went before, to a death which shall be a birth.   The
cold waters shall be as a fountain of youth from which
you shall rise, beautiful and strong, to begin an immortality of growing power.   A Christian life on earth
solves partly, a Christian life in heaven solves completely,
the problem of perpetual youth.   For those who die in
His faith and fear, "better is the end than the beginning,
and the day of one's death than the day of one's birth."
Christ keeps the good wine to the close of the feast.

> " Such is Thy banquet, dearest Lord ;
>   O give us grace, to cast
>   Our lot with Thine, to trust Thy word,
>   And keep our best till last."

WHAT MAKES A CHRISTIAN: CIRCUMCISION OR FAITH?

GALATIANS v. 6.

In Jesus Christ neither circumcision availeth anything, nor uncircumcision, but faith which worketh by love.

IT is a very singular instance of imaginative misreading of plain facts that the Primitive Church should be held up as a pattern Church. The early communities had Apostolic teaching; but beyond that, they seem to have been in no respect above, and in many respects below, the level of subsequent ages. If we may judge of their morality by the exhortations and dehortations which they received from the Apostle, Corinth and Thessalonica were but beginners in holiness. If we may judge of their intelligence by the errors into which they were in danger of falling, these first congregations had indeed need that one should teach them which were the first principles of the oracles of God. It could not be otherwise. They were but just rescued from heathenism, and we need not wonder if their spirits long bore the scars of their former bondage. If we wish to know what the Apostolic Churches were like, we have but to

look at the communities gathered by modern mission-
aries. The same infantile simplicity, the same partial
apprehensions of the truth, the same danger of being
led astray by the low morality of their heathen kindred,
the same openness to strange heresy, the same danger
of blending the old with the new, in opinion and in
practice, beset both.

The history of the first theological difference in the
early Churches is a striking confutation of the dream
that they were perfect, and a striking illustration of the
dangers to which they were exposed from the attempt,
so natural to us all, to put new wine into old bottles.
The Jewish and the Gentile elements did not coalesce.
The point round which the strife was waged was not
whether Gentiles might come into the Church. That
was conceded by the fiercest Judaizers. But it was
whether they could come in as Gentiles, without first
being incorporated into the Jewish nation by circumcision, and whether they could remain in as Gentiles,
without conforming to Jewish ceremonial and law.

Those who said "no" *were* members of the Christian
communities, and, being so, they still insisted that
Judaism was to be eternal. They demanded that the
patched and stiff leathern bottle, which had no elasti-
city or pliability, should still contain the quick fermenting
new wine of the kingdom. And certainly, if ever man
had excuse for clinging to what was old and formal,
these Judaizing Christians held it. They held by a
law written with God's own finger, by ordinances awful
by reason of Divine appointment, venerable by reason

of the generations to which they had been of absolute
authority, commended by the very example of Christ
Himself. Every motive which can bind heart and
conscience to the reverence and the practice of the
traditions of the Fathers, bound them to the Law and
the ordinances which had been Israel's treasure from
Abraham to Jesus.

Those who said "Yes" were mostly Gentiles, headed
and inspired by a Hebrew of the Hebrews. They
believed that Judaism was preparatory, and that its
work was done. For those among themselves who were
Jews, they were willing that its laws should still be obli-
gatory; but they fought against the attempt to compel
all Gentile converts to enter Christ's kingdom through
the gate of circumcision.

The fight was stubborn and bitter. I suppose it is
harder to abolish forms than to change opinions. Ceremonies stand long after the thought which they express
has fled, as a dead king may sit on his throne stiff and
stark in his golden mantle, and no one come near enough
to see that the light is gone out of his eyes, and the will
departed from the hand that still clutches the sceptre.
All through Paul's life he was dogged and tormented by
this controversy. There was a deep gulf between the
Churches he planted and this reactionary section of
the Christian community. Its emissaries were continually following in his footsteps. As he bitterly reproaches them, they entered upon another man's line
of things made ready to their hand, not caring to plant
Churches of circumcised Gentiles themselves, but starting

up behind him as soon as his back was turned, and spoiling his work.

This Epistle is the memorial of that foot-to-foot feud. It is of perennial use, as the tendencies against which it is directed are constant in human nature. Men are ever apt to confound form and substance, to crave material embodiments of spiritual realities, to elevate the outward means into the place of the inward and real, to which all the outward is but subsidiary. In every period of strife between the two great opponents, this letter has been the stronghold of those who fight for the spiritual conception of religion. With it Luther waged his warfare, and in this day, too, its words are precious.

My text contains Paul's condensed statement of his whole position in the controversy. It tells us what he fought for, and why he fought, against the attempt to suspend union to Christ on an outward rite.

I. The first grand principle contained in these words is that *Faith working by love makes a Christian.*

The antithesis of our text appears in somewhat varied forms in two other places in the Apostle's writings. To the Corinthians he says, " Circumcision is nothing, and uncircumcision is nothing, *but the keeping of the commandments of God.*" His last word to the Galatians —the gathering up into one strong sentence of his whole letter—is, "In Christ Jesus, neither circumcision availeth anything, nor uncircumcision, *but a new creature.*"

Now, all these assertions embody substantially the same opposition between the conception of Christianity as depending upon a ceremonial rite, and as being a spiritual change. And the variations in the second member of the contrast throw light on each other. In one, the essential thing is regarded from the Divine side as being not a rite performed on the body, but a new nature, the result of a supernatural regeneration. In another, the essential thing is set forth as being not an outward act, but an inward principle, which produces appropriate effects on the whole being. In yet another the essential thing is conceived as being not a mere ceremonial, but practical obedience, the consequence of the active principle of faith, and the sign of the new life. There is an evident sequence in the three sayings. They begin with the deepest, the Divine act of a new creation,—and end with the outermost, the last result and object of both the others—deeds of conformity to God's law.

This one process in its triple aspects, says Paul, constitutes a man a Christian. What correspondence is there between it, in any of its parts, and a carnal ordinance? They belong to wholly different categories, and it is the most preposterous confusion to try to mix them up together. Are we to tack on to these solemn powers and qualities, which unite the soul to Christ, this beggarly addition that the Judaizers desire, and to say, the essentials of Christianity are a new creature, faith, obedience, and circumcision? That is, indeed, sewing old cloth on a new garment, and huddling together in grotesque chaos things which are utterly diverse. It is as absurd bathos as to say, the essentials of a judge are integrity, learning, patience—and an ermine robe!

There would be less danger of being entangled in false

P 2

notions of the sort which devastated Galatia and have afflicted the Church ever since, if people would put a little more distinctly before their own minds what they mean by "religion;" what sort of man they intend when they talk about "a Christian." A clear notion of the thing to be produced would thin away a wonderful deal of mist as to the way of producing it. So then, beginning at the surface, in order to work inward, my first remark is that *religion is the harmony of the soul with God, and the conformity of the life to His law.*

The loftiest purpose of God, in all His dealings, is to make us like Himself; and the end of all religion is the complete accomplishment of that purpose. There is no religion without these elements—consciousness of kindred with God, recognition of Him as the sum of all excellence and beauty, and of His will as unconditionally binding upon us, aspiration and effort after a full accord of heart and soul with Him and with His law, and humble confidence that that sovereign beauty will be ours. "Be ye imitators of God as dear children" is the pure and comprehensive dictate which expresses the aim of all devout men. "To keep His commandments" goes deeper than the mere external deeds. Were it not so, Paul's grand words would shrink to a very poor conception of religion, which would then have its shrine and sphere removed from the sacred recesses of the inmost spirit, to the dusty Babel of the market-place and the streets. But with that due and necessary extension to the words which results from the very nature of the case— that obedience must be the obedience of a man, and not of his deeds only, and must include the submission of the will and the prostration of the whole nature before him; they teach a truth which, fully received and carried out, clears away whole mountains of theoretical confusion and practical error. Religion is no dry morality; no slavish punctilious conforming of actions to a hard law. Religion is not right thinking alone, nor right emotion alone, nor right action alone. Religion is still less the semblance of these in formal profession, or simulated feeling, or apparent rectitude. Religion is not nominal connection with the Christian community, nor participation in its ordinances and its worship. But to be godly is to be godlike. The full accord of all the soul with His character, in whom, as their native home, dwell "whatsoever things are pure, whatsoever things are lovely," and the full glad conformity of the will to His sovereign will, who is the life of our lives—this, and nothing shallower, nothing narrower, is religion in its perfection; and the measure in which we have attained to this harmony with God, is the measure in which we are Christians. As two stringed instruments may be so tuned to one key-note that, if you strike the one, a faint ethereal echo is heard from the other, which blends undistinguishably with its parent sound; so, drawing near to God, and brought into unison with His mind and will, our responsive spirits vibrate in accord with His, and give forth tones, low and thin indeed, but still repeating the mighty music of heaven. "Circumcision is nothing, and uncircumcision is nothing, but the keeping of the commandments of God."

But our text tells us, further, that if we look backwards

from character and deed to motive, *this harmony with God results from love becoming the ruling power* of our lives. The imitation of the object of worship has always been felt to be the highest form of worship. Many an ancient teacher, besides the Stoic philosopher, has said, "He who copies the gods worships them adequately." One of the prophets lays it down as a standing rule, " The people will walk every one in the name of his God." But it is only in the Christian attitude towards God that the motive power is found, which makes such imitation more than an impossible duty, even as it is only in the revealed character of God that a pattern is found, to imitate which is to be perfect. Everywhere besides, harmony with the gods meant discord with conscience, and flagrant outrages of the commonest moralities. Everywhere else, the task of copying them was one lightened by no clear confidence in their love, and by no happy consciousness of our own. But for us, the love revealed is the perfect law, and the love evoked is the fulfilling of the law.

And this is the might and nobleness of the Christian love to God; that it is no idle emotion or lazy rapture, no vague sentiment, but the root of all practical goodness, of all strenuous effort, of all virtue, and of all praise. That strong tide is meant to drive the busy wheels of life and to bear precious freightage on its bosom; not to flow away in profitless foam. Love is the fruitful mother of bright children, as our great moralist-poet learned when he painted her in the House of Holiness :—

> " A multitude of babes about her hung,
> Playing their sport that joyed her to behold.'

Her sons are Strength and Justice, and Self-control and Firmness, and Courage and Patience, and many more besides; and her daughters are Pity with her sad eyes, and Gentleness with her silvery voice, and Mercy whose sweet face makes sunshine in the shade of death, and Humility all unconscious of her loveliness; and linked hand in hand with these, all the radiant band of sisters that men call Virtues and Graces. These will dwell in our hearts, if Love their mighty mother be there. If we are without her, we shall be without them.

There is discord between man and God, which can only be removed by the sweet commerce of love, established between earth and heaven. God's love has come to us. When ours springs responsive to Him, then the schism is ended, and the wandering child forgets his rebellion, as he lays his aching head on the father's bosom, and feels the beating of the father's heart. Our souls by reason of sin are "like sweet bells jangled, harsh and out of tune." Love's master hand laid upon them restores to them their part in "the fair music that all creatures make to their great Lord," and brings us into such accord with God that

> " We on earth with undiscording voice
> May rightly answer,"

even the awful harmonies of His lips. The essential of religion is concord with God, and the power which makes that concord is love to God.

But this text leads to a still further consideration, namely, *the dominion of love to God in our hearts arises from faith.*

We thus reach the last link, or rather the staple, of the chain from which all hangs. Religion is harmony with God ; that harmony is produced by love ; and that love is produced by faith. Therefore the fundamental of all Christianity in the soul is faith. Would this sound any fresher and more obvious if we varied the language, and said that to be religious we must be like God, that to be like Him we must love Him, and that to love Him we must be sure that He loves us? Surely that is too plain to need enlarging on.

And is it not true that faith must precede our love to God, and affords the only possible basis on which that can be built? How can we love Him so long as we are in doubt of His heart, or misconceive His character, as if it were only Power and Wisdom, or awful Severity? Men cannot love an unseen person at all without some very special token of his personal affection for them. The history of all religions shows that where the gods have been thought of as unloving, the worshippers have been heartless too. It is only when we know and believe the love that God hath to us, that we come to cherish any corresponding emotion to Him. Our love is secondary, His is primary ; ours is reflection, His the original beam ; ours is echo, His the mother-tone. Heaven must bend to earth before earth can rise to heaven. The skies must open and drop down love, ere love can spring in the fruitful fields. And it is only when we look with true trust to that great unveiling of the heart of God which is in Jesus Christ, only when we can say, "Herein is love— that He gave His Son to be the propitiation for our sins," that our hearts are melted, and all their snows are dissolved into sweet waters, which, freed from their icy chains, can flow with music in their ripple, and fruitfulness along their course, through our otherwise silent and barren lives. Faith in Christ is the only possible basis for active love to God.

And this thought presents the point of contact between the teaching of Paul and John. The one dwells on faith, the other on love, but he who insists most on the former declares that it produces its effects on character by the latter; and he who insists most on the latter is forward to proclaim that it owes its very existence to the former.

It presents also the point of contact between Paul and James. The one speaks of the essential of Christianity as faith, the other as works. They are only striking the stream at different points, one at the fountain-head, one far down its course among the haunts of men. They both preach that faith must be "faith that worketh," not a barren assent to a dogma, but a living trust that brings forth fruits in the life. Paul believes as much as James that faith without works is dead, and demands the keeping of the commandments as indispensable to all true Christianity. James believes as much as Paul that works without faith are of none effect. So all three of these great teachers of the Church are represented in this text, to which each of them might seem to have contributed a word embodying his characteristic type of doctrine. The threefold rays into which the prism parts the white light blend again here, where faith, love, and work are all united in the comprehensive saying, "In Jesus Christ neither circumcision availeth anything, nor uncircumcision, but faith which worketh by love."

The sum of the whole matter is this—He who is one in will and heart with God is a Christian. He who loves God is one in will and heart with Him. He who trusts Christ loves God. That is Christianity in its ultimate purpose and result. That is Christianity in its means and working forces. That is Christianity in its starting-point and foundation.

II. But we have to consider also the negative side of the Apostle's words. They affirm that *in comparison with the essential—faith, all externals are infinitely unimportant.*

Paul's habit was always to settle questions by the widest principles he could bring to bear upon them—which one may notice in passing is the very opposite to the method, that has been in favour with many Church teachers and guides since, who have preferred to live from hand to mouth, and to dispose of difficulties by the narrowest considerations that would avail to quiet them. In our text the question in hand is settled on a ground which covers a great deal more than the existing dispute. Circumcision is regarded as one of a whole class—namely, the class of outward rites and observances; and the contrast drawn between it and faith extends to all the class to which it belongs. It is not said to be powerless because it is an Old Testament rite, but because it is a .ite. Its impotence lies in its very nature which it has in common with all external institutions, whether they be of the Old Testament or of the New, whether they be enjoined of God or invented by men. To them all the same characteristic cleaves. Compared with faith they are of no avail. Not that they are absolutely useless. They have their place, but "*in Christ Jesus*" they are nothing. Union to him depends on quite another order of facts, which may or may not exist along with circumcision, or with baptism, or with the Lord's Supper. However important these may be, they have no place among the things which bind a soul to its Saviour. They may be helps to these things, but nothing more. The rite does not ensure the faith, else the antithesis of our text were unmeaning. The rite does not stand in the place of faith, or the contrast implied were absurd. But the two belong to totally different orders of things, which may co-exist indeed, but may also be found separately; the one is the indispensable spiritual emotion which makes us Christians, the other belongs to a class of material institutions which are much as helps to, but nothing as substitutes or equivalents for, faith.

Keep firm hold of the positive principle with which we have been dealing in the former part of this sermon, and all forms and externals fall as a matter of course into their proper place. If religion be the loving devotion of the soul to God, resting upon reasonable faith, then all besides is, at the most, a means which may further it. If loving trust which apprehends the truth, and cleaves to the Person revealed to us in the Gospel, be the link which binds men to God, then the only way by which these externals can be "means of grace" is by their aiding us to understand better and to feel more the truth as it is in Jesus, and to cleave closer to Him who is the Truth. Do they enlighten the understanding? Do they engrave deeper the loved face carven on the tablets of memory, which the attrition of worldly cares is ever obliterating, and the lichens of worldly thoughts ever filling up? Do they clear out the rubbish from the channels of the heart, that the cleansing stream may flow through them? Do they, through the senses, minister to the soul its own proper food of clear thought, vivid impressions, loving affections, trustful obedience? Do they bring Christ to us, and us to Him, in the only way in which approach is possible—through the occupation of mind and heart and will with His great perfectness? Then they are means of grace, precious and helpful, the gifts of His love, the tokens of His wise knowledge of our weakness, the signs of His condescension, in that He stoops to trust some portion of our remembrance of Him to the ministry of sense. But in comparison with that faith which they cannot plant, though they may strengthen it, they are nothing; and in the matter of uniting the soul to God and making men "religious," they are of no avail at all.

And such thoughts as these have a very wide sweep, as well as a very deep influence. Religion is the devotion of the soul to God. Then *everything* besides is not religion, but at most a means to it. That is true about all Christian ordinances. Baptism is spoken about by Paul in terms which plainly show that he regarded it as "nothing" in the same sense, and under the same limitations, as he thought that circumcision was nothing.

"I baptized some of you," says he to the Corinthians; "I scarely remember whom, or how many. I have far more important work to do—to preach the Gospel." It is true about all acts and forms of Christian worship. These are not religion, but means to it. Their only value and their only test is, Do they help men to know and feel Christ and His truth? It is true about laws of life, and many points of conventional morality. Remember the grand freedom with which the same Apostle dealt with questions about meats offered to idols, and the observance of days and seasons. The same principle guided him there too, and he relegated the whole question back to its proper place with, "Meat commendeth us not to God; for neither if we eat are we the better, neither if we eat not are we the worse." "He that regardeth the day, regardeth it unto the Lord; and he that regardeth not the day, to the Lord he doth not regard it." It is true, though less obviously and simply, about subordinate doctrines. It is true about the mere intellectual grasp of the fundamental truths of God's revelation. These, and the belief of these, are not Christianity, they are helps towards it.

The separation is broad and deep. On one side are all externals, rites, ceremonies, politics, Church arrangements, forms of worship, modes of life, practices of morality, doctrines, and creeds—all which are externals to the soul: on the other is faith working through love, the inmost attitude and deepest emotion of the soul. The great heap is fuel. The flame is loving faith. The only worth of the fuel is to feed the flame. Otherwise it is of no avail, but lies dead and cold, a mass of blackness. We are joined to God by faith. Whatever strengthens that is precious as a help, but is worthless as a substitute.

III. *There is a constant tendency to exalt these unimportant externals into the place of faith.*

The whole purpose of the Gospel may be described to be our deliverance from the dominion of sense, and the transference of the centre of our life to the unseen world. This end is no doubt partly accomplished by the help of sense. So long as men have bodily organizations, there will be need for outward helps. Men's indolence, and men's sense-ridden natures, will take symbols for realities, notes for wealth. The eye will be tempted to stay on the rich colours of the glowing glass, instead of passing through these to heaven's light beyond. To make the senses a ladder for the soul to climb to heaven by, will be perilously likely to end in the soul going down the ladder instead of up. Forms are sure to encroach, to overlay the truth that lies at their root, to become dimly intelligible, or quite unmeaning, and to constitute at last the end instead of the means. Is it not then wise to minimise these potent and dangerous allies? Is it not needful to use them with the remembrance that a minute quantity may strengthen, but an overdose will kill—ay, and that the minute quantity may kill too? Christ instituted two outward rites. There could not have been fewer if there was to be an outward community at all, and they could not have been simpler; and look at the portentous outgrowth of superstition, and the unnumbered evils, religious, moral, social, and even political, which have come from the invincible tendency of human nature to corrupt forms, even when the forms are the sweet and simple ones of Christ's own appointment. What a lesson the history of the Lord's Supper, and its gradual change from the domestic memorial of the dying love of our Lord to the "tremendous sacrifice," reads us as to the dangerous ally which spiritual religion—and there is no other religion than spiritual—enlists when it seeks the help of external rites !

But remember that this danger of converting religion into outward actions has its root in us all, and is not annihilated by our rejection of an elaborate ceremonial. There is much significance in the double negation of my text, "Neither circumcision nor uncircumcision." If the Judaizers were temped to insist on the former as indispensable, their antagonists were as much tempted to insist on the latter. The one were saying, "A man cannot be a Christian unless he be circumcised." The other would be in danger of replying, "He cannot be a Christian if he is." There may be as much formalism in protesting against forms as in using them. Extremes meet ; and an unspiritual Quaker, for instance, is at bottom of the same way of thinking as an unspiritual Roman Catholic. They agree in their belief that certain outward acts are essential to worship, and even to religion. They only differ as to what these acts are. The Judaizer who says, "You must be circumcised," and his antagonist who says, "You must be uncircumcised," are really in the same boat.

And this is especially needful to be kept in mind by those who, like the most of us, hold fast by the free and spiritual conception of Christianity. That freedom we may turn into a bondage, and that spirituality into a form, if we confound it with the essentials of Christianity, and deny the possibility of the life being developed except in conjunction with it. My text has a double edge. Let us use it against all this Judaizing which is going on round about us, and against all the tendency to it in our own hearts. The one edge smites the former, the other edge the latter. Circumcision is nothing, as most of us are forward to proclaim. But, also, remember, when we are tempted to trust in our freedom, and to fancy that in itself it is good, *uncircumcision is nothing*. You are no more a Christian for your rejection of forms than another man is for his holding them. Your negation no more unites you to Christ than his affirmation. One thing alone does that,—faith which worketh by love, against which sense ever wars, both by tempting some of us to place religion in outward acts and ceremonies, and by tempting others of us to place it in rejecting the forms which our brethren abuse.

IV. *When an indifferent thing is made into an essential, it ceases to be indifferent, and must be fought against.*

Paul proclaimed that circumcision and uncircumcision were alike unavailing. A man might be a good Christian either way. They were not unimportant in all respects, but in regard of being united to Christ, it did not matter which side one took. And, in accordance with this noble freedom, he for himself practised Jewish rites ; and, when he thought it might conciliate prejudice without betraying principle, had Timothy circumcised. But when it came to be maintained as a principle that Gentiles *must* be circumcised, the time for conciliation was past. The other side had made further concession impossible. The Apostle had no objection to circumcision. What he objected to was its being *forced* upon all as a necessary preliminary to entering the Church. And, as soon as the opposite party took that ground, then there was nothing for it but to fight against them to the last. They had turned an indifferent thing into an essential, and he could no longer treat it as indifferent.

So whenever parties or Churches insist on external rites as essential, or elevate any of the subordinate means of grace into the place of the one bond which fastens our souls to Jesus, and is the channel of grace as well as the bond of union, then it is time to arm for the defence of the spirituality of Christ's kingdom, and to resist the attempt to bind on free shoulders the iron yoke. Let men and parties do as they like, so long as they do not turn their forms into essentials. In broad freedom of speech and spirit, which holds by the one central principle too firmly to be much troubled about subordinate matters,—in tolerance of diversities, which does not spring from indifference, but from the very clearness of our perception of, and from the very fervour of our adherence to, the one essential of the Christian life,—let us take for our guide the large, calm, lofty thoughts which this text sets forth before us. Let us thankfully believe that men may love Jesus, and be fed from His fulness, whether they be on one side of this undying controversy or on the other. Let us watch jealously the tendencies in our own hearts to trust in our forms or in our freedom. And whensoever or wheresoever these subordinates are made into things essential, and the ordinances of Christ's Church are elevated into the place which belongs to loving trust in Christ's love, then let *our* voices at least be heard on the side of that mighty truth that "in Jesus Christ neither circumcision availeth anything, nor uncircumcision, but faith which worketh by love.'

THE BAPTISM IN FIRE.

MATTHEW iii. 11.

He shall baptize you with the Holy Ghost, and with fire.

THERE is no more pathetic figure in Scripture than that of the forerunner of our Lord. Lonely and ascetic, charged to fight against all the social order of which he was a part, seeing many of his disciples leave him for another master; then changing the free wilderness for a prison cell, and tortured by morbid doubts; finally, murdered, the victim of a profligate woman's hate and a profligate man's perverse sense of honour: he had indeed to bear "the burden of the Lord." But perhaps most pathetic of all is the combination in his character of gaunt strength and absolute humility. How he confronts these people whom he had to rebuke, and yet how, in a moment, the flashing eye sinks in lowest self-abasement before "Him that cometh after me!" How true, amidst many temptations, he was to his own description of himself: "I am a voice"—nothing more! His sinewy arm was ever pointed to the "Lamb of God." It is given to very few to know so clearly their limits, and to still fewer,—and these men who keep very near God,—to abide so contentedly within them, and to acquiesce so thankfully in the brightening glories of one whom self-importance and ambition would prompt to take for a rival and an enemy.

The words before us signalize at once John's lofty conception of the worth of his work, and his humble consciousness of its worthlessness as compared with Christ's. "I indeed baptize you with water, but He with fire." As is the difference between the two elements, so is the difference between His ministry and mine—the one effecting an outward cleansing, the other being an inward penetrating power, which shall search men through and through, and, burning, shall purge away dross and filth. The text comes in the midst of a triple representation of our Lord's work in its relation to his, each portion of which ends with the refrain, " the fire." But these three fires are not the same. The first and last destroy, the second cleanses. These are threatenings, but this is altogether a promise. There is a fire that consumes the barren tree, and the light chaff that is whirled from the threshing floor by the wind of His fan ; but there is also a fire that, like the genial heat in some greenhouse, makes even the barren tree glow with blossom, and bends its branches with precious fruit. His coming may kindle fire that may destroy, but its merciful purpose is to plunge us into that fiery baptism of the Holy Ghost, whereof the result is cleansing and life. Looking at the words before us, then, they lead us to think of that emblem of the Spirit of God, of Christ as bestowing it, of its effects on us. I venture to offer a few considerations now on each of these points.

I. *The Holy Spirit is fire.*

It would scarcely be necessary to spend any time in illustrating that truth, but for the strange misapprehension of the words of our text which I believe to be not uncommon. People sometimes read them as if the first portion referred to those who trust in Christ, and who therefore receive the blessings of His sanctifying energy, whilst the latter words, on the other hand, were a threatening against unbelievers. Now, whatever may be the meaning of the emblem in the preceding and subsequent clauses, it can have but one meaning in our text itself—and that is, the purifying influence of the Spirit of God. Baptism with the Holy Ghost is not one thing and baptism with fire another, but the former is the reality of which the latter is the symbol.

It may be worth while to dwell briefly on the force of the emblem, which is often misunderstood. Fire, then, all over the world has been taken to represent the Divine energy. Even in heathendom, side by side with the worship of light was the worship of fire. Even that cruel Moloch-worship, with all its abominations, rested upon the notion that the swift power and ruddy blaze of fire were symbols of glorious attributes. Though the thought was darkened and marred, wrongly apprehended and ferociously worked out in ritual, it was a true thought for all that. And Scripture has from the beginning used it. It would carry us too far to enumerate the instances which might be adduced. But we may quote a few. When the covenant was made between God and Abraham, upon which all the subsequent revelation reposed, the Divine presence was represented by a smoking furnace, and a lamp of fire that passed between the divided pieces of the sacrifice. When the great revelation of the Divine Name was given to Moses, which prepared for the great deliverance from Egypt, the sign of it was a thorn-bush—one of the many dotted over the desert—burning and unconsumed. Surely the ordinary interpretation, which sees, in that undying flame, an emblem of Israel undestroyed in the furnace of bondage, is less natural than that which sees in it a sign having the same purpose and the same meaning as the awful words, " I am that I am." The Name, the revelation proper, is accompanied by the sign which expresses in figure the very same truth—the unwearied power, the undecaying life of the great self-existent God, who wills and does not change, who acts and does not faint, who gives and is none the poorer, who fills the universe and is Himself the same, who burns and is not consumed—the " I am." Then you remember how to Israel the pledge and sacramental seal of God's guardianship and guidance was the pillar which, in the fervid light of the noonday sun, seemed to be but a column of wavering smoke, but which, when the darkness fell, glowed at the heart and blazed across the sleeping camp, a fiery guard. " Who among us," says the prophet, " shall dwell with everlasting burnings?" The answer is a parallel to the description given in one of the Psalms in reply to the question, "Lord, who shall abide in Thy tabernacle?" From which parallelism, as well as from the whole tone of the passage, the conclusion is unavoidable that by "everlasting burnings" Isaiah meant a symbolic designation of God. And, passing by all other references, we remember that our Lord Himself used the same emblem, as John does, with apparently the same meaning, when, yearning for the fulfilment of His work, He said, "I am come to send fire on earth—oh that it were already kindled!" The day of Pentecost teaches the same lesson by its fiery tongues; and the Seer in Patmos beheld, burning before the throne, the sevenfold lamps of fire which are "the seven spirits of God."

Thus, then, there is a continuous chain of symbolism, according to which some aspect of the Divine nature, and especially of the Spirit of God, is set forth for us by fire. The question, then, comes to be—what is that aspect? In answer, I would remind you that the attributes and offices of the Spirit of God are never in Scripture represented as being destructive, and are only punitive, in so far as the convictions of sin, which He works in the heart, may be regarded as being punishments. The fire of God's *Spirit*, at all events, is not a wrathful energy, working pain and death, but a merciful omnipotence, bringing light and joy and peace. The Spirit which is fire is a Spirit which giveth life. So the symbol, in the special reference in the text, has nothing of terror or destruction, but is full of hope and bright with promise.

Even in its more general application to the Divine nature, the same thing is to a large extent true. The common impression is the reverse of this. The interpretation which most readers unconsciously supply to the passages of Scripture where God is spoken of as flaming fire, is that God's terrible wrath is revealed in them. I am very far from denying that the punitive and destructive side of the Divine character *is* in the symbol, but certainly that is not its exclusive meaning, nor does it seem to me to be its principal one. The emblem is employed over and over again, in connections where it must mean chiefly the blessed and joyous aspect of God's Name to men. It is unquestionably part of the felicity of the symbol that there should be in it this double force—for so is it the fitter to show forth Him who, by the very same attributes, is the life of those who love Him and the death of those who turn from Him. But, still, though it be true that the bright and the awful aspects of that Name are in themselves one, and that their difference arises from the difference of the eyes which behold them, yet we are justified, I think, in saying that this emblem of fire regards mainly the former of these and not the latter. The principal ideas in it seem to be swift energy and penetrating power, which cleanses and transforms. It is fire as the source of light and heat ; it is fire, not so much as burning up what it seizes into ashes, but rather as laying hold upon cold dead matter, making it sparkle and blaze, and turning it into the likeness of its own leaping brightness ; it is fire as springing heavenwards, and bearing up earthly particles in its shooting spires ; it is fire, as least gross of visible things ; in a word, it is fire as life, and not as death, that is the symbol of God. It speaks the might of His transforming power, the melting, cleansing, vitalizing in-fluence of His communicated grace, the warmth of His conquering love. It hath, indeed, an under side of possible judgment, punishment, and destruction, but it hath a face of blessing, of life-giving, of sanctifying power. And therefore the Baptist spake glad tidings when he said, "He shall baptize you with the Holy Ghost and with fire."

II. *Christ plunges us into this Divine fire.*

I presume that scarcely any one will deny that our version weakens the force of John's words by translating "*with* water, *with* the Holy Ghost," instead of "in water, in the Holy Ghost." One of the most accurate of recent commentators,[1] for instance, in his remarks on this verse, says that the preposition here "is to be understood in accordance with the idea of baptism, that is immersion, not as expressing the instrument with which, but as meaning 'in,' and expressing the element in which the immersion takes place." I suppose that very few persons would hesitate to agree with that state-ment. If it be correct, what a grand idea is conveyed by that metaphor of the completeness of the contact with the Spirit of God into which we are brought ! How it represents all our being as flooded with that transforming power ! But, apart from the intensity com-municated to the promise by such a figure, there is

[1] Meyer.

another important matter brought distinctly before us by the words, and that is Christ's personal agency in effecting this saturating of man's coldness with the fire from God. This testimony of John's is in full accord with Christ's claims for Himself, and with the whole tenor of Scripture on the subject. He is the Lord of the Spirit. He is come to scatter that fire on the earth. He brings the ruddy gift from heaven to mortals, carrying it in the bruised reed of His humanity; and, in pursuance of His merciful design, He is bound and suffers for our sakes, but, loosed at last from the bands by which it was not possible that He should be holden, and "being by the right hand of God exalted, He hath shed forth this." His mighty work opens the way for the life-giving power of the Spirit to dwell as an habitual principle, and not as a mere occasional gift, among men, sanctifying their characters from the foundation, and not merely, as of old, bestowing special powers for special functions. He claims to send us the Comforter. We know but little of such high themes, but we can clearly see that, while there may be many other reasons for the full bestowment of the Spirit of God following the gift of Christ, one reason must be that the measure of individual and subjective inspiration varies according to the amount of external revelation. The truth revealed is the condition and the instrument of the Spirit's working. The sharper that sword of the Spirit is, the mightier will be His power. Hence, only when the revelation of God is complete by the message of His Son, His life, death, resurrection, and ascension, was the full, permanent gift of the Spirit possible, not to make new revelations, but to unfold all that lay in the Word spoken once for all, in whom the whole Name of God is contained.

However that may be, the main thing for us, dear friends, is this—that Christ gives the Spirit. In and by Jesus, you and I are brought into real contact with this cleansing fire. Without His work, it would never have burned on earth,—without our faith in His work it will never purify our souls. The Spirit of God is not a synonym for the moral influence which the principles of Christianity exert on men who believe them ; but these principles, the truths revealed in Jesus Christ, are the means by which the Spirit works its noblest work. Our acceptance of these truths, then, our faith in Him whom these truths reveal, is absolutely essential to our possession of that cleansing power. The promise is, " of that Spirit which they that believe on Him should receive." If we have no faith in Jesus, then, however we may fancy that the gift of God can be ours by other means, the stern answer comes to our fond delusions and mistaken efforts, " Thou hast neither part nor lot in this matter." Oh ! you who are seeking for spiritual elevation, for intellectual enlightenment, for the fire of a noble enthusiasm, for the consecration of pure hearts anywhere but in Christ your Lord, will you not listen to the majestic and yet lowly voice, which blends in its tones grave and loving rebuke, gentle pity, wonder and sorrow at our blindness, earnest entreaty, and Divine authority ?—" If thou knewest the gift of God, and who it is that speaketh to thee, thou wouldst have asked of Him, and He would have given thee living water."

Here are we cold, foul, dark, dead : there is that fire of God able to cleanse, to enlighten, to give life. How is true contact to be effected between our great need and His all-sufficient energy? One voice brings the answer for every Christian soul, "*I* will send the Comforter." Brethren, let us cleave to Him, and in humble faith ask Him to plunge us into that fiery stream, which, for all its fire, is yet a river of water of life proceeding out of the throne of God and of the Lamb. "*He* shall baptize you in the Holy Ghost and in fire."

III. *That fiery baptism quickens and cleanses.*

In John's mind, the difference between the two baptisms, his and the Christ's, expresses accurately the difference between the two ministries and their effects. As has been truly and beautifully said, he is conscious of something "cold and negative" in his own teaching, of which the water of his baptism is a fit representation. His message is Divine and true, but it is hard : "Repent, do what you ought, wait for the Kingdom and its King." And, when all that has been done, his disciples come up out of Jordan, at the best but superficially cleansed, and needing that the process begun in them should be perfected by mightier powers than any which his message wields. They need more than that outward washing,—they need an inward cleansing ; they need more than the preaching of repentance and morality,—they need a gift of life ; they need a new power poured into their souls, the fiery steam of which, as it rolls along, like a lava current in the mountain forests, shall seize and burn every growth of evil in their natures. They need not water, but Spirit; not water, but Fire. They need what shall be life to their truest life, and death to all the death within, that separates them from the life of God.

So the two main effects expressed here are these: quickening and cleansing.

Fire gives warmth. We talk about ardent desires, warm hearts, the glow of love, the fire of enthusiasm, and even the flame of life. We draw the contrast with cold natures, which are loveless and unemotional, hard to stir and quicken; we talk about thawing reserve, about an icy torpor, and so on. The same general strain of allusion is undoubtedly to be traced in our text. Whatever more it means, it surely means this, that Christ comes to kindle in men's souls a blaze of enthusiastic, Divine love, such as the world never saw, and to set them aflame with fervent earnestness, which shall melt all the icy hardness of heart, and turn cold self-regard into self-forgetting consecration.

Here, then, our text touches upon one of the very profoundest characteristics of Christianity considered as a power in human life. The contrast between it and all other religions and systems of ethics lies, amongst other things, in the stress which it lays upon *love*, and on the earnestness which comes from love; whereas these are scarcely regarded as elements in virtue according to the world, and have certainly no place at all in the world's notion of "temperate religion." Christ gives fervour by giving His Spirit. Christ gives fervour by bringing the warmth of His own love to bear upon our hearts through the Spirit, and that kindles ours. Where His great work for men is believed and trusted in, there, and there only, is there excited an intensity of consequent affection to Him which glows throughout the life. It is not enough to say that Christianity is singular among religious and moral systems in exalting fervour into a virtue. Its peculiarity lies deeper—in its method of producing that fervour. It is kindled by that Spirit using as His means the truth of the dying love of Christ. The secret of the Gospel is not solved by saying that Christ excites love in our souls. *The* question yet remains—how? There is but one answer to that: He loved us to the death. That truth laid on hearts by the Spirit, who takes of Christ's and shows them to us, and that truth alone, makes fire burst from their coldness.

Here is the power that produces that inner fervour without which virtue is a name and religion a yoke. Here is the contrast, not only to John's baptism, but to all worldly religion, to all formalism and decent deadness of external propriety. Here is the consecration of enthusiasm—not of the lurid sullen heat of ignorant fanaticism, but the living glow of an enlightened nature, which flames because lighted by the inextinguishable blaze of His love who gave Himself for us. "He shall baptize you in fire."

Then, dear brethren, if we profess to have come into personal contact with Jesus Christ, here is a sharp test for us, and a solemn rebuke to much of our lives. For a Christian to be cold is sin. It can only come from our neglecting to stir up the gift that is in us. People reproach us with extravagant emotion: let us confess that we have never deserved that reproach half as much as we ought. The world's ideal of religion is decorous coldness—has not the world's idea been our practice? We are afraid to be fervent; our true danger is icy torpor. We sit frost-bitten and almost dead among the snows, and all the while the gracious sunshine is pouring down, that is able to melt the white death that covers us, and to free us from the bonds that hold us prisoned in their benumbing clasp.

No evil is more marked among the Christian Churches of this day than precisely the absence of this "spirit of burning." There is plenty of liberality and effort, there is much interest in religious questions, there is genial tolerance and wide culture, there is a high standard of morality and, on the whole, a tolerable adherence to it —but there is little love, and little fervour. "I have somewhat against thee, that thou hast left thy first love."

Where is that Spirit which was poured out on Pentecost? Where are the cloven tongues of fire, where the flame which Christ died to light up? Has it burned down to grey ashes, or, like some house-fire, lit and left untended, has it gone out after a little ineffectual crackling among the lighter pieces of wood and paper, without ever reaching the solid mass of obstinate coal? Where? The question is not difficult to answer. His promise remains faithful. He does send the Spirit, who is fire. But our sin, our negligence, and our eager absorption with worldly cares, and our withdrawal of mind and heart from the patient contemplation of His truth, have gone far to quench the spirit. Is it not so? Are our souls on fire with the love of God, aglow with the ardour caught from Christ's love? Does that love which fills our hearts coruscate and flame in our lives, making us lights in the darkness, as some firebrand caught up from the hearth will serve for a torch and blaze out into the night? " He shall baptize with fire."

> "O Thou that camest from above,
>   The pure celestial fire to impart,
> Kindle a flame of sacred love
>   On the mean altar of my heart."

Then there is another thought expressed by this symbol, namely, that this baptism gives cleansing as well as warmth, rather gives *cleansing by warmth*. Fire purifies. That Spirit, which is fire, produces holiness in heart and character, by this most chiefly among all his manifold operations, that He excites the flame of love to God, which burns our souls clear with its white fervours. This is the Christian method of making men good,—first, know His love, then believe it, then love Him back again, and then let that genial heat permeate all your life, and it will woo forth everywhere blossoms of beauty and fruits of holiness, that shall clothe the pastures of the wilderness with gladness. Did you ever see a blast-furnace? How long would it take a man, think you, with hammer and chisel, or by chemical means, to get the bits of ore out from the stony matrix? But fling them into the great cylinder, and pile the fire and let the strong draught roar through the burning mass, and by evening you can run off a glowing stream of pure and fluid metal, from which all the dross and rubbish is parted, which has been charmed out of all its sullen hardness, and will take the shape of any mould into which you like to run it. The fire has conquered, has melted, has purified. So with us. Love "shed abroad in our hearts by the Holy Ghost given unto us," love that answers to Christ's, love that is fixed upon Him who is pure and separate from sinners, will purify us and sever us from our sins. Nothing else will. All other cleansing is superficial, like the water of John's baptism. Moralities and the externals of religion will wash away the foulness which lies on the surface, but stains that have sunk deep into the very substance of the soul, and have dyed every thread in warp and woof to its centre, are not to be got rid of so. The awful words which our great dramatist puts into the mouth of the queenly murderess are heavy with the weight of most solemn truth. After all vain attempts to cleanse away the stains, we, like her, have to say, "There's the smell of the blood still—will these hands ne'er be clean?" No! never! unless there be something mightier, more inward in its power, than the water with which we can wash them, some better gospel than "Repent and reform." God be thanked there is a mightier detergent than all these—even that Divine Spirit which Christ gives, and that Divine forgiveness which Christ brings. There, and there alone, dear brethren, we can lose all the guilt of our faultful past, and receive a new and better

life which will mould our future into growing likeness
to His great purity. Oh do not resist that merciful
searching fire, which is ready to penetrate our very bones
and marrow, and burn up the seeds of death which lurk
in the inmost intents of the heart! Let Him plunge
you into that gracious baptism, as we put some poor
piece of foul clay into the fire, and like it, as you glow
you will whiten, and all the spots shall melt away before
the conquering tongues of the cleansing flame. In that
furnace, heated seven times hotter than any earthly
power could achieve, they who walk, live by the presence of the Son of Man, and nothing is destroyed but
the bonds that held them. His Spirit is fire, and that
Spirit of fire is, therefore, the Spirit of holiness.

But take one warning word in conclusion. The alternative for every man is to be baptized in the fire or to be
consumed by it. The symbol of which we have been
speaking sets forth the double thought of purifying or
destruction. Nothing which we have said as to the
former in the least weakens the completing truth that
there is in it an under side of possible terror. One of
the felicities of the emblem is its capacity to set forth
this twofold idea. There is that in the Divine nature
which the Bible calls wrath, the necessary displeasure
and aversion of holy love from sin and wrong doers.
There is in the Divine procedure even now, and here,
the manifestation of that in punishment. "The light
of Israel becomes a flaming fire."

I have no panorama of hell to exhibit, and I would
speak with all reverence on matters so awful: but this

much, at any rate, is clear, that the very same revelation of God, thankfully accepted and submitted to, is the medium of cleansing and source of joyful life, and, rejected, becomes the source of sorrow and the occasion of death. Every man sees that aspect of God's face which he has made himself fit to see. Every gift of God is to men either a savour of life unto life, or a savour of death unto death. Most chiefly is this so in regard to Christ and His gospel, who, though He came not to judge but to save, yet by reason of that very universal purpose of salvation, becomes a judge in the act of saving, and a condemnation to those in whom, by their own faults, that purpose is not fulfilled.

The same pillar of fire which gladdened the ranks of Israel as they camped by the Red Sea, shone baleful and terrible to the Egyptian hosts. The same Ark of the Covenant whose presence blessed the house of Obed-edom, and hallowed Zion, and saved Jerusalem, smote the Philistines, and struck down their bestial gods. Christ and His gospel even here hurt the men whom they do not save.

And we have only to carry that process onwards into another world, and suppose it made more energetic there, as it will be, to feel dimly in how awful a sense it may be that the same fire which gives life may be the occasion of death—and how profound a truth lies in the words—

"What maketh Heaven, that maketh Hell."

Yes! verily—to be salted with fire or to be consumed by it, to be baptized in it, or to be cast into it—is the

choice offered to us all; to thee, my brother, and to me.
Israel made its choice, and in seventy years, the Roman
standards on Zion, and the flames leaping round the
Temple, interpreted John's words in one of their halves,
while the growing energy of the fire, that was lit on Pentecost, fulfilled them in the other. Many a nation and
Church has made its choice since then. You have to
make yours. "The fire shall try every man's work, of
what sort it is." Shall our work be gold, and silver, and
precious stones, which shall gleam and flash in the light,
or wood, hay, and stubble, which shall writhe for a
moment in the blaze and perish? "Our God is a consuming fire." Shall that be the ground of my confidence
that I shall one day be pure from all my sins, or shall it
be the parent of my ghastliest fear that I may be, like
the chaff, destroyed by contact with a holy love rejected,
with a Saviour disbelieved, with a Spirit grieved and
quenched? Choose which.

THE SECRET OF TRANQUILLITY.

PSALM xxxvii. 4, 5, 7.

Delight thyself also in the Lord, and He shall give thee the desires of thine heart. Commit thy way unto the Lord. Rest in the Lord, and wait patiently for Him.

"I HAVE been young, and now am old," says the writer of this Psalm. Its whole tone speaks the ripened wisdom and autumnal calm of age. The dim eyes have seen and survived so much, that it seems scarcely worth while to be agitated by what ceases so soon. He has known so many bad men blasted in all their leafy verdure, and so many languishing good men revived, that—

> "Old experience doth attain
> To something of prophetic strain ;"

and is sure that "to trust in the Lord and do good" ever brings peace and happiness. Life with its changes has not soured but quieted him. It does not seem to him an endless maze, nor has he learned to despise it. He has learned to see God in it all, and that has cleared its confusion, as the movements of the planets, irregular and apparently opposite, when viewed from tne earth, are turned into an ordered whole, when the sun is taken for the centre. What a contrast between the bitter cynicism put into the lips of the son, and the calm cheerful godliness taught, according to our Psalm, by the father! To Solomon, old age is represented as bringing the melancholy creed, "all is vanity;" David believes, "Delight thyself in the Lord, and He shall give thee the desires of thine heart." Which style of old age is the nobler? what kind of life will lead to each?

These clauses, which I have ventured to isolate from their context, contain the elements which secure peace even in storms and troubles. I think that, if we consider them carefully, we shall see that there is a well-marked progress in them. They do not cover the same ground by any means; but each of the later flows from the former. Nobody can commit his way unto the Lord who has not begun by delighting in the Lord; and nobody can rest in the Lord who has not committed his way to the Lord. These three precepts, then, the condensed result of the old man's lifelong experience, open up for our consideration the Secret of Tranquillity. Let us think of them in order.

I. Here is *the secret of tranquillity in freedom from eager, earthly desires*—"Delight thyself in the Lord, and He shall give thee the desires of thine heart."

The great reason why life is troubled and restless lies not without, but within. It is not our changing circumstances, but our unregulated desires, that rob us of peace. We are feverish, not because of the external temperature, but because of the state of our own blood. The very emotion of desire disturbs us; wishes make us unquiet; and when a whole heart, full of varying, sometimes contradictory longings, is boiling within a man, how can he but tremble and quiver? One desire unfulfilled is enough to banish tranquillity; but how can it survive a dozen dragging different ways? A deep lesson lies in that word *distraction,* which has come to be so closely attached to *desires;* the lesson that all eager longing tears the heart asunder. Unbridled and varying wishes, then, are the worst enemies of our repose.

And, still further, they destroy tranquillity by putting us at the mercy of externals. Whatsoever we make necessary for our contentment, we make lord of our happiness. By our eager desires we give perishable things supreme power over us, and so intertwine our being with theirs, that the blow which destroys them lets out our life-blood. And, therefore, we are ever disturbed by apprehensions and shaken by fears. We tie ourselves to these outward possessions, as Alpine travellers to their guides, and so, when they slip on the icy slopes, their fall is our death. If we were not eager to stand on the giddy top of fortune's rolling wheel, we should not heed its idle whirl; but we let our foolish hearts set our feet there, and thenceforward every lurch of the glittering instability threatens to lame or kill us. He who desires fleeting joys is sure to be restless always, and to be disappointed at the last. For, even at the best, the heart which depends for peace on the continuance of things subjected to a thousand accidents, can only know quietness by forcibly closing its eyes against the inevitable; and, even at the best, such a course must end on the whole in failure. Disappointment is the law for all earthly desires; for appetite increases with indulgence, and as it increases, satisfaction decreases. The food remains the same, but its power to appease hunger diminishes. Possession brings indifference. The dose that lulls into delicious dreams to-day must be doubled to-morrow, if it is to do anything; and there is soon an end of that. Each of your earthly joys fills but a part of your being, and all the other ravenous longings either come shrieking at the gate of the soul's palace, like a mob yelling for bread, or are starved into silence; but either way there is disquiet. And then, if a man has fixed his happiness on anything lower than the stars, less stable than the heavens, less sufficient than God, there does come, sooner or later, a time when it passes from him, or he from it. Do not venture the rich freightage of your happiness in crazy vessels. If you do, be sure that, somewhere or other, before your life is ended, the poor frail craft will strike on some black rock rising sheer from the depths, and will grind itself to chips there. If your life twines round any prop but God your strength, be sure that, some time or other, the stay to which its tendrils cling will be plucked up, and the poor vine will be lacerated, its clusters crushed, and its sap bleeding out of it.

If, then, our desires are, in their very exercise, a disturbance, and in their very fruition prophesy disappointment, and if that certain disappointment is irrevocable and crushing when it comes, what shall we do for rest?

Dear brethren, there is but one answer — "Delight thyself in the Lord." These eager desires transfer them to Him; on Him let the affections fix and fasten; make Him the end of your longings, the food of your spirits. This is the purest, highest form of religious emotion—when we can say, "Whom have I but Thee? possessing Thee I desire none beside." And this glad longing for God is the cure for all the feverish unrest of desires unfulfilled, as well as for the ague fear of loss and sorrow. Quietness fills the soul which delights in the Lord, and its hunger is as blessed and as peaceful as its satisfaction.

Think how surely rest comes with delighting in God. For that soul must needs be calm which is freed from the distraction of various desires by the one master-attraction. Such a soul is still as the great river above the falls, when all the side currents and dimpling eddies and backwaters are effaced by the attraction that draws every drop in the one direction; or like the same stream as it nears its end, and, forgetting how it brawled among rocks and flowers in the mountain glens, flows "with a calm and equable motion" to its rest in the central sea. Let the current of your Being set towards God, then your life will be filled and calmed by one master-passion which unites and stills the soul.

And for another reason there will be peace : because in such a case desire and fruition go together. "He shall give thee the desires of thine heart." Only do not vulgarize that great promise by making it out to mean that, if we will be good He will give us the earthly

blessings which we wish. Sometimes we shall get th m,
and sometimes not ; but our text goes far deeper than
that.   God Himself is the heart's desire of those who
delight in Him ; and the blessedness of longing fixed
on Him is that it ever fulfils itself. They who want
God have Him. Your truest joy is in His fellowship
and His grace. If, set free from creatural delights, our
wills reach out towards God, as a plant growing in
darkness to the light—then we shall wish for nothing
contrary to Him, and the wishes which run parallel to
His purposes, and embrace Himself as their only good,
cannot be vain. The sunshine flows into the opened
eye, the breath of life into the expanding lung—so
surely, so immediately the fulness of God fills the waiting, wishing soul. To delight in God is to possess our
delight. Heart! lift up thy gates: open and raise the
narrow, low portals, and the King of Glory will stoop
to enter.

Once more : desire after God will bring peace by
putting all other wishes in their right place. The
counsel in our text does not enjoin the extinction, but
the subordination, of other needs and appetites—"Seek
ye *first* the kingdom of God." Let that be the dominant
desire which controls and underlies all the rest. Seek
for God in everything, and for everything in God. Only
thus will you be able to bridle those cravings which else
tear the heart. The presence of the king awes the
crowd into silence. When the full moon is in the
nightly sky, it makes the heavens bare of flying cloud-
rack, and all the twinkling stars are lost in the peace-

ful, solitary splendour. So let delight in God rise in our souls, and lesser lights pale before it—do not cease to be, but add their feebleness, unnoticed, to its radiance. The more we have our affections set on God, the more shall we enjoy, because we subordinate His gifts. The less, too, shall we dread their loss, the less be at the mercy of their fluctuations. The capitalist does not think so much of the year's gains as the needy adventurer, to whom they make the difference between bankruptcy and competence. If you have God for your " enduring substance," you can face all varieties of condition, and be calm, saying—

> " Give what Thou canst, without Thee I am poor,
> And with Thee rich, take what Thou wilt away."

The amulet that charms away disquiet lies here: Still thine eager desires, arm thyself against feverish hopes, and shivering fears, and certain disappointment, and cynical contempt of all things ; make sure of fulfilled wishes and abiding joys. "Delight thyself in the Lord, and He will give thee the desires of thine heart."

II. But this is not all. The secret of tranquillity is found, secondly, in *freedom from the perplexity of choosing our path.*

"Commit thy way unto the Lord "—or, as the margin says, "roll " it upon God; leave to Him the guidance of thy life, and thou shalt be at peace on the road.

This is a word for *all life*, not only for its great occasions. Twice, or thrice, perhaps in a lifetime, a man's road leads him up to a high dividing point, a water-

shed as it were, whence the rain runs from the one side
of the ridge to the Pacific, and from the other to the
Atlantic. His whole future may depend on his bearing
the least bit to the right hand or to the left, and all the
slopes below, on either side, are wreathed in mist.
Powerless as he is to see before him, he has yet to
choose, and his choice determines the rest of his days.
Certainly he needs some guidance then. But he needs
it not less in the small decisions of every hour. Our
histories are made up of a series of trifles, in each of
which a separate act of will and choice is involved.
Looking to the way in which character is made, as
coral reefs are built up, by a multitude of tiny creatures
whose united labours are strong enough to breast the
ocean ; looking to the mysterious way in which the
greatest events in our lives have the knack of growing
out of the smallest; looking to the power of habit to
make any action of the mind almost instinctive : it is of
far more importance that we should become accustomed
to apply this precept of seeking guidance from God to
the million trifles than to the two or three decisions
which, at the time of making them, we know to be
weighty. Depend upon it that, if we have not learned
the habit of committing the daily-recurring monotonous
steps to Him, we shall find it very, very hard to seek
His help, when we come to a fork in the road. So
this is a command for all life, not only for its turning-
points.

What does it prescribe ? First, the subordination—not
the extinction—of our own *inclinations*. We must begin

by ceasing from self. Not that we are to cast out of consideration our own wishes. These are an element in every decision, and often are our best helps to the knowledge of our powers and of our duties. But we have to take special care that they never in themselves settle the question. They are second, not first. " Thus I will, and therefore thus I decide ; my wish is enough for a reason," is the language of a tyrant over others, but of a slave to himself. Our first question is to be, not " What should I like?" but " What does God will, if I can by any means discover it ? " Wishes are to be held in subordination to Him. Our Will is to be master of our passions, and desires, and whims, and habits, but to be servant of God. It should silence all their cries, and itself be silent, that God may speak. Like the lawgiver-captain in the wilderness, it should stand still at the head of the ordered rank, ready for the march, but motionless, till the Pillar lifts from above the sanctuary. Yes ! " Commit thy way"—unto whom ? Conscience? No : unto Duty? No : but " unto God "—which includes all these lower laws, and a whole universe besides. Hold the will in equilibrium, that His finger may incline the balance.

Then the counsel of our text prescribes the submission of our *judgment* to God, in the confidence that His wisdom will guide us. Committing our way unto the Lord does not mean shifting the trouble of patient thought about our duty off our own shoulders. It is no cowardly abnegation of the responsibility of choice which is here enjoined ; nor any sanction of lazily taking the first vagrant impulse, wafted we know not whence, that rises in the mind, for the voice of God. But, just because we are to commit our way to Him, we are bound to the careful exercise of the best power of our own brains, that we may discover what the will of God is. He does not reveal that will to people who do not care to know it. I suppose the precursor of all visions of Him, which have calmed His servants' souls with the peace of a clearly recognised duty, has been their cry, " Lord, what wilt Thou have me to do?" God counsels men who use their own wits to find out His counsel. He speaks to us through our judgments when they take all the ordinary means of ascertaining our course. The law is : you do your best to find out your duty; you suppress inclination, and desire to do God's will, and He will certainly tell you what it is. I, for my part, believe that the Psalmist spoke a truth when he said, " In all thy ways acknowledge Him, and He shall direct thy steps." Only let the eye be fixed on Him, and He will guide us in the way. If we chiefly desire, and with patient impartiality try, to be directed by Him, we shall never want for direction.

But all this is possible only if we "delight in the Lord." Nothing else will still our desires—the voice within, and the invitations without, which hinder us from hearing the directions of our Guide. Nothing else will so fasten up and muzzle the wild passions and lusts ; "and a little child will lead them." To delight in Him is the condition of all wise judgment. For the most part, it is not hard to discover God's will concerning us, if we supremely desire to know and do it; and such supreme desire is but the expression of this supreme delight in Him. Such a disposition wonderfully clears away mists and perplexities; and, though there will still remain ample scope for the exercise of our best judgment, and for reliance on Him to lead us, yet he, whose single object is to walk in the way that God points, will seldom have to stand still in uncertainty as to what that way is. "If thine eye be single, thy whole body shall be full of light."

Thus, dear brethren, these two keys—joy in God, and trust in His guidance—open for us the double doors of the secret place of the Most High; where all the roar of the busy world dies upon the ear, and the still small voice of the present God deepens the silence, and hushes the heart. Be quiet, and you will hear Him speak—delight in Him, that you may be quiet. Let the affections feed on Him, the will wait mute before Him, till His command inclines it to decision, and quickens it into action; let the desires fix upon His all-sufficiency; and then the wilderness will be no more trackless, but the ruddy blaze of the guiding pillar will brighten on the sand a path which men's hands have never made, nor human feet trodden into a road. He will guide us with His eye, if our eyes be fixed on Him, and be swift to discern and eager to obey the lightest glance that love can interpret. Shall we be like the horse or the mule, which have no understanding, and need to be pulled with bridles and beaten with whips before they know how to go; or shall we be like some trained creature that is guided by the unseen cord of docile submission, and has learned to read the duty, which is its joy, in the glance of its master's eye, or the wave of his hand? "Delight thyself in the Lord: commit thy way unto Him.

III. Our text takes one more step. The secret of tranquillity is found, thirdly, in *freedom from the anxiety of an unknown future.* "Rest in the Lord, and wait patiently for Him." Such an addition to these previous counsels is needful, if all the sources of our disquiet are to be dealt with. The future is dim, after all our straining to see into its depths. The future is threatening, after all our efforts to prepare for its coming storms. A rolling vapour veils it all; here and there a mountain peak seems to stand out; but in a moment another swirl of the fog hides it from us. We know so little, and what we do know is so sad, that the ignorance of what may be, and the certainty of what must be, equally disturb us with hopes which melt into fears, and forebodings which consolidate into certainties. We are sure that in that future are losses, and sorrows, and death; thank God, we are sure, too, that He is in it. That certainty alone, and what comes of it, makes it possible for a thoughtful man to face to-morrow without fear or tumult. The only rest from apprehensions which are but too reasonable is "rest in the Lord." If we are sure that He will be there, and if we delight in Him, then we can afford to say, "As for all the rest, let it be as He wills, it will be well." That thought alone, dear friends, will give calmness. What else is there, brethren, for a man fronting that vague Future; from whose weltering sea such black sharp-toothed rocks protrude? Shall we bow before some stern Fate, as its lord, and try to be as stern as It? Shall we think of some frivolous Chance, as tossing its unguided waves, and try to be as frivolous as It? Shall we try to be content with an animal limitation to the present, and heighten the bright colour of the little to-day by the black background that surrounds it, saying, "Let us eat and drink, for to-morrow we die"? Is it not better, happier, nobler, every way truer, to look into that perilous uncertain future, or rather to look past it to the loving Father who is its Lord and ours, and to wait patiently for Him? Confidence that the future will but evolve God's purposes, and that all these are enlisted on our side, will give peace and power. Without it all is chaos, and we flying atoms in the anarchic mass; or else all is cold-blooded impersonal law, and we crushed beneath its chariot-wheels. Here, and here alone, is the Secret of Tranquillity.

But remember, brethren, that the peaceful confidence of this final counsel is legitimate only when we have obeyed the other two. I have no business, for instance, to expect God to save me from the natural consequences of my own worldliness or folly. If I have taken up a course from eager desires for earthly good, or from obedience to any inclination of my own without due regard to His will, I have no right, when things begin to go awry, to turn round to God, and say, "Lord, I wait upon Thee to save me." And through repentance, and forsaking of our evil ways at any point in a man's course, does ensure, through Jesus Christ, God's loving forgiveness, yet the evil consequences of past folly are often mercifully suffered to remain with us all our days. He who has delighted in the Lord, and committed his way unto Him, can venture to front whatever may be coming; and, though not without much consciousness of sin and weakness, can yet cast upon God the burden of taking care of him, and claim from his faithful Father the protection and the peace which He has bound Himself to give.

And oh, dear friends, what a calm will enter our souls then—solid, substantial,—" the peace of God,"—gift and effluence from the "God of peace"! How blessed then to leave all the possible to-morrow with very quiet heart in His hands! How easy then to bear the ignorance, how possible then to face the certainties, of that solemn future! Change and death can only thin away and finally remove the film that separates us from our delight. Whatever comes here or yonder can but bring us blessing; for we must be glad if we have God, and our wills are parallel with His, whose will all things serve. Our way is traced by Him, and runs alongside of His. It leads to Himself. Then rest in the Lord, and judge nothing before the time. We cannot criticise the Great Artist when we stand before His unfinished masterpiece, and see dim outlines here, a patch of crude colour there. But wait patiently for Him. And so, in calm expectation of a blessed future and a finished work, which will explain the past, in honest submission of our way to God, in supreme delight in Him who is the gladness of our joy, the secret of tranquillity will be ours.

THE SONG OF THE BUILDERS.

(1) LORD, remember David, and all his afflictions: (2) how he sware unto the LORD, and vowed unto the mighty God of Jacob: (3) Surely I will not come into the tabernacle of my house, nor go up into my bed; (4) I will not give sleep to mine eyes, or slumber to mine eyelids, (5) until I find out a place for the LORD, an habitation for the mighty God of Jacob. (6) Lo, we heard of it at Ephratah: we found it in the fields of the wood. (7) We will go into His tabernacles; we will worship at His footstool.

(8) Arise, O LORD, into Thy rest; Thou, and the ark of Thy strength. (9) Let Thy priests be clothed with righteousness; and let Thy saints shout for joy. (10) For Thy servant David's sake turn not away the face of Thine anointed.

(11) The LORD hath sworn in truth unto David; He will not turn from it: Of the fruit of thy body will I set upon thy throne. (12) If thy children will keep My covenant and My testimony that I shall teach them, their children shall also sit upon thy throne for evermore. (13) For the LORD hath chosen Zion; He hath desired it for His habitation. (14) This is My rest for ever: here will I dwell; for I have desired it. (15) I will abundantly bless her provision: I will satisfy her poor with bread. (16) I will also clothe her priests with salvation; and her saints shall shout aloud for joy. (17) There will I make the horn of David to bud: I have ordained a lamp for Mine anointed. (18) His enemies will I clothe with shame: but upon himself shall his crown flourish.

THE solemn prayer which King Solomon offered at the consecration of his Temple ended with words which are, at all events, closely related to a portion of

this Psalm. He said, "Now therefore arise, O LORD
God, into Thy resting place, Thou and the ark of Thy
strength; let Thy priests, O LORD God, be clothed with
salvation, and let Thy saints rejoice in goodness. O
LORD God, turn not away the face of Thine anointed;
remember the mercies of David Thy servant." It must,
however, be admitted that even this all but perfect
identity of expression does not conclusively determine
that the Psalm was composed by Solomon and used
then, for *it* may be a latter quotation and expansion of
the kingly builder's prayer. The compilers of the Book
of Psalms seem to have thought it much more modern
than his days, from their classing it along with those
"songs of degrees" which mostly refer to the Captivity
and return from exile—the time when, as one of them
says, the people of Israel "sat and wept by the rivers of
Babylon," and "were like them that dream when the
Lord turned again the captivity of Zion."

This, however, is a matter of very small consequence.
The Psalm tells it own occasion. It is plainly a hymn
for the consecration of the Temple, and whether it may
have been pealed forth in the first flush of national
triumph in the halcyon days of Solomon, or have risen up
when the voice of weeping and of thanksgiving blended
over the curtailed proportions and diminished glories of
the second house, is of little moment for our purposes.

Whilst it has this original application to the building
of the Temple, we must also regard it as being for that
very reason prophetic and Messianic. And that in two
ways—inasmuch, first, as it speaks of the rearing of the

Temple; inasmuch, also, as it speaks of the perpetual
dominion and ever-blossoming crown of the anointed
king, David's son.   The Temple in Jerusalem was itself
a prophecy.   The true abiding place of God, the true
meeting place of God and man, the true seat of the
oracle, the true place of the real sacrifice, was the
Temple of Christ's body.   The anointed king in the holy
hill of Zion was a prophecy.   The true Son of David the
everlasting King, is Jesus the Anointed.

Then, again, the New Testament teaches that besides
this one real Temple, Christ Himself, He is building
through all the ages an habitation for God—the Church.
Hence our Psalm has been universally and wisely
applied to the Church of these Christian days, and its
invocations and promises claimed as expressive of the
desires and confidences of Christian people in their
work for God.   We are God's building, and we are
God's builders too.   The Psalm is full of strength and
encouragement for us in both characters, which we shall
try to bring out by an attempt at exposition of its course
of thought.

We may call it the Song of the Builders.   It falls into
two parts—man's and God's.   In the former we have
the toil that went before the completion of the Temple,
and the prayer for the Divine blessing on it, now that
it is complete.   In the latter we have God's answer,
guaranteed by His oath, corresponding to and surpassing
all the petitions of the prayers.

For our present purpose, however, it will be most con-
v ient to divide the whole into three sections, in the

first of which, extending to the close of the seventh verse, the Church pleads with God the many thoughts and long toils that had laid the foundation for His house.

I. Let us gather from this portion some lessons touching *Preparatory Work*.

"Lord, remember David, and all his afflictions." The Psalmist looks upon the fair dwelling, reared at last for God, and goes back in thought, as all meditative and generous minds in like circumstances do, to the days when the design thus happily accomplished was first conceived. It was David's thought which was the parent of this holy and beautiful house, though Solomon was its builder; and his name springs first to the singer's lips. He asks, not that the son's toil in erecting, but that the pure desire which was in the father's heart, may be remembered of God. And if we think of Solomon himself as uttering this Psalm, what a beautiful lesson of self-oblivion there is in that tracing of all the honour of the finished work not to himself, who happened to be the instrument for its completion, but to him who, long years before, cherished the purpose which he was never allowed to execute, and gave the impulse to the work in which he himself had no part. Not the toil of hand and arm which carries out, but the mind which conceives the plan, is its true author—"Lord! remember *David*."

But look for a moment at the picture which is given us here of the aged king setting himself to his task. The historical books tell that as soon as "the Lord had given him rest from all his enemies round about," he began to think of building a house for God. The language into which his thoughts run in the narrative is but another edition of the vow which is put into his lips in the Psalm. "See now, I dwell in an house of cedar, but the ark of God dwelleth within curtains," is precisely parallel with "Surely I will not come into the tabernacle of my house till I find out an habitation for the mighty God of Jacob."

He has a sense almost of shame in thinking of his own ease and comfort while so much remained to be done. The repose which he has earned and reached at last he will not take. "God had given him rest," but he will not give it to himself, for, says he, "I will not give sleep to mine eyes, nor slumber to mine eyelids, till I find out a place for the Lord." He was an old man now, wearied with "all his afflictions," with the exhausting excitements of a stirring life that had known many a change since the far-off days, when he led his flock by still waters and into green pastures round about Bethlehem. And he had the other excuse for repose—that he had done much work, as well as suffered many changes. He might well have thought that it was enough for one man to rear such a Temple for Him who "inhabiteth the praises of Israel," as he had done in his songs—more enduring and more fragrant than the house ceiled with cedar which he planned. But not so does a true man think. Rather he will consecrate to God his leisure, as he did his active days, his old age as his youth, he will rejoice to originate work which he can never expect to see finished, and even will be glad to gather together materials which happier natures and times than his may turn to account.

He will give himself to the task which he sees before him, whatever it be, with conscious devotion, with that strenuousness of determined consecration and vehement resolve which "vows unto the Lord, and swears to the mighty God of Jacob." He will put his own comfort second; God's service—which is but the noblest name for duty—first. He will see in all his personal well-being, his wealth, his peaceful home, his exemption from carking cares perhaps, or from the engrossing anxieties which other ranks of life have to fight with, a call from God for service, the more free-hearted for his tranquillity, the more grateful for his blessings. Many of your brethren have to work, in directly religious tasks, in something of the fashion of Nehemiah's men—trowel in one hand, sword in the other; and it is oftenest from men with more than their share of troubles and trials of all sorts that the good deeds for God come. But it ought not to be so. The picture of my text may be a rebuke to the slothfulness of us all, to the feeble wavering purposes of Divine services which we languidly entertain and partially carry out, to the preference of our own comfort to God's work, which leads us all to give but the superfluity of our time, or of our means, or of our sympathy, to the service of our brethren, or, what is the same thing, to doing the work of God. But it should come with a special message to men, and emphatically to women, of comparative leisure and freedom from corroding frets and consuming toils, whose lives are only too apt to be frittered away in trifles, and dissolved in languid idleness, or corrupted by self-indulgence. To such the lesson from that picture of the old soldier-king is : Brace yourselves for continuous service, give yourselves in resolved self-dedication to it, and fling behind you your leisure and regard for your own selfish repose, that you may lay some stone in the Temple of God.

Notice, too, that *David's devotedness does make a plea with God.* The prayer goes upon the supposition that his toil and self-sacrifice will not, cannot, be all in vain. And the prayer, built upon that supposition, is answered. God does not require perfect faithfulness in us, His servants, ere He blesses us with His smile ; He does not need that the temple should be all complete ere He enters in. Neither in the first emotions of tremulous faith in the returning prodigal, nor in the continuous devotion and growing love of the believing heart, nor in the obedience and practical worship of the life, does He lay down the law that the acceptable gift must be a perfect gift. He receives, and pardons, and loves an imperfect faith ; a wandering heart He still blesses and welcomes ; stained services, in which much of the leaven of earthly motives may be fermenting, and many a taint of sloth and selfishness may be found, are not, therefore, rejected of Him. If any of us ever think, "All that I do is so poor and unworthy that He cannot take it and work it into His great purposes," let us be of good cheer. "God is not unrighteous to forget your work and labour of love which ye have showed towards His name."

And consider, too, *how God's remembrance of such preparatory work is shown.* David saw no result from all his toils to build the Temple. He got together the great store, but it was reserved for another to mould it into completeness, and to see the cloud of glory fill the house. But none the less was it true that God remembered David and all his afflictions, and accepted and crowned his work. So it is with much of every man's doings. We all receive unfinished tasks from those who go before; we all transmit unfinished tasks to them who come after. Our vocation is to advance a little the dominion of God's truth, and to be one of the long line who pass on the torch from hand to hand. "One soweth and another reapeth" is the law of the kingdom; and though we sometimes feel that this division of labour is the diminution of our joy here, let us not forget that it is the diffusion and multiplication of gladness hereafter, when "he that soweth and he that reapeth shall rejoice together," and each shall find that he has a share in the completed results, where the labours of all are represented. What does it matter in which stage of the great process our co-operation has been enlisted? Every man that has had a part in the building shall have a share in the glory. What does it matter whether we have been set to dig out the foundation, working amongst mud and wet, or have laid the lowermost courses, which are all covered up and forgotten, or happen to have been among those who bring forth the headstone with shoutings? We are all builders all the same. The main thing is that we have some work there. Never mind whereabouts it is. Never mind whether it be visible or no. Never mind whether your name is associated with it. You may never see the issues of your toils. If you can see them, they will generally not be worth looking at. We work for eternity. We may well wait for the scaffolding to be taken away. Then we shall find that preparatory work is all represented in the final issue ; even as the first film of alluvium, deposited in its delta by some mighty stream, is the real foundation for the last which, long ages after, rise above the surface and bear waving corn and the homes of men. "Lord, remember me, and all mine afflictions, and all my unfinished work, and all my unfulfilled desires," has been the half-despairing cry of many a man, who, if he will listen, may hear God Himself answering from the throne, "Surely I will never forget any of their works." If you cannot see results here in the hot working day, the cool evening hours are drawing near, when you may rest from your labours, and then they will follow you. So let us do our duty, and trust God to give the seed we sow "a body as it hath pleased Him."

The description of the preparatory work closes with a difficult verse, the various interpretations of which cannot be conveniently discussed now. "We heard of it at Ephratah, we found it in the fields of the wood." Ephratah is most probably Bethlehem. If so, the allusion is most likely to the deep obscurity in which the ark was hid during all David's youth. When he dwelt with Jesse at Bethlehem, it was but heard of, not seen, and was substantially lost for him and for the mass of the people. "The fields of the wood" is probably Kirjath-jearim (the city of the woods), where it lay for many years in a forest solitude, and whence it was at last brought by the king. Thus the whole is a brief glance at its former wanderings, to heighten the contrast of the joyful present, when, with the ark before them, they are about to pass into the tabernacles of God, and invoke His presence in the house built for His name.

II. Thus we come to the second section of our Psalm, stretching from the eighth to the tenth verse, *the prayer for God's blessing on the builders' work.*

Try to picture to yourselves the moment. The Temple is finished, shining in its new beauty on its hill top. From every corner of the land, Solomon has assembled the elders of Israel "to bring up the ark of the covenant of the Lord out of the city of David." A festal procession had swept down from the royal palace, in its midst the Levites bearing the sacred ark and the ancient vessels of the Tabernacle. Passing up before the gathered thousands, they had set it up in the Holy Place. They came forth; and at that token that the symbol of the Divine Presence was throned in the sanctuary, there bursts out the grand choral hymn, with the blare of trumpets, and the clash of cymbals, while the children of Zion rejoiced in the familiar strain, "For He is good, for His mercy endureth for ever." Then the cloud of glory, the visible manifestation of God's presence, came down and filled the house, while Solomon lifted up his voice in that wonderful prayer which ended in the words in our Psalm. "Then," says the Book of Chronicles, "the fire came down from heaven and consumed the burnt offerings and the sacrifices, and the glory of the Lord filled the house."

The Psalmist asks first that God would dwell in the completed Temple, and that the symbol of His presence may now at last, after so many wanderings, rest there. It had journeyed before the people in their wilderness marches. It had been planted in Shiloh, and had deserted that sanctuary which He once loved. It had tarried for a while at Mizpeh and at Beth-el. It had been lost on the fatal field of Aphek. It had been carried in triumph through Philistine cities, and had been sent back in their terror. It had lain for three months in the house of Obed-edom. For twenty years it had been hidden in Kirjath. It had been brought up with song and dance to David's house, and now it stands in the Holy Place. There may it abide, and go no more out. He prays that the priests may be, not merely in name and office, nor in symbolical attire, but in inmost reality, clothed with righteousness, may be pure and good as their office demands, and not, like the miserable sons of Eli, who had lost the ark at Eben-ezer, robed in violence and crime. He prays that the gathered Israel may receive such communications of God's love that their hearts and their lips may be filled with joy. And he prays, as at the beginning of the Psalm, that the memory of David may avail to bring down answers of peace to the prayer of David's son.

May we not from all this draw needful lessons for ourselves? And first as to *the one great blessing which all builders for God should desire.*

The prayer rests upon the profound conviction of the incompleteness of all our organizations and works if taken by themselves. The Temple may be finished. Solomon and Hiram, and all their architects and workmen, may have done their best; and the result of all their toils may be gleaming in the sunlight, in the first freshness of its beauty. But something more is needed. Not till the ark is in the Holiest of all, and the cloud of glory fills the house, could they say, "It is finished." And the lesson is of everlasting importance. It is true for all ages of the Church. None, perhaps, ever needed it more than our own. Our wide-spread Christian activity has the possible danger connected with it, that it shall fix our minds unduly on itself. That is the temptation of our sense-bound human nature. It is aggravated by the strong materialistic tendencies of our times. It is reinforced by the manifold examples which we have in all walks of life, of the effects of united action. We need to guard ourselves most jealously lest we come to put the instrument in the place of the power, to "burn incense to our own net, and to sacrifice to our own drag." If ever we do that, then we shall soon have to say, "We have toiled all night and caught nothing." Only when we hear His guiding voice directing us, and trust to His mighty hand to bless our work, only when in obedience to, and dependence on, Him, our motto is, "At *Thy* word we will let down the net," shall we find it filled to overflowing with the Christ-given results of Christ-trusting toil. We all think far too much of external activity, and too little of that

Spirit who must guide and fructify it; too much of the institutions, and too little of the indwelling God. Do we not always need to be driven back—back from all these outward things—to God, who alone can give them power? The great organ must be filled with the breath from the four winds of heaven, ere solemn praise can be thundered from its pipes. You may perfect your machinery; but all its nicely-fitting parts stand motionless—a dead weight; and not a spindle whirrs till the strong impulse, born of fire, rushes in. Take to yourselves the lesson of the earnest petitions of our Psalm, as it rose in the clear air on that day of completed work. Learn—would that we might never forget it!—learn that when we have done all, we have to pray, "Arise, O Lord, into Thy rest," for the temple of our rearing is not completed till the ark is in its sanctuary, and the cloud fills its courts.

That presence will surely be given, if we desire it. To think that our work is enough without Him is self-sufficient madness. To think that He will come without our work is paralysing error. To fear that perhaps He will not come to bless our work is weakening doubt. It is impossible that He should ever be absent from the poorest deed, which runs parallel with His mighty purpose, and longs for His grace to make it fruitful.

And that presence is all which we need to make ourselves strong, and our work effectual. Why does so little come of the abundant activity of this day? "Is the Spirit of the Lord straitened? Are these His doings?" Not so. Many causes may be assigned, noteworthy and true, but we can never go wrong in pressing this as the chief one—the defective measure in which we desire and have the great abiding gift of God's spirit. It is all well to devise new forms of action, and the like ; but beneath all these there must be a more profound dependence on God, a more humble depreciation of self, a more intimate personal acquaintance with the secret place of the Most High, if we would see "the pleasure of the Lord prosper in our hands." "His going forth is prepared as the morning" that breaks day by day over a dark world, flushing the heavens with tender light, wakening shrill music on every bough, and opening the folded petals of all the flowers. "He shall come unto us as the rain" freshening the grass, and giving to the moistened earth the "smell of a field which the Lord hath blessed." Such enlightening, invigorating influences He waits to breathe into our souls, and to shed over our works. Alas ! that our careless indifference should so often leave our fleeces dry, while God's dew falls in silence from His starry heaven. Brethren ! let our prayer be, "Arise, O Lord, into Thy rest ;" and His answer is swift and sure, "Lo, I am with you always."

From this fundamental petition all the other clauses of the prayer flow. Taken together, they are the sum of the Psalmist's desires for his nation, the ideal of what Israel might and should be, of what it certainly would be if God dwelt in it. And for us they trace the outlines of what the Church may be and ought to be. I can only glance hastily at them.

There is first *power*—"The ark of Thy *strength.*"

They in whom God dwells will be strong. To be weak is miserable for all men, but it is sin for Christian men. They have access to the Holiest of all, where the ark stands. How can our spiritual life be sickly, or our service languid, or our resistance to temptation feeble, unless we neglect communion with Him who is our strength?

There is next *righteousness*, with which the Psalm prays that the priests may be clothed. In the new Israel, as in the first constitution of the old, all the people are priests. Righteousness, then, is to be the robe of every Christian soul. Now, do not lose the force of this petition by thinking that "righteousness" is a hazy theological virtue, having little to do with every-day life, and small resemblance to secular morality. To be good, to be gentle and just, loving and truthful, self-forgetting and self-ruling, honest and true, kind and helpful, to live in the exercise of the virtues, which the consciences and tongues of all men call lovely and of good report, and to add to them all the consecration of reference to Him in whom these parted graces dwell united and complete— this is to be righteous, as the Psalmist conceived of it. The Gospel has taught us yet deeper thoughts associated with the word. Thank God for that "fine linen, clean and white, the righteousness" with which Christ covers our wounded nakedness. It becomes ours, though no thread of it was wrought in our looms. But remember that growing purity in life and deed is the main proof that Christ's righteousness is indeed ours. If we are to do God's work in the world, we must be good,

2ND SER.   T

true, righteous men. That robe, like the silken vest in which the knight, in the old legend, went forth to fight, is our true mail. It will turn blows, and deaden cuts, and stay thrusts that will dint and shear through and pierce every other defence. Be you equipped with the armour of righteousness, and wear for all your protection the white robes of God's priests. Be you armed with the weapons of righteousness, and use, for your assaults on evil, mainly a holy life. There is none other in all the armoury like it. The true power of the Christian soldier lies in character, character, character!

Further, the prayer desires that *gladness* from God's presence and the possession of His righteousness may burst into the shout of praise. All true religion is joyful. True, there are elements of sadness in it—a consciousness of sin, which leads to penitent confession; a sense of want, which drives to pleading supplication; a longing for the completer life, which, like all aspiration after unrealized good, has in it a tinge of melancholy which sometimes deepens into pain. But nevertheless we should be glad; and we shall be if we believe that our God is with us. What should then make us sad? True, there are enemies, but here is the ark of His strength. There are sins, but here are the garments of righteousness. There are wants, but here is the feast of the sacrifice, whereof the meek shall eat and be satisfied. There is much unreached as yet, but here is a present God. Communion with Him is not all longing: it is fruition too. Our riches are not wholly in the future: the earnest of the inheritance is already ours. Therefore if we truly possess the great gifts prayed for already, then our hearts should be full to the brim with still blessedness, which runs over in music of thanksgiving and song of joyful praise. So we shall best do our builder-work when, with hearts light, because fixed on God and filled with Him, we do it with joy. If men see on our brightened faces the sign that we " hear the joyful sound," and " walk all day long in the light of His countenance," they will be all the more ready to give heed to us, declaring with our lips what God hath done for our souls.

Finally, the Psalmist prays that the king of Israel and his people with him may be heard and accepted when they pray—being, like their great ancestor, princes who have " power with God and prevail."

Such are his desires for his nation. To be filled with God, to be pure and good, to be glad and jubilant, to have perpetual access with prayers to His mercy-seat, and large answers to the God-pleasing petitions—these are the true notes of the Church, and of the individual Christian man. What do we desire most for our brethren, and for ourselves ? Is the sum of all our hopes and wishes for both gathered in the one mighty petition, "Arise, O Lord, into Thy rest, Thou and the ark of Thy strength ?" Do we see all other gifts wrapped up in that ? Do we long for it, in the firm confidence that when He comes He will bring all that we need, that His indwelling, and it alone, at once constitutes His Church, and endows her with power, purity, and gladness ; whilst it secures that all her work shall prosper, and that the house, which she builds for God, shall stand for evermore ?

T 2

III. The final section of the Psalm contains *the Divine answer, which more than fulfils the Psalmist's desires.*

Throughout these verses there is constant allusion to the preceding petitions. The shape of the response is determined by the form of the desires, and in every case the answer is larger than the prayer. Notice the parallel between the oath of David and the oath of God with which it begins. The prayer had pointed to David's swearing to the Lord as a plea on which its petitions rested. The reply points to a mightier oath than David's, as the ground on which God's mercy is sure. The king "sware to the Lord." Yes, but "the Lord hath sworn to David." That is grander and deeper. Another parallel of the same kind occurs between the former and the latter parts of the Psalm. The one alleges David's finding out "a habitation for the Lord," as a plea. The other replies, "The Lord hath chosen Zion, *He* hath desired it for His habitation." A mightier will than David's had determined it long ago. He is throned now between the cherubim, not because of David's choice, or oath, nor because of Solomon's work, nor because of the people's prayer; but because, prior to all these, His own eternal will had settled the place of His feet, and the faithful word had gone forth from His lips. State all this in its widest form, and what does it come to but that great truth, that God's own love is the cause, and God's own promise, based upon His unchangeable nature, the guarantee, for all His merciful dealings with us? He is His own all-sufficient reason. He is not first won to dwell with us by our importunity, nor swayed by our doings. But, in the eternal depths of His own unchanging nature, in the eternal energy of His own love, lies the reason why He dwells with us unthankful. Yes, not in us, but in Him, lies the motive for His grace, and so it can never change.

Then, notice, that each single petition is enlarged in the answer to something much greater than itself. The Church asked God to arise into His rest; and He answers by adding the promise of perpetuity: "This is my rest *for ever;* here will I dwell." He adds a blessing not sought, when He promises abundance for all, and bread to fill even her poor. The Church asked for robes of righteousness for the priests; and He replies with robes of *salvation*, which is the perfecting and most glorious issue of righteousness. The Church asked that the people might shout for joy; and He replies with an emphatic reduplication of the word, which implies the *exuberance* and *continuance* of the joyful acclaim. The Church asked for favour to the king; and He replies by the promise that the horn of his power shall continually increase, that light of guidance and gladness shall be always his, that victory over all his enemies shall attend his arm, and an ever-blossoming crown be on his head.

Put this in its widest form, and what does it come to but that great law of His grace, by which He over-answers all our poor desires, and giving us more than we had expected, shames us out of our distrust? And this law holds for us, dear friends, in all our works and in all our prayers. These transcendent answers belong to us as truly as they did to the waiting multitude, who

thronged the courts of the Temple, whilst the white-robed
king stood praying on the brazen scaffold, and who saw
the cloud that had blinded Pharaoh in the Red Sea, and
guided their forefathers over many a weary mile, float
slowly down to its abiding place within the heavy veil.

We have work to do for God, and the courses of the
walls of His house are but rising yet. The day is far
distant when "God shall make the pile complete." All
seems confusion and disjointed now. So it was in that
ancient house of God. The materials were prepared at
a distance, by men separated from each other, and ignorant of one another's toils. Hiram and his Tyrians were
hewing in Lebanon, Jewish woodcutters in Carmel,
Eastern hunters and miners were gathering furs and gold
in Ophir. Each did his work, knowing little of its place
in the great whole. The plan was in Solomon's mind,
and *he* reared the Temple. We can do but little. We
have each to labour at our own isolated position. The
true builder is that greater than Solomon, of whom it was
written long ago, "Behold the Man whose Name is the
Branch—He shall build the Temple of the Lord, even He
shall build the Temple of the Lord, and He shall bear
the glory." The day shall come when the weary work of
the ages shall be accomplished, and the glory of the Lord
shall fill that wondrous House. In that lofty and glorified state of His Church, the prayers of earth shall be
surpassed by the possessions of heaven. Here we ask
that God would dwell with us, and there "the tabernacle
of God shall be with men, and God Himself shall walk
in them." Here we ask for righteousness as our gar-

ment, and there it shall be granted us to be arrayed in "fine linen, clean and white, which is the righteousness of saints." Here we ask for joy in the midst of sorrow, and there "they shall obtain joy and gladness, and sorrow and sighing shall flee away."

In that tabernacle that shall not be taken down, see that you build on the one foundation some gold and silver and precious stones, which the declaring day and the revealing fire shall manifest to have been wrought in God. Then our work, abiding, shall bring to us the endless glory with which God at last overpays the toils, even as now He over-answers the poor prayers, of his labouring servants. "Now unto Him that is able to do exceeding abundantly above all that we ask or think, according to the power that worketh in us, unto Him be glory in the Church by Christ Jesus throughout all ages, world without end. Amen."

THE SEED BY THE WAYSIDE.

MATTHEW xiii. 3, 4.

A sower went forth to sow ; and when he sowed, some seeds fell by the way side, and the fowls came and devoured them up.

THIS long series of parables, spoken by our Lord sitting in the little fishing-boat to the crowd on the beach, is bound together by a close internal connection. Their subject is the whole history of the progress of the kingdom of heaven from the beginning to the end. Various aspects of that kingdom, its methods, its corruptions, and caricatures, its growth outwardly, its growth within, the diverse ways in which men are led into it, and the great act of judgment in which the earthly form of the kingdom ends, are set forth by the parables of the sower, the tares of the field, the mustard-seed, the leaven, the merchantman seeking goodly pearls, the treasure hid in a field, and the draw-net "that gathered of every kind," and out of which the good were gathered into vessels, but the bad cast away.

Besides this internal connection, it has been pointed

out in one of our most graphic and valuable books on Palestine that the natural features of the spot where these parables were spoken are such as to suggest the greater part of them. The author tells us that, as he rose towards Gennesareth, he came upon a slight recess in the hill-side, close upon the plain, where there was a corn-field going down to the very water's edge ; that through it there ran a beaten field-path without edge or division between it and the waven ears ; that the " good soil" in it was here and there interrupted by masses of barren rock cropping up through it ; and that in the very midst of the wheat great thorn-bushes sprang up. In the corn were tares, countless birds of all kinds hover over the lake, and still a fisher or two may be seen casting the net into the waters. Beautiful to think of, how Christ laid hold of the vulgar things round about Him as the occa-sions for the utterance and moulds for the form of His precious words, and hung the teachings of His wisdom on every thorn-bush, and on every waving wheat-ear ! Do you not think that, if Christ had walked up and down our streets, He would have found just as precious and sacred lessons in things which we meet every day, and pass by as common and " of none effect ? "

This parable of the sower, of course, contains an image so natural in its application to all wisdom, that it is not on His lips only that truth has been described as "seed." There are manifold facilities about the emblem on which one may dwell for an instant. The seed has a germinat-ing power in itself that leads to endless reproduction. So every blessed word, every true word, whether of Christ's gospel or of man's wisdom, that finds its way into hearts and minds, works there, springing and growing, and bears fruit and reproduces itself—on and on again without end. My brother, take care what you sow in other hearts, for your words are living things; and we may apply in another sense to all human utterances what our Lord said of His own—"the words that we speak" to one another, "they are spirit and they are life." It is an awful thought that we may scatter abroad seeds which may take root in some hearts and may spring up a dark waving, poisonous hemlock growth. It is a blessed thought that we can sow seed which shall bear fruits of righteousness a hundred-fold.

And then, again, there are such other ideas as these : Man is but the soil. If you are to get Divine desires and a Divine life in a human heart, they must be sown there : they are not products of the soil. There needs the bringing of the seed by another. There needs the imparting of truth and righteousness and purity from a higher source and a Diviner hand. There must be the sowing before there is any right and good harvest off this soil of our sinful souls, barren but for weeds.

Then, again, man's part is accurately described by that old image of the parable—simple reception, and yet not passiveness ; simple reception, but still the co-operation, though it be only in the shape of receiving what is given —the co-operation of the Divine word and of the human soul. There is no sowing without a soil, and there is no growth without a seed. " Ye are God's husbandry ;" in your hearts, as soil, the seed must be sown ; and its growth depends upon the character of the soil wherein it is sown.

Then, again, remember that these different kinds of soil, that are spoken about here, are not unalterably and inevitably different. That does not appear in all the imagery throughout the parable, but, in reference to this portion that I have selected for my text, it does appear. The path throughout the field is not a made road, but only a beaten track. A bit of the same soil, once just like all the rest, where there was a waving harvest; but it has become hard, because men's feet have trampled it down in their busy passage. It is an acquired disposition, not a natural characteristic, that is spoken of. And that is the principal thought I have to put before you, about this seed that is sown by the way side.

In the first place, here is brought before us the *Beaten Path;* and secondly, the *Lost Seed.* "It fell by the way side, and the fowls came and devoured it up."

I. Let us think about that type of character which is here set forth under the image of "the way side." *It is a heart trodden down* by the feet that have gone across it; and, because trodden down, a heart *incapable of receiving the seed sown.* The seed falls *upon* it, not *in* it. There is no sort of contact, except the mere touch of the husk with the hard surface. It lies there exposed, and has no chance to germinate; and so, by and by, the fowls of the air come, and away it goes, and the place lies greenless and barren. Let me point out two or three ways by which the heart becomes trodden down, two or three of the passers-by whose feet trample it into unsusceptibility. The heart is trodden down by *habit and custom*. The heart is trodden down by *sin*. And, saddest of all, the heart is trodden down by *the very feet of the sower himself*.

First, the heart is trodden down by *custom and habit*. The best way of presenting before you what I mean will be to take a plain illustration. Suppose a little child, just beginning to open its eyes and unfold its faculties upon this wonderful world of ours. There you get the extreme of capacity for receiving impressions from without, the extreme of susceptibility to the influences that come upon it. Tell the little thing some trifle that passes out of *your* mind; you forget all about it; but it comes out again in the child weeks and weeks afterwards, showing how deep a mark it has made. It is the law of the human nature that, when it is beginning to grow, it shall be soft as wax to receive all kinds of impressions, and then that it shall gradually stiffen and become hard as adamant to retain them. The rock was once all fluid, and plastic, and gradually it cools down into hardness. If a finger-dint had been put upon it in the early time, it would have left a mark that all the forces of the world could not make nor can obliterate now. In our great museums you see stone slabs with the marks of rain that fell hundreds of years before Adam lived; and the footprint of some wild bird that passed accross the beach in those old, old times. The passing shower and the light foot left their prints on the soft sediment; then ages went on, and it has hardened into stone; and there they remain and will remain for evermore. That is like a man's spirit; in the childish days so soft, so susceptible to all impressions, so joyous to receive new ideas, treasuring them all up, gathering them all into itself, retaining them all for ever. And then, as years go on, habit, the growth of the soul into steadiness and power, and many other reasons beside, gradually make us less and less capable of being profoundly and permanently influenced by anything outside us; so that the process from childhood to manhood is a process of getting less impressible.

It is a matter of familiar observation, how hard it is to get a new notion into mature men's minds; how an unfamiliar idea, like a new piece of furniture in a full room, deranges the order of all the other articles, and cannot be conveniently fitted in anywhere. We uniformly get more conservative as we get older; so that really it is almost a sign of something abnormal in the mental character of a man, if he is as ready to entertain stranger thoughts, in hopes of their being angels, when he is fifty as when he was twenty. It is quite inevitable that it should be so, and it is a good thing that it is so; for, unless we have a certain kind of crust of insensibility grown over us, by our familiarity with the world, we should never come to be calm, strong men. When we were growing towards maturity, God mercifully made us open to all teachings, and susceptible to all impressions, that we might gather in the truth from every side; and when we have come to the years when we *ought* to have gathered it in, and made it our own, whether we have done so or not, God has mercifully made us hard and strong, and if you like to say so, a little obstinate and stiff in our old ways, that we "be not carried about by every wind of doctrine," like children, but may have the sturdiness and strong muscle and bone of full grown men.

So that it is a natural process, one that it is no use kicking against, one that has much good about it, by which a man's heart gets more or less into the condition that is typified by Christ here, in the image of the way side—being "trodden down" by a thousand emotions; being rammed into consolidation by the heavy wains of business and the loaded carts of traffic, and the light vehicles of pleasure and gladness; and, by all, being made steady, matured, calm, and self-possessed. And yet that may very easily come to be a disease and an evil. A man may come to be too rigid in all that he has always believed. He may come to be too callous to get new thoughts, and to have new directions given to his life from any quarter whatsoever; and then he has ceased to grow, and it is time that he were dying out of the way, and leaving his place for other people who can use better the wonderful facilities for endless growth and progress which God has given.

Now all this applies as closely to your relation to religion as to anything else. There too, a process is going on which makes it absolutely certain that, the further you advance in life, the less you will be capable of being influenced even by the Divinest truth of God's word. The heart, I say, is trodden down by the feet

of *custom*. Oh! brethren, if I were to be silent for
a minute, and ask some of you to speak, surely you
could preach a sermon on this text infinitely more im-
pressive than anything I can say; you could go back
to childhood, and remember how *then* the word of the
Lord, and the message of His grace, came to you and
touched your hearts, and could tell, in contrast, how
now the same hearts, by the traffic of business and the
tramp of the world through them, have become hardened
and unsusceptible, so that the seed, when it falls there,
only just lies upon the surface, and does not ever get
down to the conscience! Ah! some of you know that.
The "seed fell by the way side;" God grant that the
next thing may not have to be said of you, my brother,
"Immediately Satan cometh and catcheth away that
which was sown in the heart."

Let me remind you, again, that, besides this innocent
and inevitable process which goes on, and cannot but go
on, the older we get, the *heart is trodden down* too, in so
far as susceptiblity to the Gospel is concerned, *by sin.*
It is not the least sad and awful of the wide-spread
consequences of sin, that it uniformly works in the
direction of unfitting men to receive God's love. The
more we need it the less we are able to lay hold of it.
If it were presented to a pure spirit, it would be discerned for what it is, the most glorious manifestation
of God. It *is* present to purified spirits yonder, and to
them it is all glowing with beauty and glory, and they
fold it to their cleansed hearts closer than ever they
did when on earth. But the less holiness in the be-

holder the less comeliness in the Lamb whom he beholds ; and the more sin in a heart the more mist between it and Him "who takes away the sin of the world." So that wheresoever there is transgression there is need for the Gospel ; and whilst there is transgression there is the standing difficulty of receiving the Gospel.

For what is it that sin does to a man ? It averts his will from all that is good, and right, and true ; it bribes his conscience ; it impoverishes his heart of every pure affection ; it squanders and lays waste all the treasures of his immortal soul ; it gives him a bias and interest, as he fancies, in rejecting the message that comes to close quarters with him and his transgression. It makes him in love with his own passions and desires, and consequently, not in love with the pure word of the Divine truth ; just as those old Israelites with their perverted taste longed for the leeks and onions and garlick, the strong-smelling and tasting dainties that they had got down in the land of their captivity, and said, "Our soul loathes this light bread" that came from God, and had nothing in it to pamper sense and feed the flesh. Every transgression deprives us, in some degree, of power to receive the Divine word of God's truth, and making it our own. And these demons of worldliness, of selfishness, of carelessness, of pride, of sensuality, that go careering through your soul, my brother, are like the goblin horseman in the old legend ; wherever that hoof-fall strikes, the ground is blasted, and no grass will grow upon it any more for ever ! The heart is trodden down by the rebel rout of beastly sins that go storming through that once fair garden, eating up what they can, and trampling down what they cannot eat. These turn it from the field in which seed may be sown, into the hard beaten path where the seed only lies on the top, and never goes down at all.

And now, lastly, the heart is trodden down, so far as receiving the Gospel is concerned, *by the very feet of the sower*. That is a thing that chapel and church-going people want, most of all, to have preached to them. Wherever and whenever the great "Lord of the harvest," or any of the messengers He sends out to declare His word, come to you and pass across your soul, sowing "the seed of the kingdom," if that seed does not spring, then the very sowers trample down your soul. Or to put away the metaphor, every sermon that an ungodly man hears, which leaves him ungodly, leaves him, not as it found him, but harder by the passage of the word once more across his heart, harder by the rejection once more of God's grace. Dear friends, when one thinks of that, these Sunday gatherings of ours, and this poor work that I try to do, come to be tragical almost; awful at any rate, awful in their responsibility on my shoulders, and not less awful in their responsibility upon yours! If I come and sow chaff along with the "seed of the king-dom," I shall still have trodden down your hearts, and made them somewhat harder. If you, listening to these words of mine, because they are God's words in some measure, are able to turn away from them, you will be able to do it better next Sunday, and you will be able to do it easier the Sunday after that, until at last you will

2ND SER.   U

come to the position in which some of you have been standing these many years now, of utter indifference to God's voice. Will a man sow seed down our streets, and expect to get a crop there? The hearts of some of you are hard as the streets of some great city—they are beaten down by the perpetual traffic of passengers from morning till night; and almost before the last solitary wanderer has slunk from them in the darkness, the first heavy cart is out again with more supplies for the day's business, and more distractions for the souls of men. Oh, dear friends, "who is sufficient for these things?" You *hear* the word. For God's sake, for your own soul's sake, I beseech you, take heed how you hear.

II. A very few words must suffice for the second point brought into notice here—*the lost seed.*

Sown on the surface of a hardened heart, it lies there for a little while, and does nothing. But only for a little while: it is soon carried off. The parable says "by the fowls of the air;" the interpretation says by "the wicked one." He who sows tares, also roots up growing wheat, and does not neglect to sweep away the seed. His chosen instruments are those light, swift-winged, apparently innocent flocks of flying thoughts, that come swooping across your souls, even whilst the message of God's love is sounding in your ears. Yes, with most men, it is the constant succession of petty cares, the constant occupation of heart and mind with trivial subjects and passing good, much rather than any conscious fixed resolve to shut their souls against Christ and His love, that steals away the word from their memories and thoughts. Like some countless cloud of locusts, they darken our sky, and cover the face of the land, and their numbers more than make up for their individual insignificance, and their devastations are as rapid and more complete than an invading army's would be. I have no fear that many of you will say, "I am resolved to give no heed to Christ's voice of love;" but I do fear, with all but certainty of foreboding, that very many of you will simply yield yourselves to the swarm of busy thoughts that are waiting to buzz about your minds, and, without any conscious will in the matter at all, will simply lose the impression which God's truth makes upon you now. I wonder how many greedy birds are hovering up there above your heads, ready, as soon as my voice ceases, as soon as the sower's back is turned, to make their pounce and carry away each his grain of seed? I wonder what you will think about just after this sermon is over, and how long it will be before all remembrance of my poor words is clean gone from you? Five minutes on your way home will be enough for some. But if, by God's mercy, any deeper impressions than can be rubbed smooth so easily, have been made on thy soul, my brother, let me beseech you to guard them from the attrition of earthly thoughts and cares. And, above all, let me beseech you to give special heed to those thoughts that follow first after you have come in contact with the message of Christ's mercy—for that is a most weighty word in this parable, which tells us that "immediately" the fowls of the air came and devoured it up.

Surely you ought to have more control over your

minds, and the subjects which shall occupy them, than to let present cares and duties and enjoyments absolutely hide from you the truth which, you profess to believe, is of supreme importance. Surely it scarcely becomes a man to hold it with so slack a grasp that any runaway may snatch it from you as you go along. "We ought to give the more earnest heed to the things which we have heard, lest at any time we be drifted past them." Do not you be content to let your boat float along with the stream, but make fast your anchorage to that solid and abiding Truth, holding by which we are safe !

This hardness, of which our text speaks, is not unalterable. The path is of the same soil as the rest of the field, and may be made to bear corn as it does. Nothing is needed but to plough it up. God drives a deep share through many a wayside heart, and the coulter of affliction breaks up many a spirit, that it may afterwards yield "the peaceable fruit of righteousness." And if He does that for you, bless Him for His mercy ; but do not wait, for you can get rid of all this insensibility by the simple effort of your own will. Howsoever the world may have driven its traffic through your hearts and beaten them hard ; howsoever the blasting hoof of sin may have rung along the path ; howsoever the passage of the servants of the husbandman, and even the gentle footfall of Him who is the only true Sower of the seed—and comes to you as to us all—may have diminished the impression which the word, so often heard, makes on you listlessly hearing it once more—all may be changed, and your hearts may become that good soil, which brings forth fruit a hundred-fold. Do not, dear brethren, do not let yet another film of hardness be deposited on the surface of these hearts, by now again hearing and now again leaving unaccepted the offer of God's great mercy through Jesus Christ. Shake off the torpedo touch that has paralysed you. Christ Himself, my brother, speaks to you, and calls you to trust in Him, to receive His pardoning grace, His sanctifying Spirit. That voice has sounded in the tomb, and "the dull, cold ear" heard it, though stopped with clay and muffled with the napkin that bound the face, and the limbs obeyed, though stiff in death, and swathed hand and foot, and Lazarus came forth. That voice shall sound again, and "all that are in the grave shall hear," and shall arise to meet their Judge. That voice sounds now for each of us in loving invitation; and dead in sin and hardness of heart though we be, we can listen and live. Christ Himself, my brother, sows the seed now. Do you take care that it falls not on, but in, your souls. "Break up your fallow ground, for it is time to seek the Lord."

THE POWER OF FEEBLE FAITH.

MARK v. 25, 27, 28.

And a certain woman, . . . when she had heard of Jesus, came in the press behind, and touched His garment. For she said, If I may touch but His clothes, I shall be whole.

IN all the narratives of this miracle, it is imbedded in the story of Jairus's daughter, which it cuts in twain. I suppose that the Evangelists felt and would have us feel the impression of calm consciousness of power and of leisurely dignity produced by Christ's having time to pause even on such an errand, in order to heal by the way, as if parenthetically, this other poor sufferer. The child's father with impatient earnestness pleads the urgency of her case—"she lieth at the point of death;" and to him and to the group of disciples, it must have seemed that there was no time to be lost. But He who knows that His resources are infinite can afford to let her die, while He cures and saves this woman. She shall receive no harm, and her sister suppliant has as great a claim on Him. "The eyes of all wait" on His equal love; He has leisure of heart to feel for each, and

.ulness of power for all ; and none can rob another of his share in the Healer's gifts, nor any in all that dependent crowd jostle his neighbour out of the notice of the Saviour's eye.

The main point of the story itself seems to be the illustration which it gives of the genuineness and power of an imperfect faith, and of Christ's merciful way of responding to and strengthening such a faith. Looked at from that point of view, the narrative is very striking and instructive.

The woman is a poor shrinking creature, broken down by long illness, made more timid still by many disappointed hopes of cure, depressed by poverty which her many doctors had brought her to. She does not venture to stop this new Rabbi-physician, as He goes with the rich church dignitary to heal his daughter, but lets Him pass before she can make up her mind to go near Him at all, and then comes creeping up in the crowd behind, puts out her wasted, trembling hand to His garment's hem—and she is whole. She would fain have stolen away with her new-found blessing, but Christ forces her to stand out before the throng, and there, with all their eyes upon her—cold cruel eyes some of them— to conquer her diffidence and shame, and tell all the truth. Strange kindness that ! strangely contrasted with His ordinary care to avoid notoriety, and with His ordinary tender regard for shrinking weakness ! What may have been the reason ? Certainly it was not for His own sake at all, nor for others' chiefly, but for hers, that He did this. The reason lay in the incompleteness of her faith. It was very incomplete—although it was, Christ answered it. And then He sought to make the cure, and the discipline that followed it, the means of clearing and confirming her trust in Himself.

I. Following the order of the narrative thus understood, we have here first, the great lesson that *very imperfect faith may be genuine faith.* There was unquestionable confidence in Christ's healing power, and there was earnest desire for healing. Our Lord Himself recognizes her faith as adequate to be the condition of her receiving the cure which she desired. Of course, it is a very different thing from the faith which unites us to Christ, and is the condition of our receiving our soul's cure; and we shall never understand the relation of multitudes of the people in the Gospels to Jesus, if we insist upon supposing that the "faith to be healed," which many of them had, was a religious, or, as we call it, "saving faith." But still, the trust which was directed to Him, as the Giver of miraculous temporal blessings, is akin to that higher trust into which it often passed, and the principles regulating the operation of the loftier are abundantly illustrated in the workings of the lower.

The imperfections, then, of this woman's faith were many. It was intensely *ignorant* trust. She dimly believes that, somehow or other, this miracle-working Rabbi will heal her, but the cure is to be a piece of magic, secured by material contact of her finger with His robe She has no idea that Christ's will, or His knowledge, much less His pitying love, have anything to do with it. She thinks that she may get her desire furtively, and may carry it away out of the crowd, and He, the source of it, be none the wiser, and none the poorer, for the blessing which she has stolen from Him. What utter blank ignorance of Christ's character, and way of working! What complete misconception of the relation between Himself and His gift! What low, gross, superstitious ideas! Yes, and with them all what a hunger of intense desire to be whole; what absolute assurance of confidence that one finger-tip on His robe was enough! Therefore she had her desire, and her Lord recognized her faith as true, foolish and unworthy as were the thoughts which accompanied it!

Thank God! the same thing is true still, or what would become of any of us? There may be a real faith in Christ, though there be mixed with it many and grave errors concerning His work, and the manner of receiving the blessings which He bestows. A man may have a very hazy apprehension of the bearing and whole scope of even Scripture declarations concerning the profounder aspects of Christ's person and work, and yet be holding fast to Him by living confidence. I do not wish to underrate for one moment the absolute necessity of clear and true conceptions of revealed truth, in order to a vigorous and fully developed faith; but, while there can be no faith worth calling so, which is not based upon the intellectual reception of truth, there may be faith based upon the very imperfect intellectual reception of very partial truth. The power and vitality of faith is not measured by the comprehensiveness and clearness of belief. The richest soil may bear shrunken and barren ears; and on the arid sand, with the thinnest layer of earth, gorgeous cacti may bloom out, and fleshy aloes lift their sworded arms, with stores of moisture to help them through the heat. It is not for us to say what amount of ignorance is destructive of the possibility of real confidence in Jesus Christ. But for ourselves, feeling how short a distance our eyesight travels, and how little, after all our systems, the great bulk of men in Christian lands know lucidly and certainly of theological truth, and how wide are the differences of opinion amongst us, and how soon we come to towering barriers, beyond which our poor faculties can neither pass nor look, it ought to be a joy to us all, that a faith which is clouded with such ignorance may yet be a faith which Christ accepts. He that knows and trusts Him as Brother, Friend, Saviour, in whom he receives the pardon and cleansing which he needs and desires, may have very much misconception and error cleaving to him, but Christ accepts him. If at the beginning His disciples know but this much, that they are sick unto death, and have tried without success all other remedies, and this more, that Christ will heal them; and if their faith builds upon that knowledge, then they will receive according to their faith. By degrees they will be taught more; they will be brought to the higher benches in His school; but, for a beginning, the most cloudy apprehension that Christ is the Saviour of the world, and my Saviour, may become the foundation of a trust which will bind the heart to Him and knit Him to the heart in eternal union. This poor woman received her healing, although she said, "If I may touch but the hem of His garment, I shall be whole."

Her error was akin to one which is starting into new prominence again, and with which I need not say that I have no sort of sympathy,—that of people who attach importance to externals as means and channels of grace, and in whose system the hem of the garment and the touch of the finger are apt to take the place which the heart of the wearer and the grasp of faith should hold. The more our circumstances call for resistance to this error, the more needful is it to remember that, along with it and uttering itself through it, may be a depth of devout trust in Christ, which should shame us. Many a poor soul that clasps the base of the crucifix clings to the cross; many a devout heart, kneeling before the altar, sees, through the incense smoke, the face of the Christ. The faith that is tied to form, though it be no faith for a man, though in some respects it darken God's Gospel, and bring it down to the level of magical superstition, may yet be, and often is, accepted by Him whose merciful eye recognized, and whose swift power answered, the mistaken trust of her who believed that healing lay in the fringes of His robe, rather than in the pity of His heart.

Again, her trust was very *selfish.* She wanted health; she did not care about the Healer. She thought much of the blessing in itself, little or nothing of the blessing as a sign of His love. She would have been quite contented to have had nothing more to do with Christ if she could only have gone away cured. She felt but little glow of gratitude to Him whom she thought of as unconscious of the good which she had stolen from Him. All this is a parallel to what occurs in the early history of many a Christian life. The first inducement to a serious contemplation of Christ is, ordinarily, the consciousness of one's own sore need. Most men are driven to Him as a refuge from self, from their own sin, and from the wages of sin. The soul, absorbed in its own misery, and groaning in a horror of great darkness, sees from afar a great light, and stumbles towards it. Its first desire is deliverance, forgiveness, escape; and the first motions of faith are impelled by consideration of personal consequences. Love comes after, born of the recognition of Christ's great love to which we owe our salvation; but faith precedes love in the natural order of things, however closely love may follow faith; and the predominant motive in the earlier stages of many men's faith is distinctly self-regard. Now, that is all right, and as it was meant to be. It is an overstrained and caricatured doctrine of self-abnegation, which condemns such a faith as wrong. The most purely self-absorbed wish to escape from the most rudely-pictured hell may be, and often is, the beginning of a true trust in Christ. Some of our superfine modern teachers who are shocked at Christianity, because it lays the foundation of the loftiest, most self-denying morality in "selfishness" of that kind, would be all the wiser for going to school to this story, and laying to heart the lesson it contains; how a desire no nobler than to get rid of a painful disease was the starting-point of a moral transformation, which turned a life into a peaceful, thankful surrender of the cured self to the service and love of the mighty Healer.

But while this faith, for the sake of the blessing to be obtained, is genuine, it is undoubtedly imperfect. Quite legitimate and natural at first, it must grow into something nobler when it has once been answered. To think of the disease mainly is inevitable before the cure, but, after the cure, we should think most of the Physician. Self-love may impel to His feet; but Christ-love should be the moving spring of life thereafter. Ere we have received anything from Him; our whole soul may be a longing to have our gnawing emptiness filled; but when we have received His own great gift, our whole soul should be a thank-offering. The great reformation which Christ produces is, that He shifts the centre for us from ourselves to Himself; and whilst He uses our sense of need and our fear of personal evil as the means towards this, He desires that the faith, which has been answered by deliverance, should thenceforward be a "faith which worketh by love." As long as we live, either here or yonder, we shall never get beyond the need for the exercise of the primary form of faith, for we shall ever be pressed by sore needs, and dependent for all help and blessedness on Him; but as we grow in experience of His tender might, we should learn more and more that His gifts cannot be separated from Himself. We should prize them most for His sake, and love Him more than we do them. We should be drawn to Him as well as driven to Him.

Faith may begin with desiring the blessing rather than the Christ. It must end with desiring Him more than all besides, and with losing self utterly in His great love. Its starting-point may rightly be, "Save, Lord, or I perish." Its goal must be, "I live, yet not I, but Christ liveth in me."

Again, here is an instance of real faith weakened and interrupted by much *distrust*. There is not a full, calm reliance on Christ's power and love. She dare not appeal to His heart, she shrinks from meeting His eye. She will let Him pass, and then put forth a tremulous hand. Cross-currents of emotion agitate her soul. She doubts, yet she believes; she is afraid, yet emboldened by her very despair; too diffident to cast herself on His pity, she is too confident not to resort to His healing virtue.

And so is it ever with our faith. Its ideal perfection would be that it should be unbroken, undashed by any speck of doubt. But the reality is far different. It is no full-orbed completeness, but, at the best, a growing segment of reflected light, with many a rough place in its jagged outline, prophetic of increase; with many a deep pit of blackness on its silver surface; with many a storm-cloud sweeping across its face; conscious of eclipse and subject to change. And yet it is the light which He has set to rule the night of life, and we may rejoice in its crescent beam. We are often tempted to question the reality of faith in ourselves and others, by reason of the unbelief and disbelief which co-exists with it. But why should we do so? May there not be an

inner heart and centre of true trust, with a nebulous
environment of doubt, through which the nucleus shall
gradually send its attracting and consolidating power,
and turn it, too, into firm substance? May there not
be a germ, infinitesimal, yet with a real life throbbing in
its microscopic minuteness, and destined to be a great
tree, with all the fowls of the air lodging in its branches?
May there not be hid in a heart a principle of action,
which is obviously marked out for supremacy, though
it has not yet come to sovereign power and manifestation in either the inward or the outward being? Where
do we learn that faith must be complete to be genuine?
Our own weak hearts say it to us often enough; and
our lingering unbelief is only too ready to hiss into our
ears the serpent's whisper, "You are deceiving yourself;
look at your doubts, your coldness, your forgetfulness:
you have no faith at all." To all such morbid thoughts,
which only sap the strength of the spirit, and come from
beneath, not from above, we have a right to oppose the
first great lesson of this story—the reality of an imperfect
faith. And, turning from the profitless contemplation
of the feebleness of our grasp of Christ's robe to look
on Him, the fountain of all spiritual energy, let us cleave
the more confidently to Him for every discovery of our
own weakness, and cry to Him for help against ourselves,
that He would not quench the smoking flax; for the
old prayer is never offered in vain, when offered, as
at first, with tears, "Lord, I believe; help Thou mine
unbelief."

II. The second stage of this story sets forth a truth

involved in what I have already said, but still needing to be dealt with for a moment by itself—namely, that *Christ answers the imperfect faith.*

There was no real connection between the touch of His robe and the cure, but the poor ignorant sufferer thought that there was; and, therefore, Christ stoops to her childish thought, and allows her to prescribe the path by which His gift shall reach her. That thin wasted hand stretched itself up beyond the height to which it could ordinarily reach, and, though its highest point fell far short of Him, He lets His blessing down to her level. He does not say, "Understand Me, put away thy false notion of healing power residing in My garment's hem, or I heal thee not." But He says, "Dost thou think that it is through thy finger on My robe? Then, through thy finger on My robe, it shall be. According to thy faith, be it unto thee."

And so it is ever. Christ's mercy, like water in a vase, takes the shape of the vessel that holds it. On the one hand, His grace is infinite, and "is given to every one of us according to the measure of the gift of Christ"—with no limitation but His own unlimited fulness; on the other hand, the amount which we practically receive from that inexhaustible store is, at each successive moment, determined by the measure and the purity and the intensity of our faith. On His part there is no limit but infinity, on our sides the limit is our capacity, and our capacity is settled by our desires. His word to us ever is, "Open thy mouth wide, and I will fill it." "Be it unto thee even as thou wilt."

A double lesson, therefore, lies in this thought for us
all. First, let us labour that our faith may be enlightened, importunate, and firm : for every flaw in it will
injuriously affect our possession of the grace of God.
Errors in opinion will hinder the blessings that flow from
the truths which we misconceive or reject. Languor of
desire will diminish the sum and enfeeble the energy of
the powers that work in us. Wavering confidence, crossed
and broken, like the solar spectrum, by many a dark line
of doubt, will make our conscious possession of Christ's
gift fitful. We have a deep well to draw from. Let us
take care that the vessel with which we draw is in size
proportionate to *its* depth and *our* need, that the chain
to which it hangs is strong, and that no leaks in it let the
full supply run out, nor any stains on its inner surface
taint and taste the bright treasure.

And the other lesson is this. There can be no faith
so feeble that Christ does not respond to it. The most
ignorant, self-regarding, timid trust may unite the soul to
Jesus Christ. To desire is to have ; and whoever will,
may "take of the water of life freely." If you only come
to Him, though He have passed, He will stop. If you
come trusting and yet doubting, He will forgive the
doubt and answer the trust. If you come to Him,
knowing but that your heart is full of evil which none
save He can cure, and putting out a lame hand—or
even a tremulous finger-tip—to touch His garment, be
sure that anything is possible rather than that He should
turn away your prayer, or His mercy from you.

III. The last part of this miracle teaches us that

Christ corrects and confirms an imperfect faith by the very act of answering it.

Observe how the process of cure and the discipline which followed are, in Christ's loving wisdom, made to fit closely to all the faults and flaws in the suppliant's faith.

She had thought of the healing energy as independent of the Healer's knowledge and will. Therefore His very first word shows her that He is aware of her mute appeal, and conscious of the going forth from Him of the power that cures—" Who touched me ?" As was said long ago, " the multitudes thronged Him, but the woman touched." Amidst all the jostling of the unmannerly crowd that trod with rude feet on His skirts, and elbowed their way to see this new Rabbi, there was one touch unlike all the rest ; and, though only the finger-tip of a poor woman, wasted to skin and bone with twelve years' weakening disease, He knew it ; and His will and love sent forth the " virtue" which healed. May we not fairly apply this lesson to ourselves ? There is Christ, as most of us, I suppose, believe, Lord of all creatures, administering the affairs of the universe ; the steps of His throne and the precincts of His court are thronged with dependants whose eyes wait upon Him, who are fed from His stores ; and yet my poor voice may steal through that chorus-shout of petition and praise, and His ear will detect its lowest note, and will separate the thin stream of my prayer from the great sea of supplication which rolls to His seat, and will answer *me*. My hand uplifted among the millions of empty and imploring palms that are raised towards the heavens will receive into its clasping fingers the special blessing for my special wants.

Again, she had been selfish in her faith, had not cared for any close personal relation with Him ; and so she was taught that He was in all His gifts, and that He was more than all His gifts. He compels her to come to His feet that she may learn His heart, and may carry away a blessing not stolen, but bestowed.

> " With open love, not secret cure,
>   The Lord of hearts would bless."

And thus is laid the foundation for a personal bond between her and Christ, which shall be for the joy of her life, and shall make of that life a thankful sacrifice to Him, the Healer.

Thus it is with us all. We may go to Him, at first, with no thought but for ourselves. But we have not to carry away His gift hidden in our hands. We learn that it is a love token from Him. And so we find in His answer to faith the true and only cure for all self-regard ; and, moved by the mercies of Christ, are led to do what else were impossible—to yield ourselves as living sacrifices to Him.

Again, she had shrunk from publicity. Her womanly diffidence, her enfeebled health, the shame of her disease, all made her wish to hide herself and her want from His eye, and to hide herself and her treasure from men. She would fain steal away unnoticed, as she hoped she had come. But she is dragged out before all the thronging multitude, and has to tell the whole. The answer to her faith makes her bold. In a moment she is changed from timidity to courage : she stretched out her hand, a tremu-lous invalid ready to creep into any corner to escape notice—the instant after, she knelt at His feet in the spirit of a confessor. This is Christ's most merciful fashion of curing our cowardice, not by rebukes but by giving us, faint-hearted though we be, the gift which out of weakness makes us strong. He would have us testify to Him before men, and that for our own sakes, since faith unacknowledged, like a plant in the dark, is apt to become pale and sickly, and bears no bright blossoms nor sweet fruit. But, ere He bids us own His name, He pours into our hearts, in answer to our secret appeal, the health of His own life, and the blissful consciousness of that great gift which makes the tongue of the dumb sing. Faith at first may be very timid, but faith will grow bold to witness of Him and not be ashamed, in the exact pro-portion in which it is genuine, and receives from Christ of His fulness.

And then—with a final word to set forth still more clearly that she had received the blessing from His love, not from His magical power, and through her confidence not through her touch,—" Daughter ! thy faith"—not thy finger—" hath made thee whole ; go in peace and *be* whole "—Jesus confirms by His own authoritative voice the furtive blessing, and sends her away perhaps to see Him no more, but to live in tranquil security, and in her humble home to guard the gift which He had bestowed on her imperfect faith ; and to perfect—we may hope—

the faith which He had enlightened and strengthened by the over-abundance of His gift.

Dear friends, this poor woman represents us all. Like her, we are sick of a sore sickness, we have spent our substance in trying physicians of no value, and are "nothing the better, but rather the worse." Oh, is it not strange that you should need to be urged to go to the Healer to whom she went? Do not be afraid, my brother, of telling Him all your pain and pining—He knows it already. Do not be afraid that your hand may not reach Him for the crowd, or that your voice may fail to fall on His ear. Do not be afraid of your ignorance, do not be afraid of your wavering confidence and many doubts. All these cannot separate you from Him who Himself took our infirmities and bare our sickness. Fear but one thing—that He pass on to carry life and health to other souls, ere you resolve to press to His feet. Fear but one thing, that whilst you delay, the hem of the garment may be swept beyond the reach of your slow hand. Imperfect faith may bring salvation to a soul: hesitation may ruin and wreck a life.

THE PRIEST OF THE WORLD AND KING OF MEN.

ZECHARIAH vi. 13.

He shall build the temple of the Lord . . . and He shall be a priest
upon His throne.

A HANDFUL of feeble exiles had come back from
their captivity. "The holy and beautiful house
where their fathers praised Him was burned with fire."
There was no king among them, but they still possessed
a representative of the priesthood, the other great office
of Divine appointment. Their first care was to rear
some poor copy of the Temple ; and the usual difficulties
that attend reconstruction of any sort, and dog every
movement that rests upon religious enthusiasm, beset
them—strong enemies, and half-hearted friends, and
personal jealousies weakening still more their weak
forces. In this time of anarchy, of toil with inadequate
resources at a great task, of despondency that was
rapidly fulfilling its own forebodings, the prophet, who
was the spring of the whole movement, receives a word in
season from the Lord. He is bidden to take from some
of the returned exiles the tribute-money which they had

brought, and, having made of it golden and silver crowns
—the sign of kingship—to set them on the high priest's
head, thus uniting the sacerdotal and regal offices, which
had always been jealously separated in Israel. This
singular action is explained, by the words which he is
commanded to speak, as being a symbolic prophecy of
Him who is "the Branch"—the well-known name that
older prophets had used for the Messiah—indicating that
in Him was the reality which the priesthood shadowed,
and the rule which was partly delegated to Israel's king
as well as the power which should rear the true temple
of God among men.

It is in accordance with the law of prophetic development from the beginning, that the external circumstances
of the nation at the moment should supply the mould
into which the promise is run. The earliest of all
Messianic predictions embraced only the existence of
evil, as represented by the serpent, and the conquest of it
by one who was known but as a son of Eve. When the
history reaches the patriarchal stage, wherein the family
is the predominant conception, the prophecy advances
proportionately to the assurance, "In thy seed shall all
the families of the earth be blessed." When the life of
Moses had made the people familiar with the idea of a
man who was the medium of revelation, then a further
stage was reached—"a prophet shall the Lord your God
raise up unto you, of your brethren, like unto me." The
kingdom of David prepared the way for the prediction
of the royal dignity of the Messiah, as the peaceful reign
of Solomon for the expectation of one who should bring

peace by righteousness. The approach of national
disaster and sorrow was reflected in Isaiah's vision of the
suffering Messiah, and that prophet's announcements of
exile had for their counterpoise the proclamation of Him
who should bring liberty to the captive. So, here, the
kingless band of exiles painfully striving to rear again
"the tabernacle which had fallen down," are heartened
for their task by the thought of the priest-king of the
nation, the builder of an imperishable dwelling-place
for God.

To-day we need these truths not less then Zechariah's
contemporaries did. And, thank God! we can believe
that, for every modern perplexity, the blessed old words
carry the same strength and consolation. If kings seem
to have perished from among men, if authorities are
dying out, and there are no names of power that can
rally the world—yet there is a Sovereign. If old institutions are crumbling, and must still further decay ere
the site for a noble structure be cleared, yet He shall
build the Temple. If priest be on some lips a name of
superstitious folly, and on others a synonym for all that
is despised as effete in religion, yet this Priest abideth
for ever, the guide and the hope for the history of
humanity and for the individual spirit. Let us, then, put
ourselves under the prophet's guidance, and consider the
eternal truths which he preaches to *us* too.

I. *The true hope of the world is a priest.*

The idea of priesthood is universal. It has been
distorted and abused ; it has been made the foundation
of spiritual tyranny. The priest has not been the

teacher nor the elevator of the people. All over the world he has been the ally of oppression and darkness, he has hindered and cramped social and intellectual progress. And yet, in spite of all this, there the office stands, and wherever men go, by some strange perversity they take with them this idea, and choose from among themselves those who, being endowed with some sort of ceremonial and symbolic purity, shall discharge for their brethren the double office of representing them before God, of representing God to them. That is what the world means, with absolute and entire unanimity, by a priest—one who shall be sacrificer, intercessor, representative; bearer of man's worship, channel of God's blessing. How comes it, that, in spite of all the cruelties and lies that have gathered round the office, it lives, indestructible, among the families of men? Why, because it springs from, and corresponds to, real and universal wants in their nature. It is the result of the universal consciousness of sin. Men feel that there is a gulf betwixt them and God. They know themselves to be all foul. True, as their knowledge of God dims and darkens, their conscience hardens and their sense of sin lessens; but, as long as there is any notion of God at all, there will be a parallel and corresponding conviction of moral evil. And so, feeling that, and feeling it, as I believe, not because they are rude and barbarous, but because, though rude and barbarous, they still preserve some trace of their true relation to God, they lay hold upon some of their fellows, and say, "Here! be thou for us this thing which we cannot be for ourselves—stand thou there in front of us, and be at once the expression of our knowledge that we dare not come before our gods, and likewise, if it may be, the medium by which their gifts may come on us, unworthy."

That is a wide-spread and all but universally expressed instinct of human nature. Argue about it as you like, explain it away how you choose, charge the notion of priesthood and sacrifice with exaggeration, immorality, barbarism, if you will—still the thing remains. And I believe for my part that, so far from that want being one which will be left behind, with other rude and savage desires, as men advance in civilization—it is as real and as permanent as the craving of the understanding for truth, and of the heart for love. When men lose it, it is because they are barbarized, not civilized, into forgetting it. On that rock all systems of religion and eminently all theories of Christianity, that leave out priest and sacrifice, will strike and split. The Gospel for the world must be one which will meet all the facts of man's condition. Chief among these facts is this necessity of the conscience as expressed by the forms in which for thousands of years the worship of mankind has been embodied—all but everywhere with an altar, and a priest standing by its side.

I need not pause to remind you how this Jewish people, who have at all events taught the world the purest Theism, and led men up to the most spiritual religion, had this same institution of a priesthood for the very centre of its worship. Nor need I dwell at length on the fact that the New Testament gives-in its full adhesion to the same idea. We are told that all these sacerdotal allusions in it are only putting pure spiritual truth in the guise of the existing stage of religious development — the husk not the kernel. It seems to me much rather that the Old Testament ceremonial—temple, priesthood, sacrifice—was established for this along with other purposes, of being a shadow of things to come. Christ's office is not metaphorically illustrated by reference to the Jewish ritual; but the Jewish ritual is the metaphor, and Christ's office the reality. He is the priest.

And what is the priest whom men crave?

The first requisite is oneness with those whom he represents. Men have ever felt that one of themselves must fill this office, and have taken from among their brethren their medium of communication with God. And we have a priest who, "in all things, is made like unto His brethren," having taken part of their flesh and blood, and being "in all points tempted like as we are." The next requisite is that these men, who minister at earth's altars, should, by some lustration, or abstinence, or white robe, or other external sign, be separated from the profane crowd, and possess, at all events, a symbolic purity—expression of the conviction that a priest must be cleaner and closer to God than his fellows. And we have a Priest who is holy, harmless, undefiled, radiant in perfect purity, lustrous with the light of constant union with God.

And again, as in nature and character, so in function, Christ corresponds to the widely expressed wants of men, as shown in their priesthoods. They sought for one who should offer gifts and sacrifices on their behalf, and we have one who is "a merciful and faithful High Priest to make reconciliation for the sins of the people." They sought for a man who should pass into the awful presence, and plead for them while they stood without, and we lift hopeful eyes of love to the heavens, "whither the Forerunner is for us entered, even Jesus, made an High Priest for ever." They sought for a man who should be the medium of Divine blessings bestowed upon the worshippers, and we know who hath gone within the veil, having ascended up on high, that He might give gifts unto men.

The world needs a priest. Its many attempts to find such show how deep is the sense of need, and what he must be who shall satisfy them. We have the Priest that the world and ourselves require. I believe that modern Englishmen, with the latest results of civilization colouring their minds and moulding their characters, stand upon the very same level, so far as this matter is concerned, as the veriest savage in African wilds, who has darkened even the fragment of truth which he possesses, till it has become a lie and the parent of lies. You and I, and all our brethren, alike need a brother who shall be holy and close to God, who shall offer sacrifices for us, and bring God to us. For you and me, and all our brethren alike, the good news is true, "we have a great High Priest that is passed into the heavens, Jesus, the Son of God." That message quenches the fire on every other altar, and strips the mitre from every other head.

It, and it alone, meets fully and for ever that strange craving, which, though it has been productive of so many miseries and so many errors, though it has led to grinding tyranny, and dark superstitions, though it has never anywhere found what it longs for, remains deep in the soul, indestructible and hungry, till it is vindicated and enlightened and satisfied by the coming of the true Priest, "made not after the law of a carnal commandment, but after the power of an endless life."

II. Our text tells us, secondly, that *the priest of the world is the king of men.* "He shall be a priest upon His throne."

In Israel these two offices were jealously kept apart, and when one monarch, in a fit of overweening self-importance, tried to unite in his own person, the kingly and the priestly functions, "the leprosy rose up in his forehead," even as he stood with the censer in his hand, and "Uzziah the king was a leper unto the day of his death." And the history of the world is full of instances, in which the struggles of the temporal and spiritual power have caused calamities only less intolerable than those which flowed from that alliance of priests and kings which has so often made monarchy a grinding tyranny, and religion a mere instrument of statecraft. History being witness, it would seem to be a very doubtful blessing for the world that one man should wield both forms of control without check or limitation, and be at once king and priest. If the words before us refer to any one but to Christ, the prophet had an altogether mistaken notion about what would be good for men, politically and ecclesiastically, and we may be thankful that his dream has never come true. But if they point to the Son of David who has died for us, and declare that because he is Priest, He is therefore King—oh! then they are full of blessed truth concerning the basis, and the nature, and the purpose of His dominion, which may well make us lift up our heads and rejoice that in the midst of tyranny and anarchy, of sovereignties whose ultimate resort is force, there is another kingdom—the most absolute of despotisms and yet the most perfect democracy, whose law is love, whose subjects are every one the children of a King, the kingdom of that Priest-ruler on whose head is Aaron's mitre, and more than David's crown.

He does rule. "The kingdom of Christ" is no unreal fanciful phrase. Take the lowest ground. Who is it that, by the words He spoke, by the deeds he did, by the life He lived, has shaped the whole form of moral and religious thought and life in the civilized world? Is there one among "the great of old, the dead yet sceptred sovrans, who still rule our spirits from their urns," whose living power over thought and heart and deed, among the dominant races of the earth, is to be compared with his? And beyond that, we believe that, as the result of his mighty work on earth, the dominion of the whole creation is His, and He is King of kings, and Lord of lords, that His will is sovereign and His voice is absolute law, to which all the powers of nature, all the confusions of earth's politics, all the unruly wills of men, all the pale kingdoms of the dead, and all the glorious companies of the heavens, do bow in real though it be sometimes unconscious and sometimes reluctant obedience.

The foundation of His rule is His sacrifice. Or in other words, no truer, though a little more modern in their sound—men will do anything for Him who does *that* for them. Men will yield their whole souls to the warmth and light that stream from the Cross, as the sunflower turns itself to the sun. He that can give an anodyne, which is not an opiate, to my conscience—He that can appeal to my heart and will, and say, " I have given Myself for thee," will never speak in vain to those who accept His gift, when He says, " Now give thyself to Me."

Brethren, it is not the thinker who is the true king of men, as we sometimes hear it proudly said. We need one who will not only show but be the Truth; who will not only point, but open and be, the Way; who will not only communicate thought, but give, because He is, the Life. Not the rabbi's pulpit, nor the teacher's desk, still less the gilded chairs of earthly monarchs, least of all the tents of conquerors, are the throne of the true king. He rules from the Cross. The one dominion worth naming, that over men's inmost spirits, springs from the one Sacrifice which alone calms and quickens men's inmost spirits. " Thou art the King of Glory, O Christ," for Thou art " the Lamb of God, which taketh away the sins of the world."

His rule is wielded in gentleness. Priestly dominion has ever been fierce, suspicious, tyrannous. " His

words were softer than oil, yet were they drawn swords"
But the sway of this merciful and faithful High Priest is
full of tenderness. His sceptre is not the warrior's
mace, nor the jewelled rod of gold, but the reed—
emblem of the lowliness of his heart, and of authority
guiding by love. And all His rule is for the blessing of
His subjects, and the end of it is that they may be made
free by obedience, emancipated in and for service,
crowned as kings by submission to the King of kings,
consecrated as priests by their reliance on the only Priest
over the house of God, whose loving Will rests not until
it has made all His people like Himself.

Then, dear brethren, amid all the anarchic chaos of this
day, when old institutions are crumbling or crashing into
decay, when the whole civilized world seems slowly and
painfully parting from its old moorings, and, like some
unwieldy raft, is creaking and straining at its chains as it
feels the impulse of the swift current that is bearing it
to an unknown sea, when venerable names cease to have
power, when old truths are flouted as antiquated, and
the new ones seem so long in making their appearance,
when a perfect Babel of voices stuns us, and on every
side are pretenders to the throne which they fancy
vacant; let us joyfully welcome all change, and hope-
fully anticipate the future. Lifting our eyes from the
world, let us fix them on the "likeness of a throne above
the firmament that is above the cherubs," and rejoice
since there we behold "the likeness as the appearance of
a man upon it." "Shout, O daughter of Jerusalem;
behold, thy King cometh unto thee."

III. Our text still further reminds us that *the Priest-King of men builds among men the Temple of God.*

The prophet and his companions had become familiar in their captivity with the gigantic palaces and temples which Assyrian and Babylonian monarchs had a passion for rearing. They had learned to regard the king as equally magnified by his conquests and by his buildings. Zechariah foretells that the true King shall rear a temple more lasting than Solomon's, more magnificent than those which towered on their marble-faced platforms over the Chaldean plain.

Christ is Himself the true Temple of God. Whatsoever that shadowed Christ is or gives. In Him dwelt all the fulness of the Godhead. "The glory" which once dwelt between the cherubim, "tabernacled among us" in His flesh. As the place of sacrifice, as the place where men meet God, as the seat of revelation of the Divine will, the true tabernacle which the Lord hath pitched is the Manhood of our Lord.

Christ builds the temple. By faith, the individual soul becomes the abode of God, and into our desecrated spirits there comes the King of Glory. "Know ye not that ye are the temples of God?" By faith, the whole body of believing men "are builded together for an habitation of God through the Spirit."

Christ builds this temple because He is the temple. By His incarnation and work, He makes our communion with God and God's dwelling in us possible. By His death and sacrifice He draws men to Himself, and blends them in a living unity. By the gift of His Spirit and

2ND SER. Y

His life, He hallows their wills, and makes them par-takers of His own likeness; so that "coming to Him, we also are built up a spiritual house."

Christ builds the temple, and uses us as His servants in the work. Our prophecy was given to encourage faint-hearted toilers, not to supply an excuse for indolence. Beneath all our poor labours, and blessing them all, is the power of Christ. We may well work diligently who work in the line of His purposes, after the pattern of His labours, in the strength of His power, under the watchfulness of His eye. The little band may be few and feeble; let them not be fearful, for He, the throned priest, even *He*, and not they with their inadequate resources, shall build the temple.

Christ builds on through all the ages, and the prophecy of our text is yet unfulfilled. Its fulfilment is the meaning and end of all history. For the present, there has to be much destructive as well as constructive work done. Many a wretched hovel, the abode of sorrow and want, many a den of infamy, many a palace of pride, many a temple of idols, will have to be pulled down yet, and men's eyes will be blinded by the dust, and their hearts will ache as they look at the ruins. Be it so. The finished structure will obliterate the remembrance of poor buildings that cumbered its site. This Emperor of ours may indeed say, that He found the city of brick and made it marble. Have patience if His work is slow; mourn not if it is destructive; doubt not, though the unfinished walls, and corridors that seem to lead no-where, and all the confusion of unfinished toils puzzle you, when you try to make out the plan. See to it, my brother, that you lend a hand and help to rear the true temple, which is rising slowly through the ages, at which successive generations toil, and from whose unfinished glories they dying depart, but which shall be completed, because the true Builder "ever liveth," and is "a priest for ever after the order of Melchizedek." Above all, brethren, take heed that you are yourselves builded in that temple. Travellers sometimes find in lonely quarries, long abandoned or once worked by a vanished race, great blocks squared and dressed, that seem to have been meant for palace or shrine. But there they lie, neglected and forgotten, and the building for which they were hewn has been reared without them. Beware lest God's grand temple should be built up without you, and you be left to desolation and decay. Trust your souls to Christ, and He will set you in the spiritual house, which the King greater than Solomon is building still.

In one of the mosques of Damascus, which has been a Christian church, and before that was a heathen temple, the portal bears, deep cut in Greek characters, the inscription, "Thy kingdom, O Christ, is an everlasting kingdom, and Thy dominion endureth throughout all generations." The confident words seem contradicted by the twelve centuries of Mohammedanism on which they have looked down. But, though their silent prophecy is unheeded and unheard by the worshippers below, it shall be proved true one day, and the crescent shall wane before the steady light of the Sun of Righteousness. The words are carven deep over the portals of the temple which Christ rears ; and though men may not be able to read them, and may not believe them if they do, though for centuries traffickers have defiled its courts, and base-born usurpers have set up their petty thrones, yet the writing stands sure, a dumb witness against the transient lies, a patient prophet of the eternal truth. And when all false faiths, and their priests who have oppressed men and traduced God, have vanished ; and when kings that have prostituted their great and godlike office to personal advancement and dynastic ambition are forgotten ; and when every shrine reared for obscene and bloody rites, or for superficial and formal worship, has been cast to the ground, then from out of the confusion and desolation shall gleam the temple of God, which is the refuge of men, and on the one throne of the universe shall sit the Eternal Priest—our brother, Jesus the Christ.

REVELATION xxi. 1.

And there was no more sea.

" I JOHN," says the Apocalypse at its commencement, "was in the isle that is called Patmos, for the testi mony of Jesus." In this, the one prophetic book of the New Testament, we find the same fact that meets us in the old prophecies, that the circumstances of the prophet colour, and become the medium for, the representation of the spiritual truths that he has to speak. All through the book we hear the dash of the waves. There was "a sea of fire mingled with glass before the throne." The star Wormwood fell "upon the sea." Out of the sea the beast rises. When the great angel would declare the destruction of Babylon, he casts a mighty stone into the ocean, and says, "Thus suddenly shall Babylon be destroyed." And when John hears the voice of praise of the redeemed, it is "like the voice of many waters," as well as like the voice of "harpers harping on their harps." And then, when there dawns at the close of the vision, the bright and the blessed time which has yet to

come, the "new heavens and the new earth" are revealed to him; and that sad and solitary and estranging
ocean that raged around his little rock sanctuary has
passed away for ever. I suppose I need not occupy
your time in showing that this is a symbol; that it does
not mean literal fact at all; that it is not telling us anything about the geography of a future world, but that it
is the material embodiment of a great spiritual truth.

Now what is meant by this symbol is best ascertained
by remembering how the sea appears in the Old Testament. The Jew was not a sailor. All the references in
the Old Testament, and especially in the prophets, to
that great ocean are such as a man would make who
knew very little about it, except from having looked at
it from the hills of Judea, and having often wondered
what might be lying away out yonder at the point where
sky and sea blended together. There are three main
things which it shadows forth in the Old Testament. It
is a symbol of mystery, of rebellious power, of perpetual
unrest. And it is the promise of the cessation of these
things which is set forth in that saying, "There was no
more sea." There shall be no more mystery and terror.
There shall be no more "the floods lifting up their
voice," and the waves dashing with impotent foam
against the throne of God. There shall be no more
the tossing and the tumult of changing circumstances,
and no more the unrest and disquiet of a sinful heart.
There shall be the "new heavens and the new earth."
The old humanity will be left, and the relation to God
will remain, deepened and glorified and made pure. But

all that is sorrowful and all that is rebellious, all that is mysterious and all that is unquiet, shall have passed away for ever.

I. Let us then by way of illustrating this great and blessed promise consider it first as the revelation of *a future in which there shall be no more painful mystery*.

"Thy way is in the sea, and thy path in the great waters, and thy footsteps are not known." "Thy judgments are a mighty deep." "O the depth of the riches both of the wisdom and of the knowledge of God! How unsearchable are His judgments, and His ways past finding out!" Such is the prevailing tone of expression when the figure appears either in the Old or in the New Testament.

Most natural is it. There are two sources of obscurity there. We look out upon the broad ocean, and far away it seems to blend with air and sky. Mists come up over its surface. Suddenly there rises on the verge of the horizon a white sail that was not there a moment ago ; and we wonder, as we look out from our hills, what may be beyond these mysterious waters. And to these ancient peoples there were mysteries which we do not feel. Whither should they come, if they were to venture on its untried tides? And then, what lies in its sunless caves that no eye has seen? It swallows up life and beauty and treasure of every sort, and engulphs them all in its obstinate silence. They go down in the mighty waters and vanish as they descend. What would it be if these were drained off! What revelations—wild sea-valleys and mountain gorges ; the dead that are in it, the power that lies there, all powerless now, the wealth that has been lost in it! What should we see if depth and distance were annihilated, and we beheld what there is out yonder, and what there is down there?

And is not our life, brethren, ringed round in like manner with mystery? And, alas! wherever to a poor human heart there is mystery, *there* will be terror. The unknown is ever the awful. Where there is not certain knowledge, imagination works to people the waste places with monsters. There is a double limitation of our knowledge. There are mysteries that come from the necessary limitation of our faculties; and there are mysteries that come from the incompleteness of the revelation which God has been pleased to make. The eye is weak and the light is dim. There is much that lies beyond the horizon which our eyes cannot reach. There is much that lies covered by the deeps, which our eyes *could* reach if the deeps were away. We live—the wisest of us live—having great questions wrestling with us like that angel that wrestled with the patriarch in the darkness till the morning broke. We learn so little but our own ignorance, and we know so little but that we know nothing. There are the hard and obstinate knots that will not be untied; we bend all our faculties to them, and think they are giving a little bit, and they never give; and we gnaw at them, like the viper at the file, and we make nothing of it, but blunt our teeth!

Oh! to some hearts here, surely this ought to come as not the least noble and precious of the thoughts of what that future life is—" there shall be no more sea;"

and the mysteries that come from God's merciful limitation of our vision, and some of the mysteries that come from God's wise and providential interposition of obstacles to our sight, shall have passed away. It is no dream, my brethren! Why, think how the fact of dying will solve many a riddle! how much more we shall know by shifting our position! "There must be wisdom with great Death," and he "keeps the keys of all the creeds." Try to conceive how some dear one that was beside us but a moment ago, perhaps but little conscious of his own ignorance, and knowing but little of God's ways, thinking as we did, and speaking as we did, and snared with errors as we were, has grown at a bound into full stature, and how a flood of new knowledge and divine truth rushes into the heart the moment it passes the grave!—If they were to speak to us, perhaps we should not understand their new speech, so wise have *they* become who have died.

What mysteries have passed into light for them? I know not. Who can tell what strange enlargement of faculty this soul of ours is capable of? Who can tell how much of our blindness comes from the flesh that clogs us, from the working of the animal nature that is so strong in us? Who can tell what unknown resources and what possibilities of new powers there lie all dormant and unsuspected in the beggar on the dung-hill, and in the idiot in the asylum? This, at least, we are sure of: we shall "know, even as also we are known." God, will not be fathomed, but God will be known. God will be incomprehensible, but there will be no

mystery in God, except that most blessed mystery of
feeling that the fulness of His nature still surpasses our
comprehension.   Questions that now fill the whole
horizon of our minds will have shrunk away into a mere
point, or been answered by the very change of position.
How much of the knowledges of earth will have ceased
to be applicable, when the first light-beam of heaven
falls upon them! Those problems which we think so
mysterious—why God is doing this or that with us and
the world; what is the meaning of this and the other
sorrow—what will have become of these? We shall
look back and see that the bending line was leading
straight as an arrow-flight, home to the centre, and that
the end crowns and vindicates every step of the road.
Something of the mystery of God will have been resolved, for man hath powers undreamed of yet, and "we
shall see Him as He is."   Much of the mystery of man,
and of man's relation to God, will have ceased; for then
we shall understand all the way, when we have entered
into the true sanctuary of God.

Men that love to know, let me ask you, where do you
get the fulfilment, often dreamed of, of your desires,
except here? Set this before you, as the highest truth
for us; Christ is the beginning of all wisdom on earth.
Starting thence I can hope to solve the remaining mysteries when I stand at last, redeemed by the blood of the
Lamb, in the presence of the great light of God.

Not that we shall know everything, for that were to
cease to be finite. And if ever the blasphemous boast
come true that tempted man once, "Ye shall be as gods,

knowing good and evil," there were nothing left for the soul that was filled with all knowledge but to lie down and pant its last. It needs, by our very nature, and for our blessedness, that there should be much unknown. It needs that we should ever be pressing forward. Only, the mysteries that are left will have no terror nor pain in them. "There shall be no more sea," but we shall climb ever higher and higher up the mountain of God, and as we climb see further and further into the blessed valleys beyond, and "shall know even as we are known."

II. Secondly, the text tells us of a state that is to come, when *there shall be no more rebellious power.* In the Old Testament the floods are often compared with the rage of the peoples, and the rebellion of man against the Will of God. "The floods have lifted up, O Lord, the floods have lifted up their voice. The Lord on high is mightier than the noise of many waters; yea, than the mighty waves of the sea." "Thou stillest the noise of the waves, and the tumult of the people." In like manner that symbolic reference surely supplies one chief meaning of Christ's miracle of stilling the tempest; the Peace-bringer bringing to peace the tumults of men. Here, then, the sea stands as the emblem of untamed power. It is lashed into yeasty foam, and drives before it great ships and huge stones like bulrushes, and seems to have a savage pleasure in eating into the slow-corroding land, and covering the beach with its devastation.

"There shall be no more sea." God lets people work against His kingdom in this world. It is not to be always so, says my text. The kingdom of God *is* in the earth, and the kingdom of God admits of opposition. Strange! But the opposition, even here on earth, all comes to nothing. "Thou art mightier than the noise of many waters;" the floods "have lifted up their voice;" but Thou "sittest upon the floods, yea, Thou sittest king for ever." Yes, it is an experience repeated over and over again, in the history of individuals and in the history of the world. Men, fancying themselves free, resolved to be rebellious, get together and say, mutteringly at first, and then boldly and loudly, "Let us break His bands asunder, and cast away His cords from us." And God sits in seeming silence in His heavens, and they work on, and the thing seems to be prospering, and some men's hearts begin to fail them for fear. The great Armada comes in its pride across the waters—and the motto that our England struck upon its medal, when that proud fleet was baffled, serves for the epitaph over all antagonism to God's kingdom, "The Lord blew upon them, and they were scattered." The tossing sea, that rages against the will and purpose of the Lord, what becomes of all its foaming fury? Why, this becomes of it—the ark of God "moves on the face of the waters," and though wild tempests howl to beat it from its course, yet beneath all the surface confusion and commotion, there is, as in the great mid-ocean, a silent current that runs steady and strong, and it carries the keel that goes deep enough down to rest in it, safely to its port. Men may work against God's kingdom, the waves may rave and rage; but beneath them there is a mighty tidal sweep, and God's purposes are wrought out, and God's ark comes to "its desired haven," and all opposition is nugatory at the last.

But there comes a time, too, when there shall be no more violence of rebellious wills lifting themselves against God. Our text is a blessed promise that, in that holy state to which the Apocalyptic vision carries our longing hopes, there shall be the cessation of all strife against our best Friend, of all reluctance to wear *His* yoke whose yoke brings rest to the soul. The opposition that lies in all our hearts shall one day be subdued. The whole consent of our whole being shall yield itself to the obedience of sons, to the service of love. The wild rebellious power shall be softened into peace, and won to joyful acceptance of His law. In all the regions of that heavenly state, there shall be no jarring will, no reluctant submission. Its "solemn troops and sweet societies" shall move in harmonious concent of according hearts, and circle His throne in continuousness of willing fealty. There shall be One will in heaven. "There shall be no more sea;" for "His servants serve Him," and the noise of the waves has died away for ever.

Before I pass on, let me appeal to you, my friend, on this matter. Here is the revelation for us of the utter hopelessness and vanity of all opposition to God. Oh ! what a thought that is, that every life that sets itself against the Lord is a futile life, that it comes to nothing at last, that none hardens himself against God and prospers ! It is true on the widest scale. It is true on the narrowest. It is true about all those tempests that have risen up against God's Church and Christ's Gospel,

like "waves of the sea foaming out their own shame,"
and never shaking the great rock that they break against.
And it is true about all godless lives; about every man
who carries on his work, except in loving obedience to
his Father in heaven.   There is one power in the world,
and none else.   When all is played out, and accounts
are set right at the end, you will find that the power that
seemed to be strong, if it stood against God, was weak
as water and has done nothing, and is nothing!   Do not
waste your lives in a work that is self-condemned to be
hopeless!   Rather ally yourselves with the tendencies of
God's universe, and do the thing which will last for ever,
and live the life that has hope of fruit that shall remain.
Submit yourselves to God!   Love Christ!   Do His will!
Put your faith in the Saviour to deliver you from your
sins; and when the wild tossing of that great ocean of
ungodly power and rebellious opposition is all hushed
down into dead silence, you and your work will last and
live hard by the stable throne of God.

III. Lastly, the text foretells a state of things in which
there is no more disquiet and unrest.   The old, old figure
which all the world, generation after generation in its
turn, has spoken, is a scriptural one as well, and enters
into the fulness of the meaning of this passage before us.
Life is a voyage over a turbulent sea; changing circumstances come rolling after each other, like the undis-
tinguishable billows of the great ocean.   Tempests and
storms rise.   There is wearisome sailing, no peace, but
"ever climbing up the climbing wave."   *That* is life!
But for all that, friends, there is an end to it some day;

and it is worth while for us to think about our "island
home, far, far beyond the sea." Surely some of us have
learned the weariness of this changeful state, the weariness of the work and voyage of this world. Surely
some of us are longing to find anchorage whilst the
storm lasts, and a haven at the end. There *is* one, if
only you will believe it, and set yourselves towards it.
There is an end to all "the weary oar, the weary wandering fields of barren foam." On the shore stands the
Christ; and there is rest *there*. *There* is no more sea,
but unbroken rest, unchanging blessedness, perpetual
stability of joy, and love in the Father's house. Are *we*
going there? Are *we* living for Christ? Are *we* putting
our confidence in the Lord Jesus? Then, "He brings
us to the desired haven."

One thing more: not only does unrest come from the
chaos of changing circumstances, but besides that, there
is another source of disquiet, which this same symbol
sets forth for us. "The wicked is like the troubled sea
which cannot rest, whose waters cast up mire and dirt."
That restless, profitless working of the great homeless,
hungry, moaning ocean—what a picture it is of the heart
of a man that has no Christ, that has no God, that has
no peace by pardon! A soul all tossed with its own
boiling passion, a soul across which there howl great
gusts of temptation, a soul which works and brings forth
nothing but foam and mire! Unrest, perpetual unrest is
the lot of every man that is not God's child. Some of
you know that. Well, then, think of one picture. A
little barque pitching in the night, and one figure rises

quietly up in the stern, and puts out a rebuking hand, and speaks one mighty word, "Peace! be still." And the word was heard amid all the hurly-burly of the tempest, and the waves crouched at his feet like dogs to their master.   It is no fancy, brethren, it is a truth.   Let Christ speak to your hearts, and there is peace and quietness.   And if He do that, then your experience will be like that described in the grand old Psalm, "Though the waters roar and be troubled, and though the mountains shake with the swelling thereof, yet will we not fear," for the City stands fast, in spite of the waves that curl round its lowest foundations.   Death, death itself, will be but the last burst of the expiring storm, the last blast of the blown-out tempest.   And then, the quiet of the green inland valleys of our Father's land, where no tempest comes any more, nor the loud winds are ever heard, nor the salt sea is ever seen ; but perpetual calm and blessedness ; all mystery gone, and all rebellion hushed and silenced, and all unrest at an end for ever ! "No more sea," but, instead of that wild and yeasty chaos of turbulent waters, there shall be "the river that makes glad the city of God," the river of water of life, that "proceeds out of the throne of God and of the Lamb."

THE END.